D0796507

Kings and Presidents

Kings

and

Presidents

Saudi Arabia and the United States
since FDR

BRUCE RIEDEL

BROOKINGS INSTITUTION PRESS
Washington, D.C.

Copyright © 2019
THE BROOKINGS INSTITUTION
1775 Massachusetts Avenue, N.W., Washington, D.C. 20036
www.brookings.edu

All rights reserved. No part of this publication may be reproduced or transmitted in any form or by any means without permission in writing from the Brookings Institution Press.

The Brookings Institution is a private nonprofit organization devoted to research, education, and publication on important issues of domestic and foreign policy. Its principal purpose is to bring the highest quality independent research and analysis to bear on current and emerging policy problems. Interpretations or conclusions in Brookings publications should be understood to be solely those of the authors.

Library of Congress Cataloging-in-Publication data are available.
ISBN 978-0-8157-3715-5 (paperback : alk. paper)
ISBN 978-0-8157-3138-2 (ebook)

9 8 7 6 5 4 3 2 1

Typeset in Fournier MT

Composition by Westchester Publishing Services

To Gloria

Contents

Preface to the Paperback Edition

Jamal Khashoggi sat in the front row of the Brookings Institution's Falk Auditorium in the fall of 2017 when Brookings first launched this book. He had become a fixture at Brookings events on Saudi Arabia and the Middle East. Born in Medina, Khashoggi had made his name as a journalist covering the mujahedin in Afghanistan in the 1980s, during the war in which America and Saudi Arabia had secretly conspired to destroy the Soviet Union. He interviewed the most famous Saudi volunteer in the war, Osama bin Laden. Later he became an adviser to Prince Turki bin Faisal, the head of Saudi intelligence during the war and subsequently Saudi ambassador to first the United Kingdom and then the United States. Khashoggi became disillusioned when Muhammad bin Salman began accumulating power in 2016, disturbed by the prince's reckless decision making in Yemen and elsewhere and his brutal repression of any criticism at home. Khashoggi began writing opinion pieces for the *Washington Post*, always affirming his loyalty to the monarchy and his country but despairing of the young prince's dangerous policies. His last essay was a damning indictment of the crown prince's signature policy initiative, the war in Yemen, which had become a quagmire.

On October 2, 2018, Khashoggi was murdered in the Saudi consulate in Istanbul, Turkey. He had gone there to acquire documents for his upcoming wedding. The Saudi ambassador to the United States, Prince Kamal bin Salman, had apparently sent Khashoggi to Istanbul for the documents. Inside the consulate a team of more than a dozen assassins was waiting. Jamal was tortured, murdered, and then dismembered. The assassins included members of the Royal Guard Regiment, the intelligence service, and the crown prince's office. They almost certainly were there on the orders of Crown Prince Muhammad bin Salman, who wanted his most visible critic permanently silenced.

At first the Saudis denied that Khashoggi was dead, claiming he had left the consulate alive. An inchoate cover-up story was put out piecemeal that the murder had been a rogue operation carried out on the orders of the deputy chief of Saudi intelligence. The Central Intelligence Agency concluded instead that the crown prince had ordered the premeditated murder and had monitored the operation while it was under way, according to senators briefed by the CIA director on the issue. Jamal's body has yet to be recovered. The Turkish defense minister Hulusi Akar has said publicly that parts of the body were probably conveyed to the Kingdom by the assassins using diplomatic immunity.

Since ascending to the number two position in the Kingdom, Muhammad bin Salman has undertaken the most repressive purge in the country's modern history. Saudi Arabia has never had a good human rights record, but the level of repression has increased noticeably since Muhammad bin Salman became crown prince. On November 4, 2017, almost four hundred prominent Saudis were detained without charge at the Ritz Carlton Hotel in Riyadh, held incommunicado, and forced to hand over substantial financial assets to the crown prince. Allegedly part of an anticorruption campaign, it was in fact a moblike shakedown of the rich and important in the Kingdom. No doubt many of those detained were corrupt, but the process lacked accountability and transparency. The commander of the Saudi Arabian National Guard (SANG), Prince Mitab bin Abdullah, was among those detained and was released only after being removed from command of the SANG and giving up a billion dollars. His brother, Prince Turki bin Abdullah, formerly governor of Riyadh, is still in detention. Both are sons of the late King Abdullah. About fifty of the four hundred are still detained.

Some of the detainees were tortured, and at least one was killed. It was an unprecedented act of brutal coercion by the Saudi state. While fostering an atmosphere of fear and intimidation, the episode also resulted in a widespread alienation of the Saudi establishment from the crown prince. He lives in fear of assassination from the many enemies he has made, spending much of his time on his luxury yacht in the Red Sea, where his protection is maximized.

Women activists, including many who had lobbied for decades for the right to drive, were arrested and detained in 2018, often accused of terrorism. Some were tortured. When Canada complained about the detention of one dual national woman, the crown prince expelled the Canadian ambassador and ordered thousands of Saudi students in Canada to return home immediately.

The war in Yemen, Muhammad bin Salman's signature policy commitment, continued through 2018. It is the worst humanitarian catastrophe in the world today, according to the United Nations. Some 14 million Yemenis are in a state of extreme malnourishment, and at least 85,000 children have already starved to death. The war costs Saudi Arabia at least $50 billion a year. By contrast, Iran, which supports the Houthi rebels, spends a pittance. The Houthis have fired ballistic missiles at Riyadh and other Saudi cities. The prince's stated goal, the return of President Abdrabbu Mansour Hadi and his government to power in Sana'a, is nowhere in sight; Hadi almost never leaves Riyadh.

The economic reforms that the crown prince has proposed in his Saudi Vision 2030 program are stalled. The much-touted opening of Aramco was postponed indefinitely, and the king dismissed the project. Foreign investment has fallen and capital flight has increased, the Ritz Carlton shakedown having degraded confidence in the rule of law in the Kingdom.

Yet Donald Trump has supported the crown prince slavishly. He tweeted support for the shakedown at the Ritz, backed the war in Yemen, and tried to ignore Khashoggi's murder and the cover-up in Istanbul. He has openly dismissed the CIA's conclusions. He welcomed the crown prince to a Group of Twenty summit in Buenos Aires in December 2018. The White House issued a statement, clearly written by the president, defending the prince and suggesting that the question of his involvement in the murder was irrelevant. Trump's son-in-law, Jared Kushner, is the crown prince's biggest booster in the White House.

The American media, especially the *Washington Post*, and Congress have been much more critical of the young prince. Many have called him unfit to lead the Kingdom. The Senate passed a bill invoking the War Powers Act to cut off American support for the war in Yemen: an unprecedented rebuke of the Kingdom. It also unanimously condemned the crown prince for the murder of Khashoggi. The outcry is not likely to go away. Many of those who hailed the crown prince as a "revolutionary" only months before Khashoggi's murder have now changed their tune. The chorus is now demanding accountability for aggressive actions in the region and brutal repression at home. Indeed, it is likely the crown prince will conduct more reckless and impulsive acts, leading to further calls for his removal from the line of succession as unfit for the job. Beneath the surface, the Kingdom is in turmoil, more unstable today than at any time since 1958, when King Saud was stripped of his powers by the royal family and the Wahhabi clerical establishment and Faisal was appointed to run the country. The episode is illuminating: it took Faisal another half dozen years to consolidate his power and finally oust Saud completely. Quarrels over succession are the Achilles' heel of absolute monarchs. It is not a sign of stability when the heir apparent is changed twice in three years with no reason.

Concern about Crown Prince Muhammad bin Salman's judgment and future has led to mounting anxiety in the region. One of his fellow monarchs, King Muhammad of Morocco, even refused to meet with the crown prince on his return from the G-20 summit. Oman's Sultan Qaboos has shunned him as well. Turkish president Recep Tayyip Erdogan seems determined to keep the pressure on Riyadh for a full and complete explanation of Khashoggi's murder; he certainly has more evidence to reveal. The Iranians are crowing about crown prince's setbacks. They especially welcome having their Sunni rival bogged down in his own Vietnam in Yemen.

For now, King Salman gives his son his legitimacy and political cover. Without the king, the crown prince would never have achieved the consolidation of power he has. The king leaves day-to-day governance to his son but lays out the Kingdom's position on the big issues. He has been particularly adamant about Saudi Arabia's interest in Jerusalem. When Trump moved the American embassy in Israel from Tel Aviv to Jerusalem, King Salman turned the annual Arab summit in Dhahran into the "Jerusalem summit" in April

2018, condemning the move and affirming that East Jerusalem should be the capital of an independent Palestinian state. The king made the defense of Palestinian rights the "foremost" objective of Saudi policy in his speech to the nation in November 2018, and the Gulf Cooperation Council summit in December reiterated the priority of Jerusalem. The king's strong position on Jerusalem reflects his decades of commitment to the issue and sends a clear signal to his son and others not to compromise or water down the Saudi position. It was also a reminder that the Palestinian issue remains a point of friction in the U.S.-Saudi relationship.

The Saudi-American partnership turned seventy-five in 2018. As I wrote in the 2018 edition of this book, the relationship has had its ups and downs. Some of the downs, such as the 1973 oil embargo, were near-death experiences for the partnership, but it has endured nonetheless. Common interests, not common values, kept it alive in 2001 and 2011.

This time is in one sense profoundly different. The issues raised by Khashoggi's murder and the ongoing carnage in Yemen are more about personality than about policy; they are really about the crown prince. That makes them much harder to resolve through compromise. In the worst case it is possible, though not likely, that the U.S.-Saudi relationship will collapse. If so, its demise will be more troubling for the Kingdom than for the United States. The Kingdom will lose its security blanket in an especially turbulent and dangerous time in the region. America doesn't need Saudi oil any more, though the global economy does. The security-for-oil bargain that FDR negotiated with Ibn Saud in 1943 is antiquated and may be unraveling.

It is also possible the royal family will change the line of succession. The transition from the sons of Ibn Saud to his grandsons was always going to be a test of the Kingdom's monarchy. After Faisal assumed the throne, the succession process was predictable and stable. King Salman has changed that by twice removing a sitting crown prince without explanation since 2015. The rise of his favorite son and now his third crown prince has made the next succession more unpredictable than any in modern Saudi history. The king has not chosen a deputy crown prince. The Kingdom is in uncharted waters, and its future is uncertain. It is now even more important than ever to understand the complex interactions between Saudi kings and American presidents.

Prologue

It was a bitterly cold day in December 2001. The terrible tragedy of September 11 was still fresh in our minds. The attack on America by al Qaeda had stunned the world. It had also created a crisis in America's relations with its oldest ally in the Middle East and the Islamic World. Fifteen of the nineteen terrorists were Saudi citizens and the leader of al Qaeda was another Saudi, Osama bin Laden. Indeed, bin Laden had wanted to create a crisis between Americans and Saudis and deliberately chose his countrymen to attack the World Trade Center, the Pentagon, and the Capitol to damage the relationship.

My wife, Elizabeth, and I were going to the Virginia residence of the Saudi ambassador to the United States, His Royal Highness Prince Bandar bin Sultan bin Abdul Aziz, for lunch. I was leaving the White House after almost five years on the National Security Council staff under Presidents Bill Clinton and George Bush for another assignment with the Central Intelligence Agency. For more than a decade I had worked closely with Prince Bandar, and he wanted to host us for a farewell lunch. His wife, Haifa bint Faisal, the daughter of the former king of Saudi Arabia, was joining us.

The son of the late crown prince Sultan bin Abdul Aziz al Saud, Bandar is a graduate of the Royal Air Force College in Cranwell in the United Kingdom. Bandar later received additional military training in the United States and a master's degree from the Johns Hopkins University School for Advanced International Studies (as did Elizabeth). King Fahd appointed him defense attaché to the United States in 1982 and then ambassador in October 1983. He served in that post until 2005; his twenty-two years in office were longer than any other current ambassador, and this made him the dean of the diplomatic corps in Washington.

His skills as a diplomat, conspirator, and spymaster are legendary. A colleague of mine called Bandar the "greatest show in Washington" for his ability to insinuate himself into American decisionmaking and to influence American foreign policy toward policies that the Kingdom wanted. He worked with five American presidents, ten secretaries of state, and eleven national security advisers during his two decades as the king's man in Washington. The king provided him with his own four-engine wide-bodied Airbus 3000, fitted out with three bedrooms and a lounge so the ambassador could travel quickly and in comfort around the world.[1]

Of course Bandar also had his setbacks and detractors. A plane accident during his Royal Saudi Air Force flying days left him with chronic back pain, which often led to lengthy rehabilitation absences from his job. He sometimes exaggerated his ability to influence his boss's thinking and over-reached beyond his brief. Even his critics admitted, however, that he was a major player both in Washington and Riyadh.

Our lunch was served in a small room in the residence decorated to remember the Battle of Britain, the RAF's historic victory over the Luftwaffe in 1940 that saved England from Nazi invasion. Much of our lunch was a social occasion. Over more than a decade I had spent considerable time with Bandar at his homes in America, England, Switzerland, and in the Saudi kingdom. We had dined on fine meals at luxury restaurants as well as on McDonald's Big Macs, a shared passion, in his residence and at the Saudi embassy. I briefed him in August 1990 on the Iraqi threat after the invasion of Kuwait, shared meetings with three presidents and two Saudi monarchs together, and even stood by him to help explain to his father, then Defense Minister Prince Sultan, why a Saudi conspiracy to divide Yemen had failed. Bandar had sent flowers to celebrate our wedding and had attended a party after it, so we had had previous social encounters. He wanted to wish Elizabeth and me well in our next assignment in London.

Bandar is a great storyteller. He regaled us with one story about a trip he and Haifa took to a spa in England a few years earlier to detoxify their systems with healthy food and country air. After a few days of the regime, Haifa and Bandar slipped out one night to the local Chinese restaurant and indulged in a food binge. They both giggled like teenagers at the memory of their little adventure.

But inevitably work and 9/11 came into the conversation. Bandar was highly agitated that his years of trying to bring the Kingdom and America together as allies were jeopardized by al Qaeda's murderous attack. Bandar had spent his life seeking to persuade Americans, especially American presidents, that the Kingdom is America's most reliable and influential ally in the Islamic world— an ally that could deliver on issues ranging from fighting the Soviet Union in Afghanistan in the 1980s; stopping Saddam's aggression in Kuwait in the 1990s; and helping make peace between Arabs and Israelis over many decades to ensuring the reliable and affordable supply of oil to the world market.

Bin Laden's attack on America jeopardized all of Bandar's work. Instead of an ally, the Kingdom suddenly appeared to many Americans as an enemy. Saudi Arabia was increasingly portrayed in the American media as a hothouse of terrorism, an extremist Islamic state that provided the ideological base for al Qaeda, and a fertile recruiting ground for terrorists. The Kingdom's many enemies were quick to jump on the bandwagon of Saudi phobia. A prominent Israeli author, for example, quickly wrote a book titled *Hatred's Kingdom: How Saudi Arabia Supports the New Global Terrorism*. A former CIA officer wrote another, *Sleeping with the Devil: How Washington Sold Our Soul for Saudi Crude*. There were demands that Washington investigate the Saudi role in allegedly sponsoring al Qaeda in general and to determine what role it played in the 9/11 conspiracy itself. Haifa, Bandar's wife, was even accused of helping to finance the plot.

Bandar found himself accused of being the enemy. A man who had spent decades working with America in the Oval Office, a super fan of "America's team," the Dallas Cowboys, and a generous supporter of many humanitarian causes in the United States, now was suspected of being secretly in bed with America's worst enemy.

Ambassador Prince Bandar bin Sultan greeting the author and his wife,
September 8, 2001, just days before the events of 9/11. (Author's collection)

His problems were not only in Washington, D.C. In Riyadh the royal family was in denial about al Qaeda. Most of the senior princes simply refused to believe a band of Arab and Muslim terrorists in Afghanistan could be so formidable as to attack the American heartland. Two key princes, the minister of interior, Prince Nayef, and the governor of Riyadh, Prince Salman (who became king in 2015), blamed the Israeli secret intelligence service, the Mossad, for the attack. The American ambassador in Saudi Arabia had to get a CIA briefer to Riyadh to show the princes compelling evidence of al Qaeda's culpability.[2]

All this was especially painful for Bandar because just days before 9/11 he had appeared to have helped resolve a falling out between his boss Crown

Prince Abdallah, who was ruling the Kingdom because his brother Fahd had suffered a major stroke, and President George W. Bush. The president had been eager to have the crown prince visit the White House since his inauguration in January, but the crown prince was angry at American support for Israel. Bandar had repeatedly told Bush and his aides the crown prince would not come to Washington as long as Bush did not take a stand supporting a Palestinian state. Secretary of State Colin Powell and I had met with Abdallah in Paris in the summer at the George V Hotel. The Saudi prince gave the secretary a photo book of dead Palestinian children killed in the intifada, or uprising, that was raging in the occupied West Bank and Gaza Strip. He accused Israel of war crimes and America of abetting them. Visibly angry, he categorically refused to see Bush until American policy changed. Our ambassador in Riyadh later characterized the crown prince as "livid" and "bitter" toward Bush due to the Palestinian issue.[5]

At Bandar's suggestion Bush wrote the crown prince in August 2001 and pledged American support for a two-state solution to the Israeli-Palestinian conflict. He promised to make his pledge public at the next session of the United Nations General Assembly, in September. The letter broke the impasse with Abdallah, and he agreed to a future visit to the United States. Then the al Qaeda attacks intervened, the General Assembly was postponed, and the immediate prospect for movement on the Palestinian issue was lost. Bush did promise American support for an independent Palestine at the UN General Assembly when it was rescheduled in November, but for Bandar his success in persuading the Bush administration to be the first to publicly call for a Palestinian state was entirely overshadowed by 9/11. Now Bandar was trying to put back together the Saudi-American alliance under enormous pressure from American public opinion, which saw Saudi Arabia as the root source of terrorism.

There is a basic conundrum at the core of the American relationship with Saudi Arabia. It has always been an uneasy alliance between two very different countries. America is a superpower democracy that aspires to be a tolerant home to a diverse multiethnic and multireligious population, all of whom are equal in the eyes of the law. Saudi Arabia is the world's last absolute monarchy and also is a theocracy with a fundamentalist religious faith, dominated by a Wahhabi clergy that is intolerant and suspicious of outsiders.

This book seeks to tell the story of this conflicted partnership from its origins in 1943 to today. It is not a diplomatic history of the relationship or a comprehensive study of all their interactions. Rather, it focuses on a select number of case studies of interaction between American presidents and Saudi kings to illustrate the nature of the uneasy alliance. For example, it begins with the famous meeting between President Franklin Delano Roosevelt and the founder of the modern Kingdom of Saudi Arabia, King Abdul Aziz al Saud, better known as Ibn Saud, on Valentine's Day in 1945 that forged the American-Saudi entente. That meeting focused heavily on American support for Zionism, the movement advocating the creation of a Jewish state, which FDR supported and the king adamantly opposed. The meeting was a success of sorts. The two men established a personal bond and agreed on an alliance that eventually was based on American security assistance and access to Saudi oil. The contradictions inherent in the partnership have been managed since that meeting by American presidents and Saudi kings for decades. This book focuses on the presidents and kings who have been the managers of the relationship—and how they managed the tensions in the alliance.

This book also looks at the fundamental areas of common interests and differences between Washington and Riyadh that create the dynamic of the alliance. It seeks to answer these questions: Is Saudi Arabia a force for order in the world or a force for chaos? Is the Kingdom an ally in promoting stability and order in the world? Does it promote peace between nations and the goals of the United Nations for a peaceful world order? Or is it a force for chaos, whose Wahhabi ideology is a root base of the global jihad? To try to answer these questions we must begin with an exploration of the Kingdom's origins and the unique alliance between the House of Saud and the al Shaykh family, the successors of Muhammad Ibn 'Abd al Wahhab, the founder of Wahhabism. That story begins two centuries earlier than the American-Saudi alliance, back to 1744 in the Nejd region of the Arabian Peninsula.

The book also looks to the future. Saudi Arabia today is in the midst of a complex generational transition. The sons of Ibn Saud have ruled the Kingdom since his death for over a half-century; now they are preparing to transfer power to his grandsons. It is a potentially destabilizing period. The Kingdom also is surrounded by a region in profound turmoil, with civil wars, failed states, and terrorism on the rise. In the United States a new president, Donald

Trump, is advocating what he calls an "America First" foreign policy, which is significantly different from the policies of any of his predecessors. The Kingdom has a new swashbuckling ambassador in Washington, Prince Khalid bin Salman, another former Royal Saudi Air Force pilot in his late twenties, who also is the son of the current king. Thus, it is a propitious moment to reexamine the American-Saudi relationship and assess its future.

Many of my colleagues at Brookings have been generous with their time and thoughts as I researched and drafted this book. Strobe Talbott, Martin Indyk, Bruce Jones, Michael O'Hanlon, Tamara Wittes, Suzanne Maloney, Kenneth Pollack, Bradley Porter, and Shaqaiq Birashk were all tremendously helpful. The staff of the Brookings library made my life much easier with their assistance. The Brookings Institution Press was, as always, a pleasure to work with and is a fine, professional institution. My wife, Elizabeth, was a constant companion and inspiration.

Any errors of fact or interpretation are solely my responsibility. The Central Intelligence Agency has reviewed the manuscript to ensure there is no inadvertent disclosure of classified information. The views in this book do not represent the views of the CIA or the United States government, nor does the CIA validate any facts or judgments in the book. This does not constitute an official release of CIA information. All statements of fact, opinion, or analysis are those of the author and do not reflect the official positions or views of the Central Intelligence Agency or any other U.S. government agency. Nothing in the contents should be construed as asserting or implying U.S. government authentication of information or CIA endorsement of the author's views. This information has been reviewed solely for classification.

There are many Saudis who contributed to my thinking about their country over many decades. They will know who they are, and I thank them for their insights and friendship.

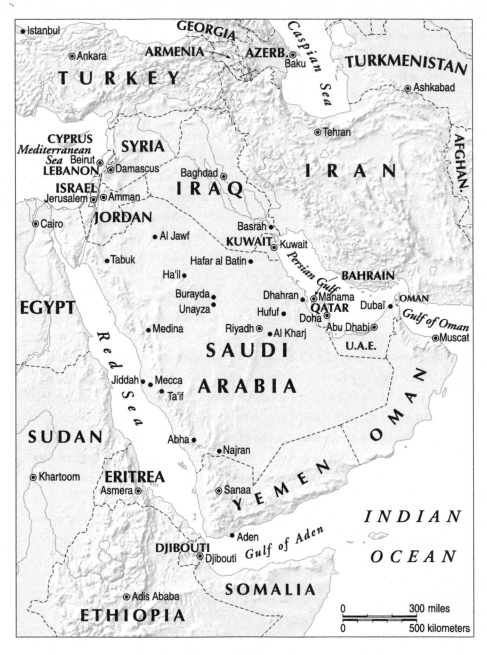

Saudi Arabia and its neighbors

Chapter One

FDR AND IBN SAUD,
1744 TO 1953

I t was an extraordinary meeting during an extraordinary trip. On January 22, 1945, President Franklin Delano Roosevelt left the White House secretly by train for Newport News, Virginia, where he boarded an American naval cruiser, the USS *Quincy*. Ten days later, on February 2, the *Quincy* docked in Malta, where the president transferred to the first presidential aircraft, the *Sacred Cow*, to fly to Yalta in the Crimea for a top-secret conference with Soviet leader Joseph Stalin and British prime minister Winston Churchill. FDR hoped this meeting would build a new world order to prevent another global catastrophe like the Second World War. The Yalta summit finished on February 11 and FDR flew to Cairo for one more vital meeting.[1]

On February 14, 1945, as the Second World War was coming to an end, President Roosevelt met with King Abdul Aziz bin Abdul Rahman al Saud in Egypt, and the two forged a partnership that has endured, despite occasional severe strains, for the last seventy years. Even today, every Saudi official recalls the meeting vividly. Photos of the two leaders together are ubiquitous in

Franklin Roosevelt and Ibn Saud meeting aboard the USS Quincy,
February 14, 1945. (FDR Presidential Library)

Saudi embassies, and the American ambassador's residence in Riyadh is named
after the cruiser on which the two held their summit.

The American-Saudi summit meeting was a closely held secret for security reasons; only a handful on each side knew it was coming. Germany was in
the final agony of defeat, but it still had sharp claws, U-boats and jet fighters
that could surprise an unwary opponent. FDR and Ibn Saud, as the king was
known in the world by 1945, met on the USS *Quincy*, the cruiser that brought
FDR across the Atlantic and then back again to America, in the Great Bitter
Lake along the Suez Canal.

Roosevelt's health was very poor and he had only a few weeks to live. The
trip was grueling and dangerous; FDR would travel 13,842 miles through a
chaotic war zone. Churchill would later write that FDR "had a slender contact
with life." His blood pressure was 260 over 150.[2] The USS *Quincy* was surrounded
by other cruisers and destroyers with an air cap overhead of fighter planes.
German U-boat submarines were a constant menace. The president stayed in
constant contact with the White House map room by cable, and through the map
room's cables he was kept up-to-date on the progress of the war.

Ibn Saud had come from Jidda on an American destroyer, the USS *Murphy*,
with an entourage of bodyguards, cooks, and slaves, plus an astrologer, a for-

tuneteller, and other retainers—and some sheep. The *Murphy* was the first-ever American Navy vessel to visit Jidda. The Navy's only available charts dated from 1834. The king only reluctantly agreed to leave his wives behind in Jidda when he was told their privacy could not be assured in the crowded space of a destroyer. His brother Saud accompanied him as well as his son, Crown Prince Saud, and his interpreter. A senior member of the *ulema*, or clergy, was also in the king's party. Another son, Prince Faisal, stayed behind in Jidda to run affairs and communicated with the king's party every hour by radio to assure Ibn Saud that all was well in the Kingdom. It was the king's first trip outside the Arabian Peninsula aside from a brief visit to Basra in Iraq and his first time to travel at sea.

The two leaders were remarkably different. FDR was the scion of one of America's most famous families. He had grown up in the most modern country in the world and the oldest democracy. After a failed run at vice president in 1920 and a paralyzing polio attack in 1921 he had gone on to win four elections for the presidency. He had led America out of the Great Depression and then through the fire of World War II. He had traveled the world and was, in 1945, undoubtedly the most powerful man in the world.

Ibn Saud had been born in the deserts of the Arabian Peninsula, one of the most backward and impoverished lands in the world. He, too, was a scion of a famous family, but it had fallen on hard times and was living in exile in Kuwait. Ibn Saud had restored his family's rule in the Arabian Peninsula, fought numerous battles, and had gone on to expand the borders of the Kingdom of Saudi Arabia to dominate the peninsula. He had a prodigious sex life, producing forty-three acknowledged sons and at least fifty-five daughters. He told a confidant, the Englishman Harry St John Philby, that he had "married no fewer than 135 virgins."[3] His kingdom was an absolute monarchy, desperately poor but sitting on incredible riches in oil. FDR was the first foreign head of state Ibn Saud had ever met. In 1945 there were only 400 foreigners in all of Saudi Arabia, about one hundred of whom were Americans in the oil fields near Dhahran.[4]

FDR came to the Great Bitter Lake to see Ibn Saud as part of the mission that had taken him to Yalta, fashioning the postwar world. At Yalta he had focused on creating the United Nations to provide the framework for the new political order that would come after the worst war in human history. In the

Suez Canal he was seeking to ensure Saudi support for that order through a bargain that would trade American security guarantees for access to Saudi oil, and Saudi political support for stability in the Middle East.

Oil was very much on Roosevelt's mind. The huge armies, air forces, and navies of the Second World War were fueled by oil—no longer by coal and horsepower, as their predecessors had been. At the peak of military operations in 1944 in Europe, for example, the daily requirement of oil for the U.S. Army and Air Force in just that theater of the global conflict was fourteen times the total amount of gasoline shipped to Europe in the First World War. By 1945, some 7 billion barrels of petroleum had been required to support the allied war effort. American domestic production provided two-thirds of the global output and American refineries almost the entire refined product. Already American experts believed Saudi Arabia would prove to be the home of vast quantities of as yet unproven oil reserves. The Kingdom mattered enormously for postwar energy.[5]

Oil was also on the king's mind. He and his country were broke. The depression and the war had hurt Saudi Arabia badly. The British had been subsidizing the Saudis for years, but they, too, were broke. Only the United States had the resources to help the Saudi economy cope until oil production grew sufficiently to make the Kingdom solvent. Americans had found oil in Saudi Arabia and were exploring for more.

The king was also worried about the Kingdom's security as well as its economy. The Middle East was a rough neighborhood then and remains so now, and the king was well aware of his many enemies. The Hashemites, who ruled Jordan and Iraq and claimed their lineage had a direct family connection to the Prophet Muhammad, longed to recover the two holy cities of Mecca and Medina that Ibn Saud had seized from them two decades earlier. Yemen was a constant source of tension; Ibn Saud had taken territory from its rulers, as well. Even his putative ally Great Britain was an avaricious empire that might yet want Saudi oil. The Kingdom was vulnerable and needed an ally.

Roosevelt and Ibn Saud agreed to work together to ensure stability in the postwar Middle East. The United States would ensure security for the Kingdom, and the Saudis would ensure access to their oil fields. The United States acquired use of Dhahran air base for operations in the Middle East; U.S. oil companies were already operating in the Kingdom. Saudi Arabia declared war on Nazi Germany and Imperial Japan two weeks later, thus securing a seat in the United Nations.

The *Quincy* summit was carefully planned in advance. Ibn Saud's son Prince Faisal, the future king, had visited the United States in November 1943 to begin the courtship. Faisal flew from the Kingdom through Africa to arrive in Miami before heading to Washington. Prince Faisal and his brother Prince Khalid, another future king, stayed at Blair House while meeting with President Roosevelt and senior executive and legislative officials. Faisal was only thirty-seven, but he had been serving as his father's top diplomat since 1919, when he was twelve and had traveled to London to discuss the future of the region after the First World War. After visiting Washington, Faisal and Khalid traveled to Texas, New Mexico, Arizona, California, Colorado, Michigan, New York, New Jersey, and Maryland before flying to London. It was during Faisal's visit that the plans for the Dhahran air base were agreed upon and the United States began providing military assistance to the Kingdom.[6] By the end of the war American lend-lease assistance to the Kingdom amounted to almost $100 million.[7] An American chargé d'affaires arrived in the Kingdom in 1943, the first American diplomat accredited to Saudi Arabia.[8]

Aboard the USS *Murphy* the king and his entourage slept and ate on the deck. They slaughtered a lamb they had brought with them and prayed five times a day, relying on the destroyer captain to tell them the direction to Mecca. Ibn Saud was introduced to apple pie à la mode and loved it. The king saw his first movie, *The First Lady*, a documentary about the aircraft carrier USS *Yorktown* fighting in the Pacific against the Japanese Imperial Navy. The one-hour Technicolor film had exciting scenes of aerial dogfights and crashes on the flight deck. Another American movie was shown to the king's entourage later, *Best Foot Forward*, a Lucille Ball musical comedy that featured a scene where her dress was ripped off. Ibn Saud's sons decided it was not fitting for their father.

Also on board the USS *Murphy* was America's consul to Saudi Arabia, Colonel William Eddy, a Marine hero of World War I. Eddy was born in Lebanon and spoke fluent Arabic. After his service in the First World War he taught at Dartmouth College and the American University of Cairo, then went on to be a college president. At the start of World War II he returned to active duty in the Marines and was assigned as naval attaché, first in Cairo and then in Tangier. After the creation of the Office of Strategic Services (OSS), the forerunner of the Central Intelligence Agency, Eddy was assigned to the OSS. He played a central role in collecting intelligence in French North Africa before the Allied invasion in 1942, but his proposals to arm the Arab population against the French Vichy colonial government were regarded as too dangerous by the Allied military command, which did not want to encourage Arab nationalism.[9] He acquired a reputation for espionage daring and expertise in Arabia. In 1943 Eddy was assigned to Saudi Arabia and in November 1944 he was promoted to the position of American chargé to the kingdom. After the war Eddy would play a part in the early development of the Central Intelligence Agency.

Eddy's account of the summit on the *Quincy* is the principle firsthand source of what happened there. On board the *Murphy* and the *Quincy* Eddy had the difficult duty of reconciling two strong traditions, those of the U.S. Navy and the House of Saud. He did so brilliantly.

On February 14 the two ships came together and Ibn Saud transferred to the USS *Quincy*. FDR sent his daughter Anna Roosevelt Boettiger, who was traveling with him, to Cairo for the day to shop, telling her that "this king is a Muslim, a true believer with lots of wives. As a Muslim he will not permit women in his presence when he is talking to other men."[10] No guns were fired to salute the king, to maintain the secrecy about the meeting, and the two men began an informal discussion on the deck.

The king raised one issue at the start. He had received a message that British prime minister Winston Churchill wanted to see him in Egypt. Churchill had learned from FDR on the final day of the Yalta summit of FDR's upcoming visit to see Ibn Saud. Churchill was determined that the Middle East remain the sole preserve of the British Empire when the war ended, and he was not going to let FDR get a jump on London. The Saudis had had a difficult relationship with the British for decades, largely because the British backed their Arab rivals, the Hashemites, and sought domination of the Arabian Peninsula. Ibn Saud wanted FDR's advice: Should he meet with Churchill? The president, who increasingly regarded Churchill as a Victorian imperialist antique wedded to keeping the empire intact, told the king to see Churchill. He was, undoubtedly, confident that Churchill would misplay his meeting with the Saudis and only reinforce Ibn Saud's inclination to tilt to Washington.

Ibn Saud told the president that the two of them shared much in common, including infirmity. The king could walk only with difficulty, due to his age and many war wounds. FDR was paralyzed from the waist down. FDR gave Ibn Saud one of his extra wheelchairs on the spot to assist the king. It was to become a prized possession even though the king was too large to fit comfortably in the chair.

Lunch was served in the captain's mess below decks. On the way down in the elevator, FDR stopped the lift and smoked two cigarettes, having refrained from smoking in the king's presence. Lunch was prepared by the president's Filipino chefs from the White House. On the menu were curried lamb, rice, grapefruit, eggs, raisins, tomatoes, olives, pickles, chutney, and coconut. The king was so pleased that he asked if he could be given the chef as a gift. In the Kingdom, royal chefs were slaves. FDR cleverly told the king the chef had a contract with the U.S. Navy and could not break it.

After lunch the two went back on deck for a four-hour meeting with only Eddy present as the translator. Now that the two had established a personal connection and agreed that America and Saudi Arabia should be allies in the postwar world, Roosevelt wanted to raise another issue: the fate of Europe's Jewish survivors of the Holocaust and of a Jewish homeland in Palestine.

In Yalta the president had told Stalin he was going to see Ibn Saud and raise the question of a Jewish homeland for the survivors of the German concentration camps. Stalin said the Soviets had tried to create a Jewish homeland in Birobidzhan in Siberia. Stalin had created the Jewish Autonomous Oblast of Birobidzhan in 1934 as a bid to increase support for the Soviet Union among Russia's Jews, but the idea had never gotten much support, in part because Stalin was a notorious anti-Semite. FDR told Stalin he was a Zionist and that he hoped to convince Ibn Saud to support a Jewish homeland in Palestine.[11]

In 1945 Saudi Arabia and Yemen were the only independent countries in the Arab world. The rest were colonies or protectorates of Britain, France, or Italy, their governments pawns of the European imperial powers. Egypt, for example, had a king put in power by the British army. FDR did meet with King Farouk on his trip to the Suez Canal, but Farouk had no credibility as an Arab leader and was rightly regarded as a British puppet.

Ibn Saud, on the other hand, was a credible defender of Arab and Islamic interests. He was not under British protection, although London liked to regard itself as the preeminent power in the peninsula, and as a Wahhabi Muslim Ibn Saud was rightly seen as a "true believer," as FDR had told his daughter Anna. If Ibn Saud could be persuaded to support a Jewish homeland in Palestine, it would be a major diplomatic coup for Zionism and for Roosevelt.

The president opened by saying he wanted to get the king's advice on the question of Palestine and the Jews' desire for a state there. The Auschwitz concentration camp in Poland had been liberated by the Red Army three weeks earlier, and the full extent of the Nazis' mass murder was now becoming clear to the world. FDR argued the survivors should go to Palestine, where the Zionist movement had been building the basis for a Jewish homeland for decades.

The king was firm in his reply. "The Jews should return to live in the lands from which they were driven. The Jews whose homes were completely destroyed and who have no chance of livelihood in their homelands should be given living space in the Axis countries which oppressed them." Roosevelt argued the Jews of Europe did not want to live in Germany. The king was unpersuaded, saying, "make the enemy and the oppressor pay; that is how we Arabs wage war. Amends should be made by the criminal, not by the innocent bystander. What injury have the Arabs done to the Jews of Europe? It is the Christian Germans who stole their homes and lives. Let the Germans pay."[12]

Roosevelt tried another tack. The Arabs were numerous and their lands extensive; the Jews were few in number and sought only Palestine. The king looked FDR in the eye and quietly uttered one word: "No."[13] Then the president tried an idea that Churchill had suggested, that the Jews could build their state in Libya. Libya had been an Italian colony before the war and had a small population. Once again Ibn Saud rejected the notion of any part of the Arab world being ceded to the Jews. It would not be fair to the Libyan Arabs. "Give them [the Jewish survivors] and their descendants the choicest lands and homes of the Germans who oppressed them."[14]

FDR decided to end this part of the conversation with a commitment to the king. He told Ibn Saud that as president "he wished to assure His Majesty that he would do nothing to assist the Jews against the Arabs and would make no move hostile to the Arab people." His government "would make no change in its basic policy in Palestine without full and prior consultation with both Jews and Arabs."[15] The king was pleased with the president's commitment.

The conversation finished with a discussion of the future of Syria and Lebanon, French trusteeships since 1919. Roosevelt assured the king that the United States would press the French to give them independence just as the United States was giving the Philippines its independence after the war. Ibn Saud said: "The USA never colonizes nor enslaves."[16]

The meeting then almost collapsed into failure. Roosevelt said he must start his voyage home (it would take sixteen days to sail back to Virginia). The king was appalled. Under Arab custom it was imperative that the king now host the president for a meal on the USS *Murphy*. The president had hosted him for lunch, now honor demanded the king host the president.

Always astute to the needs of his interlocutors, FDR said for security reasons the USS *Quincy* must leave. Ibn Saud turned to Eddy and blamed him for this insult, not the last time an ambassador was to take the blame for a decision he had no role in making. Then the king suggested a compromise: he would serve the president Arabian coffee. Two coffee servants appeared in minutes and poured the king and president cardamom-scented Arabian coffee.

Gifts were exchanged. The king gave FDR four complete sets of Arab robes, a solid gold knife, and a vial of perfume. His retainers also gave Anna and Eleanor Roosevelt Arab gowns, perfumes, bracelets, anklets, rings, pearl earrings, and belts. Roosevelt gave the king a gold medal and told him that he was also arranging for a twin engine DC3 to be provided to the Kingdom with an American crew for the king's use. When it arrived later it had a swivel throne chair so the king could always face Mecca while airborne. Finally, the president's navy physician gave the king's doctor a small box containing the new medicine penicillin. The king's doctor asked if it would cure venereal disease, and the physician said it would. The king was very impressed.[17]

Despite his poor health, FDR had been a masterful host. He used his famous charm with the king, he engaged intensively on the issues, and was keen to make a connection with the king. Eddy said later the president was in fine form although the strains of his years in office were also clear.[18]

When the two-day voyage ended, the king gave the *Murphy*'s captain a gold dagger, the other officers' Arab robes and watches engraved with Ibn Saud's name, and every member of the crew money in sterling. In return the destroyer's captain gave the king two submachine guns and a pair of Navy binoculars. It was a small start to America's arms relationship with the Saudis.

There was one final moment of drama. After the president's party had departed and the king was transferred to Cairo, his personal physician approached Eddy to report that the king's medicines had been inadvertently left on the *Murphy*. They had to be retrieved. Eddy immediately sent word to get them and also asked the chief medical officer of the U.S. Army in Cairo to review the list of medicines and see if they could be reproduced from U.S. military stocks. The army doctor reviewed the list and reported 210 of the 240 items on the list were aphrodisiacs, most of which were entirely phony and unavailable. Fortunately, the crew of the USS *Murphy* found the original medicines on the ship and they were returned without the king ever knowing of their loss. His doctor went on to be Saudi Arabia's ambassador to France.[19]

FDR found Ibn Saud to be a fascinating figure but a tough negotiator. After the five-hour meeting the president told his special adviser Bernard Baruch that "among all the men that I had to deal with during my lifetime, I have met no one than this Arab monarch from whom I could extricate so little: the man has an iron will."[20] In April, just a week before he died in Georgia, FDR wrote Ibn Saud a letter reaffirming his promise that he "would take no action, in my capacity as Chief of the Executive Branch of this Government, which might prove hostile to the Arab people." He promised full consultation on Palestine. The king believed Roosevelt's promise was binding on the American government.[21]

After the king and his entourage went back to the USS *Murphy*, they traveled to see Churchill in Egypt. The two met at the Hotel Auberge du Lac on the shore of Lake Karoun fifty miles south of Cairo. The meeting took place over lunch. During their luncheon Churchill smoked and drank champagne, and the Saudis felt insulted. Churchill's aides had told him smoking and drinking alcohol were offensive, but the prime minister responded, "No, I won't pull down the flag. I feel as strongly about smoking as His Majesty feels about not smoking." He told the king, "My religion prescribes as an absolute sacred rite smoking cigars and drinking alcohol before, after and if need be during all meals and intervals between them." The king offered Churchill a glass of water from a well in Mecca.[22]

The Anglo-Saudi summit's substance was as troubled as its ambiance. Churchill also pressed for Saudi support for a Jewish state in Palestine. The prime minister told the king that the British Empire had been his ally for twenty years, subsidizing the Kingdom for many of those years, and now wanted Saudi help as it dealt with the difficult situation in Palestine, which had been a British trusteeship since 1919. Churchill had helped implement Britain's commitment to a Jewish state in Palestine when he was minister for colonial affairs in the 1920s—indeed he had designed the British Empire's domination of the Middle East at a conference in Cairo in 1921.

As he had been with FDR, the king was blunt. He told Churchill that "promotion of Zionism from any quarter must indubitably bring bloodshed, widespread disorder in the Arab lands with certainly no benefit to Britain or anyone else." Instead of agreeing to help smooth the way to a Jewish state, Ibn Saud asked for assurances from London that Jewish immigration to Palestine be stopped completely.[23]

The king told Consul Eddy later that he was impressed at "the contrast between the President and Mr. Churchill. Mr. Churchill speaks deviously, evades understanding and changes the subject to avoid commitment, forcing me repeatedly to bring him back to the point. The President seeks understanding in conversations, his effort is to make the two minds meet, to dispel darkness and shed light upon this issue." He concluded, "I have never met the equal of the President in character, wisdom and gentility."[24]

Even the British-Saudi parting was unpleasant. The king gave Churchill a sword and dagger set with jewels and a large diamond for Mrs. Churchill. Churchill gave the king a Rolls Royce automobile, but it was a right-hand drive. The king liked to sit in the front when he rode in a car, but if he sat to the left of the driver, in Arab culture he would be dishonored. The king never used the car. He also complained that the food on the British Royal Navy cruiser that took him home to Jidda was unpalatable.[25]

Overall, Roosevelt's trip to Egypt to meet Ibn Saud was a success despite the differences over Palestine. The king's meetings with FDR and Churchill, in retrospect, can be seen as the initial passing of the torch of power in the Middle East from the United Kingdom to the United States. It would mark the beginning of the U.S. alliance with the Kingdom, America's oldest ally in the Middle East. Every king and every president since 1945 has reaffirmed the partnership begun on the *Quincy*.

The most concrete result of the summit on the *Quincy* was the construction of an American airfield in Dhahran. The formal agreement to build the base was signed on August 5, 1945, by Eddy. The United States Air Force built more than fifty buildings, all air-conditioned, including a restaurant, hospital, movie theater, and housing for 500 personnel. The original agreement leased the Dhahran base to the USAF for three years. It also provided for the American civilian airline TWA to use the airfield for commercial air traffic on the New York-Cairo-Bombay route. It was the first American military facility in the Arabian Peninsula, previously the exclusive preserve of the British Empire.[26]

FDR's genius was to see the future. In the midst of a global war, the president looked to the future and recognized Saudi Arabia's huge potential importance not only for oil but for what we now call soft power in the Islamic world. Roosevelt sought to harness that importance to America, detaching it from Britain, as America prepared to be the guardian of the postwar peace. It is unlikely any other American in 1945 was as far-sighted as FDR.

The meeting on the *Quincy* also illustrated what has become the fundamental paradox in the relationship. Aside from commerce Saudi Arabia and the United States have few values in common. The Kingdom is an absolute monarchy named after the ruling family; the United States is a vibrant democracy. Saudi Arabia is one of the most intolerant countries in the world regarding religious freedom; the United States prizes freedom of religion. Saudis cannot criticize the king or the ruling family; Americans exercise their freedom of speech. Absent a bedrock of shared values, the alliance has always been defined primarily by shared threats and enemies. Even the first summit was dominated by argument over Palestine's future. It has always been an uneasy partnership.

The Kingdom's Origin

The beginnings of what was to become today's Kingdom of Saudi Arabia can be traced to 1744. The heart of the kingdom's leadership is an alliance of two families. One is the al Saud family, which has provided political leadership in an absolute monarchy since 1744. The second is the al Shaykh family, which has provided religious leadership and spiritual guidance for the kingdom since 1744, when the two families sealed an agreement to work together as partners in building a state in the Arabian Peninsula. This partnership between a governing royal family and a family with its own special claim to a set of theological beliefs is the crucial glue in the political and religious chemistry that makes Saudi Arabia.

Two men created Saudi Arabia. Muhammad ibn Saud, the founder of the dynasty of the House of Saud, was, in the mid-eighteenth century, the amir of Diriyya, a town in the Nejd, the center of the Arabian Peninsula. The Nejd was a barren backwater of the Islamic world, so poor that no outsider wanted to waste the resources to govern it. It was divided among a number of local leaders. Muhammad ibn Saud was one of many local potentates.[27]

But Muhammad ibn Saud would prove to be more than just another Arabian potentate. Between 1744 and his death in 1765 he gradually expanded Saudi control beyond the agricultural town of Diriyya to most of the Nejd, including the town of Riyadh, today the Kingdom's capital. He is now remembered as the founder of the first Saudi kingdom, and the Imam Muhammad ibn Saud Islamic University in Riyadh is named in his honor.

Central to Muhammad ibn Saud's success in conquering the Nejd was his alliance with the second key figure, Muhammad ibn 'Abd al Wahhab. Wahhab is one of the most controversial figures in the history of Islam. To devout Saudis he is the man who restored Islam to its origins, a preacher who taught the right path for believers. The current king, Salman, has created a center for the study of Wahhab's life and preachings on the site of the original Saudi capital, Diriyya; Salman's personal palace is nearby. The center has museums depicting life in the first Saudi state, a library of books by Wahhab and his descendants, and a Memorial Hall illustrating his contribution to Islam. At the center of the complex is a reconstruction of the first house of worship Wahhab built.[28] King Salman's son Sultan, Saudi Arabia's only astronaut, has been the driving force behind the reconstruction of Diriyya at his father's behest.[29] Qatar, also a Wahhabi state, named its state mosque after him, the Muhammad ibn 'Abd al Wahhab mosque in Doha.

To his many enemies, Wahhab is the archvillain of intolerance and the spiritual father of al Qaeda and the Islamic State. Efforts have been made to paint him as a tool of British imperialism, with one conspiracy theory alleging that he was recruited by a British spy in Basra to encourage conflict between Muslims.[30] Even the name of his movement is controversial. Wahhabis generally do not like to be called Wahhabis because it elevates Muhammad ibn 'Abd al Wahhab to the rank of a prophet or a holy figure, an elevation that borders on the idolatry that Wahhab preached against his entire life. They prefer to be called Unitarians or *muwahiddun*, or just Muslims.

Because of his central role in the creation of Saudi Arabia and its ideology, it is crucial to study Muhammad ibn 'Abd al Wahhab in some depth. More than any other figure, Wahhab set the ideological base for what Saudi Arabia stands for. He lived in a backwater of Arabia on the edge the Ottoman Empire, and his life story has many gaps and uncertainties. His enemies vilified him effectively. Only recently has Muhammad ibn 'Abd al Wahhab been the subject of a detailed biography by a British scholar, who drew on original sources to paint a portrait of one of the most revolutionary and radical figures in the history of Islam.

Muhammad Ibn 'Abd al Wahhab was born in the Nejd in 1703, the son of a local preacher and judge. He traveled to Mecca and Medina to perform the holy pilgrimage and to study. His first mentor was an Indian scholar, Muhammad Hayat al Sindhi, who emphasized a return to the original sources of Islam, the Quran, and the early accounts of the prophet's life. In the middle 1730s Ibn 'Abd al Wahhab traveled to Basra, a major city in southern Iraq. Basra was much more cosmopolitan then than any city in Arabia and was home to a large Shia population, as well as many Persians. Christians and Jews lived in Basra as well as traders and merchants from India. Representatives of the English and Dutch East India Companies were engaged in global trading deals there. The city was under the nominal control of the Ottoman Empire but was often threatened by the Safavid Empire in neighboring Iran.

Basra had an important impact on Wahhab's thinking and development. He may have begun writing his first book during his time in Basra. He certainly began preaching against the diversity of Islamic practice while in the city. Ibn 'Abd al Wahhab denounced the worship of Ali, the nephew of Muhammad, who is the central figure in Shia Islam. He also denounced the practice of worshipping local Muslim saints and clerics; he spoke against mystical Sufism and the veneration of the tombs of respected Muslim clerics. He was expelled from the city at some point in the 1730s and moved to what is now the Eastern Province of Saudi Arabia, also known as al Ahsa or al Hasa. This region along the Persian Gulf has a significant Shia presence and, like Basra, apparently played an important part in Wahhab's hostility to Shi'ism. He was expelled from al Hasa for his views and returned to the Nejd.

He did not travel outside that region for the rest of his life.[31] Some biographies claim Wahhab traveled much further, perhaps to Damascus, Baghdad, and even into Persia. The best recent scholarship, by Michael Crawford, a British scholar whose biography is the most credible to date, dismisses these reports as inaccurate and invented by Wahhab's detractors.[32]

In the Nejd, Wahhab aligned himself at first with the ruler of his own native town. Again he spoke out against what he called polytheists who venerated local tombs and even trees. He destroyed these false idols with help from his followers. He said that Arabia had fallen out of grace since the death of the prophet and had returned to the state of ignorance that had preceded Muhammad's prophecy in the seventh century. He ordered stoned to death a woman who publicly announced her adultery. He was expelled from the community and left for Diriyya, where he came under the protection of Abdul Aziz.

The eldest son of Muhammad al Saud, Abdul Aziz had already become a follower of Ibn 'Abd al Wahhab, as were several of his brothers and probably his favorite wife. Taking in the radical preacher was a dangerous move because it put the small Saudi community at war with its neighbors and the Ottoman Empire itself. For the rest of Muhammad al Saud's life he was engaged in battles to defend Diriyya and, ultimately, expand his realm to seize Riyadh and the rest of the Nejd. After his father's death, Abdul Aziz continued the process of expanding the borders of what is now called the first Saudi kingdom.

Muhammad ibn 'Abd al Wahhab's most important book is *Kitab al Tawhid*, and it deals with the central message of his preaching. Wahhab taught that the oneness of God, *tawhid*, is the most important essence of Islam. By this he meant two things. First, God is the sole creator, provider, giver of life and death, and orderer of affairs in the universe. Second, God alone should be the addressee of prayers, supplications, sacrifices, and all other forms of worship. There should be no intermediary between a believer and God, no intercessor to appeal to for help with prayer or devotion. The Prophet Muhammad, as important as he is to Islam, should not be worshipped. Those who pray to Ali (Shia) or Jesus (Christians) or some local, venerated Muslim cleric or saint are infidels even if they claim to be Muslims.

From his perspective almost all Muslims in the world were, thus, infidels or at least polytheists and idol worshippers. The illiterate nomads of Arabia, the Bedouin, were especially ignorant in Wahhab's view because they knew nothing about their beliefs other than what their local cleric told them and often venerated trees or sacred tombs. The Shia were especially ignorant, with their elaborate ceremonies celebrating the struggles of Ali and his son Husayn, their veneration of senior clerics called ayatollahs, and their failure to understand the importance of *tawhid*. Wahhab's own experiences in Basra and al Hasa had bred a deep antagonism toward all Shia. When the first Saudi state conquered al Hasa after his death, the Saudis tried to convert the Shia population to the new Wahhabi viewpoint or at least destroy any vestige of Shi'ism in the mosques and public space.

Given the centrality of *tawhid* in the narrative of Ibn 'Abd al Wahhab it was inevitable that a second major element of his thinking concerned the nature of the Wahhabi community. It must be a community apart, separated from the ignorant. It was essential that infidels not be allowed to travel in the community because they would corrupt it. Equally important, the believers should not travel among the ignorant, again because they might be corrupted. Thus the early version of Wahhabi Islam was very xenophobic and aloof from the outside world. It guarded its righteousness by staying apart from the unbelievers. The believers must be isolated from the infidels.[33]

A final key principle was the importance of jihad or holy warfare to expand the community of the faithful. It was incumbent on every believer, and especially those in positions of leadership, to expand the boundaries of the believers and defeat the ignorant. As a result, "the obligation to wage jihad was absolute" for the community and the Saudi leadership especially.[34] War between the Saudis and the Ottomans was virtually inevitable.

After the conquest of Riyadh, Muhammad Ibn 'Abd al Wahhab largely retired from everyday public life and devoted himself to writing and preaching. He wrote an extended biography of the Prophet Muhammad and several other books about the teachings of other key Islamic figures. He died in June 1792 at the age of eighty-five. He left six sons who would continue his work and founded the al Shaykh family dynasty that is the al Saud family's most crucial partner.

Muhammad Ibn 'Abd al Wahhab did not try to develop a concept of an Islamic political order or of a state. Such concepts were simply unknown in the Nejd in the eighteenth century. He was content to leave governance to the Saudi family. He did not call for the creation of an Islamic caliphate or an empire uniting all Muslims. Wahhab's vision was rather simple: the power of *tawhid* was the basis for understanding everything else. The contradictions between a simple and radical worldview and the realities of governance and diplomacy were challenges for Wahhab's successors, not for the first Saudi state. The first Saudi state made no compromises with the ignorant and waged war relentlessly against them.

In the last decade of the eighteenth century the first Saudi state grew to become much larger than the current Kingdom of Saudi Arabia. At its peak in 1808 it included all the territory that is today Saudi Arabia except for the port of Jidda, which remained an outpost of the Ottoman Empire. It also included what is today Qatar, Bahrain, the United Arab Emirates, and parts of northern Oman. The Hadramawt region in south Yemen was a Saudi vassal. Only two parts of the peninsula with unique Islamic sects of their own, Zaydi Shia Yemen and Ibadi Oman, held out against the Saudi state. Mecca and Medina were under Saudi control, an enormous humiliation to the Ottomans who regarded themselves as the true defenders of Islam and the holy cities. In the north, Saudi armies raided Iraq, capturing the wealthy Shia holy city of Kerbala and destroying the tomb of Husayn. They also laid siege to Najaf and Basra in Iraq and Sana'a in Yemen. For a brief moment it appeared the Saudis would dominate the entire Arabian Peninsula. At its peak, the first Saudi state ruled some 2.4 million people.[35]

The Ottoman Empire, meanwhile, had been under attack from Napoleon and France. The French had invaded Egypt in 1798 and marched into Palestine. The French threat was not fully defeated until late in 1801, and even then the Ottomans were preoccupied with the Napoleonic wars in Europe for several more years. The Ottomans, in 1811, dispatched an army from Egypt, which regained control of Mecca and the Hijaz. In 1818 they marched into the Nejd and captured Diriyya. The senior members of the Saud family that survived the siege and capture of their capital were imprisoned and sent to Cairo. King 'Abd Allah al Saud was sent on to Istanbul where he was executed. After storming out of the Nejd and creating a state, the House of Saud's fortunes had collapsed and the family was all but destroyed.[36]

The Second Saudi Kingdom

The Turkish-Egyptian army that destroyed the first Saudi state did not stay long in Arabia. Political challenges at home required the use elsewhere of the resources that had conquered Arabia. In the 1820s the Ottomans withdrew the bulk of their forces from the Nejd. One of the surviving members of the House of Saud, Turki ibn Abdallah, began to rebuild the Saudi empire. Turki recovered Riyadh from the Turks in 1824. He was assassinated by a cousin in 1834, and his son Faisal bin Turki al Saud succeeded him. The current Saudi leadership are direct descendants of Faisal.

Faisal was forced into exile in 1838 by another Ottoman army, only to return in 1843 to resume Saudi rule of Riyadh and the Nejd. He was successful in bringing the bulk of central Arabia back under Saudi and Wahhabi rule. His forces retook control of the Eastern Province, or al Hasa, from the Turks. Most of what is today the United Arab Emirates and all of Qatar also fell under the control of the second Saudi state. In 1861 Faisal threatened to seize Bahrain, as well, but the British Royal Navy intervened to protect the island from Saudi conquest. The British raj in India felt keeping Bahrain out of the orbit of the Saudis was in the interest of the empire.

Otherwise Faisal was careful not to provoke the British. Unlike the first Saudi state, the second did not try to reach beyond the Arabian Peninsula into Iraq or to fight the Ottomans for the Hejaz and the British in the Gulf states. The Saudis had learned there were some limits to their power and that accommodation with the dominant powers of the day was a necessary constraint enabling their survival. The British gradually consolidated their influence all along the southern shore of the Persian Gulf from Kuwait to Oman, leaving only al Hasa out of their orbit.

Faisal died in December 1865. Infighting among his four sons was the hallmark of the next thirty years of the second Saudi state. Each claimed the right to the throne, and some were prepared to make tactical alliances with the Turks to defeat their brothers. Power and control of Riyadh passed from one to another. In 1871 the Turks recovered control of al Hasa, and in 1887 the Saudis were driven out of Riyadh. By 1893 the House of Saud was in exile in Kuwait where the amir gave them sanctuary.

Between 1744 and 1893 there were fourteen successions in the House of Saud, as power passed from one king to another. The first two, from Muhammad bin Saud to his son Abdul Aziz and then to his son Saud, were smooth and uncontested. The three kings ruled from 1744 to 1814, and they oversaw the great growth of the first Saudi Kingdom. The next twelve successions witnessed eleven power struggles within the family as power was transferred from one monarch to another. Of fourteen successions in the first two Saudi states, eleven were contested. The founders avoided succession struggles; the generations that followed were consumed with them.[37]

The long history of the first and second Saudi states is largely unknown in America. The intricacies of their rise and fall has not been taught by many American scholars, even to students of the region. For Saudis, of course, the history of their kingdom is very much a part of their national identity, and the narrative of the rise, fall, rise, fall, and rise again of their state is central to their worldview. Saudis look back on their past, as all nations do, and see lessons learned—or in some cases, lessons learned but later forgotten or set aside.

If Saudis today study the first Saudi state for inspiration about their faith and their roots in the eighteenth century, the second state is a lesson in the dangers of family disharmony. Surrounded by powerful enemies like the Ottomans and the British, the family prospered when its enemies were distracted and the family was united. When the regional powers were able to deploy forces into Arabia and the family was split, the House of Saud was on the defensive if not defeated. The nineteenth century was a time of peril for the family and their Wahhabi ally because the royal family was divided and let the door open to foreign conspiracy against them. In the twentieth century the Saudis would not repeat this mistake.

Ibn Saud and the Third Saudi State

Abd al Aziz ibn Saud was born in Riyadh in 1880. The city was anarchic during much of his childhood as the various factions of the al Saud family competed for power. As one biography notes, "The young Abd al Aziz was aware of an all pervading atmosphere of insecurity and sense of impermanence during his early years."[38] It was a searing experience that guided him through the rest of his life.

In 1891 under pressure from the Turks and their Arab allies, his father Abd al Rahman al Saud took the family out of Riyadh and into exile. At first they tried to survive in the harsh desert of the Rub al Khali, a huge expanse in what is now southern Saudi Arabia. In 1894 they moved to Kuwait. The local amir in Kuwait was constantly trying to balance the strength of his more powerful neighbors, and giving the Saudis protection in the mid-1890s was temporarily in the interest of the Ottomans who claimed Kuwait as their territory and did not want the rivals of the al Sauds to get too powerful in Arabia.

Kuwait was a much more cosmopolitan place than Riyadh, with merchants from around the world trading and dealing in the port. Ibn Saud was tutored by the members of the al Shaykh family who accompanied the Saudi exiles. The young Ibn Saud was exposed to a world much more complex than that of the Nejd, and he befriended up-and-coming members of the Kuwaiti royal family. The port of Kuwait was also a sought-after prize in the competition between the rival European empires of the late nineteenth century, including Germany and Britain. The British won the battle, and Ibn Saud maneuvered deftly between factions in the Kuwaiti ruling family and backed the group aligned with the British.

With the support of Kuwait, Ibn Saud decided to return to Riyadh and re-establish Saudi control of the Nejd. With a handful of supporters he captured the central fort in the town on January 15, 1902. Ibn Saud's elderly father Abd al Rahman came back from Kuwait and presented his son with a sword that had belonged to Muhammad ibn 'Abd al Wahhab and had been handed down from one Saudi leader to the next for generations. Abd al Rahman would nominally serve as the ceremonial leader of the new Saudi state until his death in 1928, but in practice Ibn Saud ran the kingdom. He fought in over fifty battles between 1902 and 1932.

In the dozen years after taking Riyadh, Ibn Saud gradually restored Saudi authority over the Nejd. He also began a dialogue with the British consul in Kuwait, Captain William Henry Irvine Shakespear, a fluent Arabist and adventurer who reported to the British viceroy in India who had responsibility for Persian Gulf affairs in the empire. Shakespear took the first photographs of Ibn Saud, and the two forged a strong friendship. Ibn Saud was interested in a dialogue with the British to deter the Turks and his other enemies. In this he was breaking with the Saudi and Wahhabi tradition of seeing all foreigners as infidels who could not be dealt with. It was dramatic evidence that the third Saudi state was going to be a more pragmatic and realistic state than its two predecessors.

In 1913 the Saudis invaded and occupied al Hasa, which had been an Ottoman province. Preoccupied with wars in the Balkans and Libya, the Turks had no resources to defend a faraway desert province. The local Shia community was suppressed, although Ibn Saud granted some local notables in the main Shia towns of Qatif and al Hasa a measure of local rule. Saudi discrimination against the Shia minority (perhaps as many as 10 to 15 percent of Saudis today) is deeply entrenched in the Wahhabi faith. No Shia has ever been a minister in the Kingdom, and only once has a Shia been a Saudi ambassador (to Iran in 1999–2003). The region was renamed the Eastern Province.[39]

With the outbreak of the First World War in August 1914, Ibn Saud's fledgling state found itself in the middle of a global power struggle. When the Ottomans joined the war on the side of the Germans, the allies began planning to carve up the Turkish Empire between them. The British were eager to get the Saudis on their side. Shakespear offered Ibn Saud a treaty guaranteeing Saudi independence under the protection of the viceroy of India and the British Empire. In return Ibn Saud would not support Ottoman calls for a Muslim jihad against the allies. Saud agreed to the proposed treaty, which was dispatched to India and London for review.

Before an answer was returned, Shakespear was killed in a battle between the Saudis and a rival pro-Turkish tribe, the Rashids, in January 1915. His death removed the urgency behind British dealings with Ibn Saud. The Saudi file receded into the background for the British, and they, instead, found a different Arab ally in the sharif of Mecca and his Hashemite family that ruled the Hejaz, the area of current-day Saudi Arabia bordering the Red Sea. The British did, ultimately, sign a treaty with Ibn Saud in 1916 and provided him with some rifles and a small monthly stipend to pay his supporters, but the main focus of British policy in Arabia shifted from the Saudis to the Hashemites.

Ibn Saud stayed on the British side in the war and greatly expanded his territory at the expense of the pro-Turkish Rashid tribe. When the war ended, the Saudis and Hashemites fought their own war to determine control of Arabia. Ibn Saud relied on his tribal army's shock troops, called the *Ikhwan*, or brothers. These were extreme supporters of Wahhabism who were dedicated to expanding the borders of the Saudi-Wahhabi state, much like the early Muslims had in the golden age of Islam or the Wahhabi armies of the first Saudi state in the eighteenth century. They were settled in oases and practiced a stern and extreme puritanism.

In 1925 Ibn Saud's Ikhwan army took Mecca and Medina. The Hashemites were expelled from the Hejaz, although thanks to their British connection they remained in Jordan and Iraq. In Mecca and Medina the Saudis purged the holy cities of what they considered idols. Mosques or other structures built to remember members of Muhammad's family or those of his key supporters were destroyed. In particular, the Jannat al Baqi cemetery in Medina—the burial site adjacent to the prophet's mosque for many of his family members, close companions, and other central figures of early Islam—was leveled, destroying many sites revered especially by Shia. The site also had been destroyed by the first Saudi state and then restored by the Ottomans. The destruction of the Baqi cemetery remains an outstanding source of friction between the Saudis and Shia today.

In January 1926 Ibn Saud was proclaimed king of the Nejd and Hejaz. The British negotiated a new treaty with Ibn Saud a year later, recognizing him as an independent king and accepting his conquest of the Hejaz. In return Ibn Saud accepted British control of the Gulf emirates and their position in Jordan and Iraq. He also accepted the transfer of part of the northern Hejaz to Jordan, especially the cities of Aqaba and Ma'an, which had historically been ruled as part of the Hejaz. In addition, Ibn Saud ceded claims to the narrow eastern wing of Jordan that connects it to Iraq.[40] Relations with the Hashemite monarchs in Amman and Baghdad remained strained well into the 1950s.

The Ikhwan were dissatisfied with Ibn Saud's decision to accept British primacy in the region and to halt the expansion of the Saudi state further to the north and east. After a bloody two-year-long rebellion, they were crushed as a military force. The British Royal Air Force helped Ibn Saud defeat the Ikhwan by bombing its raiding parties whenever they moved close to Jordan or Kuwait. The Wahhabi clerical establishment stayed loyal to the Saudi monarchy, and in return its hegemony over domestic and social issues was confirmed.[41]

While the Ikhwan was crushed, another institution of the Wahhabi establishment flourished. These were the religious police, or *mutawween*. These were official enforcers of the religious rules and rituals of Wahhabi Islam. No one was beyond their authority. Most mutawween were Nejdis even in the Hejaz and al Hasa, where they were brought in to enforce discipline. Later they were given the official title of the Committee for the Propagation of Virtue and the Prohibition of Vice.[42]

The Saudis fought another war in 1934 with the only other independent state in the Arab world, Yemen. After the nominal Ottoman control of Yemen ended in 1918, the Zaydi Shia monarchy proclaimed the country's independence. The Wahhabi and Zaydi monarchies were uncomfortable neighbors. In the war Ibn Saud's forces defeated the Yemenis and then took several border regions in the resulting peace agreement, expanding the Saudi state to the southwest. Many Yemenis have never accepted the outcome of the 1934 war as legitimate.

The Kingdom of Saudi Arabia was formally proclaimed in 1932. The conquest of the Hejaz had made Ibn Saud the defender of the holy cities and provided a modest income from fees paid by pilgrims coming to the holy cities, especially during the annual Hajj. But the Great Depression of the 1930s sharply reduced the number of pilgrims each year with a resulting significant decline in the Kingdom's income. In the boom years of the 1920s, about 100,000 pilgrims came each year for the Hajj; by 1940 the number had dropped to only 37,000.[43]

Ibn Saud was increasingly desperate for another source of income. Oil had been discovered decades earlier in Iran, Bahrain, and Iraq, and the global oil companies were eager to explore the Kingdom, especially al Hasa, now known as the Eastern Province. The king in 1933 turned to an American oil company, Standard Oil Company of California, and signed a deal for exploration. This signing took place in his new palace in Riyadh, which had just been built for him by a young emigrant from the Hadramawt in Yemen, Muhammad bin Laden.[44]

The Americans found oil in 1938. Ibn Saud had chosen Standard Oil in large part because it was American and he did not want a British or other European oil company exploring the Kingdom for fear it would lead to the British or French trying to gain political control of the Kingdom. The Saudi fear of British imperialism was deeply rooted. Ibn Saud and others knew they needed to accommodate London, but they had no faith that Britain had abandoned plans for the further expansion of the empire, especially if there was oil to be gained.

In the Second World War Ibn Saud was officially neutral but, in fact, tilted toward the Allied cause. Surrounded by the British Empire, he had little choice. Italy inadvertently bombed Dhahran in October 1940; the intended target had been British bases in nearby Bahrain.[45] The Germans tried to tempt Faisal to join their side. In early 1941 a pro-German coup took place in Iraq; the Germans suggested Ibn Saud support the coup but he refrained. In April 1941 Adolf Hitler sent Ibn Saud a personal, private message suggesting that if Saudi Arabia joined the Axis powers against Britain, Berlin would recognize Ibn Saud as "King of all the Arabs." The message was sent via the Saudi ambassador in Switzerland. Ibn Saud not only rejected Hitler's offer, he recalled the ambassador in Bern for dealing with the Nazis.[46] As we have seen, near the end of the war Saudi Arabia officially declared war on both Germany and Japan.

In the postwar era Saudi oil income and wealth gradually expanded, but for the majority of the residents the Kingdom remained a desperately impoverished backwater through the remainder of Ibn Saud's life. He did consolidate power in his own hands. He had demonstrated a pragmatic foreign policy much more sophisticated than his predecessors in the first two Saudi states, making treaties with the British and welcoming American oil prospectors. Ibn Saud had total power over life and death in his kingdom. His alliance with the United States sealed on the USS *Quincy* on Valentine's Day 1945 further strengthened his posture as the undisputed master of Arabia. On his death on November 9, 1953, Ibn Saud's legacy was firm: the third Saudi state was an absolute monarchy rooted in its commitment to practicing Wahhabi Islam.

The American "Betrayal" of Ibn Saud

The last years of Ibn Saud's life were as tumultuous as the earlier years. After 1945 the British, French, and Italian empires in the Middle East were in retreat. Arab states like Egypt, Syria, and Iraq gradually got their independence. The Zionist movement triumphed in Palestine and created the state of Israel, with important support from Roosevelt's successor, Harry S. Truman. For Ibn Saud and his family the latter was a betrayal of the promise the king thought he had secured aboard the USS *Quincy*. This Saudi sense of betrayal would have a longstanding and bitter residue in U.S.-Saudi relations.

As noted earlier in this chapter, President Roosevelt sent the king a letter after the summit in Egypt in response to a message from the king dated March 10, 1945. FDR's April 5, 1945, letter was addressed to GREAT AND GOODFRIEND. It stated. "Your majesty will recall that on previous occasions I communicated to you the attitude of the American government towards Palestine and made clear our determination that no decision be taken with respect to the basic situation in that country without full consultation with both Arabs and Jews . . . and that I would take no action, in my capacity as Chief of the Executive Branch of this Government, which might prove hostile to the Arab people." The letter concluded with FDR reassuring Ibn Saud that those commitments were "unchanged."[47]

Great Britain, exhausted by the cost of the world war, turned Palestine's future over to the United Nations to decide. A UN special commission recommended in 1947 that the country be partitioned between the Jews and the Arabs. The Arabs rejected the recommendation and requested, instead, full independence for a unified Palestine, which would elect its own government. Since Arabs were still a majority in the area, that would have been an Arab government.

President Truman, for a variety of reasons, including domestic politics but also a keen sense of responsibility to assist the survivors of Hitler's Holocaust, chose to support the UN recommendation. In 1947 the United States lobbied the UN Security Council to endorse the partition plan. Both the State Department and the military pressed Truman not to support partition, because they feared it would provoke an Arab, especially Saudi, backlash. But Truman's White House advisers told him, accurately, that the Saudis needed the American oil companies and their oil income too much to afford to take any action against Washington. Clark Clifford, Truman's legal counsel, argued, "The fact of the matter is the Arab states must have oil royalties or go broke. Military necessity, political and economic self preservation will compel the Arabs to sell their oil to the United States. Their need of the United States is greater than our need of them."[48]

The Saudis were deeply angered by Truman's decision, which they saw, right or wrong, as a repudiation of the FDR commitment to take no action harmful to the Arabs. The Roosevelt letter was not a personal communication, as the language in it makes clear it was an official commitment of the presidency and the government. Prince Faisal, who had been the architect of the American-Saudi alliance in 1943, now urged his father to cut diplomatic relations with the United States. Ibn Saud did not, largely because he needed the income from the American oil company in the Eastern Province. Instead, Ibn Saud instructed all provincial governors to raise volunteers to fight in Palestine alongside the other Arab armies. At least a thousand joined the war in 1947–48, the first instance of Saudi volunteers going abroad to fight for a Muslim cause.[49]

The American role in the creation of Israel left a bitter residue in the minds of many influential Saudis, especially Faisal. For Faisal and others in the royal family, Truman had betrayed Roosevelt's commitments and the Kingdom was too dependent on America to do anything about it. This would prove to have lasting implications.

Chapter Two

FAISAL, KENNEDY, JOHNSON, AND NIXON, 1953 TO 1975

The Great Mosque of Brussels is set in one of Belgium's most beautiful and monumental parks, Le Parc Cinquantenaire or Jubelpark, which opened on the fiftieth anniversary of Belgium's independence in 1880. Originally the mosque was the Oriental Pavilion in the complex of museums built throughout the park to mark the anniversary. It was not a house of worship but a museum to teach Belgians about Islam and the Middle East. For many years after the celebrations in 1880 the building was neglected and deteriorated.

In 1967 King Baudouin of Belgium gave the building as a gift to King Faisal bin Abdul Aziz of Saudi Arabia who was on a goodwill visit to Europe. Faisal had become king three years earlier as the result of a protracted succession struggle with his brother Saud. The Saudi Wahhabi clergy, the *ulema*, had been critical to Faisal's victory in the power struggle, and Faisal was eager to demonstrate his piety and religious devotion to Wahhabi Islam to keep the favor of the clerics.

Over the next decade Faisal and then his successor, King Khalid, provided generous funding to restore the original building and turn it into a major religious center in Brussels, the Centre Islamique et Culturel de Belgique. It officially opened its doors to the faithful in 1978 at a ceremony presided over by Khalid and Baudouin. Today it is the largest and most influential mosque in the capital of the European Union. It propagates Saudi Islamic values, notably the religion of Wahhab, including its intolerance. The director of the Centre Islamique and most of the staff are Saudis. Indeed, the Belgian authorities in April 2012 quietly asked Riyadh to replace the director with another Saudi because his views were so extreme.[1] The mosque is only a few hundred meters away from the EU's headquarters in the city. My own home for more than three years was directly across the street from the mosque, on Avenue de la Renaissance, giving me a close-up view.

The mosque in Brussels is symbolic of King Faisal's decisive influence on both the Kingdom of Saudi Arabia and the Islamic world more broadly. It was during his reign that the Kingdom began aggressively exporting its own brand of Islam around the world. Faisal commissioned great mosques in many countries, from Belgium to Pakistan, to help spread the faith as practiced in the Kingdom. The Kingdom's rapidly expanding oil revenues paid for this export of the faith. Faisal rightly is regarded as the architect of modern Saudi diplomacy based on the "legacy of strong puritan Islamic values maintained by descendants of Wahhabi reformers with the al Shaykh" family, as his biographer wrote. Indeed Faisal's mother was an al Shaykh, a direct descendant of Muhammad Ibn 'Abd al Wahhab, the founder of Wahhabism. Faisal literally embodied the unity of the two great families that created the Kingdom, the Sauds and the al Shaykhs.[2]

Faisal's oil-funded export of Saudi Islamic values helped strengthen Muslim communities around the world. Much of his work benefited the global community of Islam, the *umma*, providing schools, hospitals, and mosques for many faithful. But it also fueled the least tolerant and most extreme elements within the *umma*. Within the puritanical version of Islam that Saudi Arabia values so much, some have exploited their faith for political purposes to justify global jihad and terrorism. Osama bin Laden is only the most famous Saudi to make the journey from faithful citizen of Saudi Arabia to mass murderer. Faisal would undoubtedly denounce bin Laden and al Qaeda if he were alive, but his propagation of an intolerant version of faith cannot escape some culpability for the problems besetting Islam today.

Belgium has become a hotbed of Islamic militancy and extremism. The small Muslim community at the time of Faisal's visit in 1967 has grown enormously with the arrival of migrants, mostly from Morocco—from 100,000 to more than 600,000 in 2017. Perhaps a quarter of the city's population is now Muslim. More Belgians have joined groups like al Qaeda and the Islamic State per capita than in any other country in Europe. The district of Molenbeek, across the city from le Parc Cinquantenaire, has achieved dubious fame as "jihad central" in Europe.[3] The mosque Faisal created is still the center of Islamic teaching in the city. Ninety-five percent of the courses offered on Islam for Muslims in Brussels are operated by young preachers trained in Saudi Arabia under the mosque's supervision, according to a European think tank based in Brussels.[4]

Faisal was the architect of modern Saudi Arabia. He inherited a still-impoverished kingdom with an almost medieval government and turned it into a modern state with a global reach. He ensured that out of the ashes of a dangerous succession struggle, the passage of power from one of his brothers to another would provide stability in the Kingdom for fifty years. That stability provides the basis for the Kingdom's remarkable achievements.

Three American presidents dealt with Faisal as king: John F. Kennedy, Lyndon Johnson, and Richard Nixon. The interaction of each with the king illustrates the contradictions and complexity of the uneasy alliance.

For all his importance in the history of the Kingdom, Faisal has been the subject of little rigorous scholarly research in English to date. One scholar stands out, Joseph A. Kechichian, whose biography, *Faysal: Saudi Arabia's King for All Seasons*, is considered by the king's heirs as the most authoritative, and it benefits from unique access to his papers. Prince Turki al Faisal, the son who became head of Saudi intelligence and ambassador to both the United States and the United Kingdom, recommended it to me. Indeed when he graciously came to speak to my class studying Middle East history at Georgetown University, he gave every student a copy.

*President John F. Kennedy meets with Crown Prince Faisal bin Abdul Aziz
in Washington, D.C., September 1962. (Diomedia)*

Training for the Job

Faisal bin Abdul Aziz al Saud was born April 9, 1906, in Riyadh, the third son
of Ibn Saud. His mother was Tarfah bint al Shaykh, a direct descendant of
Muhammad Ibn 'Abd al Wahhab. Faisal was the only son born of this mar-
riage; Tarfah died in 1912. The young Faisal was raised by the al Shaykhs, so

he epitomized the union of the House of Saud and the al Shaykh Wahhabi *ulema* more than any other modern Saudi monarch. His upbringing under the tutelage of his maternal grandfather, Abdallah bin Abdukl Latif al Shaykh, anchored him firmly in the Kingdom's faith.[5]

Ibn Saud recognized his son's talents early and put him to work as the Kingdom's diplomat. At the age of twelve Faisal was sent by his father in 1919 to London to represent Saudi interests as the allies prepared to divide the Ottoman Empire among them. The king believed Faisal was a good choice for the mission in part because his impeccable Wahhabi credentials ensured he would not be accused of selling out to Western influence. Ibn Saud called Faisal the *walad* of the al Shaykh, the boy from the al Shaykh family.[6] The young prince toured the United Kingdom, France, and Belgium, meeting with British and French diplomats, visiting the battlefields of Flanders, and experiencing the modern world of Europe as no Saudi had ever before. He visited armaments factories, watched plays, climbed the Eiffel Tower, and became a symbol for the Kingdom.[7] It was an extraordinary change from the early Wahhabis, who shunned the outside world as evil.

Upon his return Faisal was appointed commander of Saudi forces fighting in Asir, a southern province bordering Yemen. Then he commanded the year-long siege of Jidda, where the Hashemites were finally defeated and ousted from the peninsula for good. His father made him the viceroy of the Hejaz in August 1926. He traveled again to Europe to secure diplomatic recognition of the Saudi conquest of the Hejaz from Britain, France, and the Netherlands, the three countries with diplomatic legations in Jidda.

A third trip to Europe in 1932 included stops in Italy, Switzerland, France, Britain, Holland, Germany, Poland, and Russia. In Moscow Faisal met with senior officials of the Union of Soviet Socialist Republics after the USSR recognized Saudi Arabia and opened a consulate in Jidda. On the way home Faisal visited Turkey, Iran, Iraq, and Kuwait. Just twenty-six years old, Faisal was, without question, the most experienced and widely traveled Saudi prince.[8]

So it was no surprise that Ibn Saud sent Faisal to Washington in 1943 to lay the foundation for the Saudi alliance with America two years before the famous meeting on the USS *Quincy*. The prince met with President Roosevelt twice, stayed in Blair House, met with many members of Congress, and then toured the country to California and back. He visited Princeton and met with American Arabists.

Two years later he was back in the United States to attend the San Francisco conference establishing the United Nations. Saudi Arabia became one of the original signers to the UN Charter, and Faisal gave a speech hailing Roosevelt's leadership in securing the Allied victory in World War II. In 1947 Faisal represented the Kingdom in the deliberations of the UN Palestine committee in New York; as noted earlier he was profoundly disappointed in Truman's support for the establishment of Israel.

Troubled Transition

On November 9, 1953, Ibn Saud passed away in Taif. His eldest son Saud succeeded him as king with Faisal as crown prince. This began what would become a decade-long transition as the two brothers engaged in a prolonged power struggle for the crown. This succession struggle took place against the backdrop of a deeply troubled Middle East and the American-Soviet Cold War. Within the Arab world, the independent states recently freed from European colonial rule fought with each other over their individual regional ambitions, and they fought with Israel. The Arab Cold War, as it was called, pitted the revolutionary Arab nationalist republics against the conservative monarchies. The Arab states also became pawns in the Cold War, and at the same time exploited the war to secure favors from the Americans and Russians.

King Saud had difficulty maneuvering in these tricky waters. It did not help that he lacked good financial judgment and spent the Kingdom's oil wealth on too much luxury for himself and his cronies. The national debt more than doubled between 1953 and 1958, from $200 million to $480 million despite increased oil exports and earnings. Like his father he was a prodigious father, with fifty-three sons and fifty-four daughters.[9] He was torn between his commitment to the conservative values of his father and the new wealth of the oil boom. He was also torn between the appeal of Arab nationalism and the reality of heading an absolute monarchy. Saud also placed his sons in important cabinet positions, like defense minister, before they had experience, suggesting that he might try to have a son succeed him as king. This alienated many of his important brothers, who were also sons of Ibn Saud and who had their own aspirations for higher office and more experience and qualifications for office than did Saud's sons.

In the end Faisal would win the power struggle because he had strong support from the *uloma*, the Wahhabi establishment, as well as the backing of most of the royal family. The struggle between Saud and Faisal inevitably involved Washington, as well, not just as an important observer but as an occasional participant. Saudi Arabia was firmly in the anti-communist camp during the Cold War, not just because it is a deeply Islamic country, which regards atheist communism as anathema, but also because the House of Saud recognized that only the United States could provide security against the Soviet Union, British imperialism, revolutionary Arab nationalists, and other perceived threats.

Saud turned to the United States in November 1955 to secure a five-year military training program for the Saudi military. The training mission was linked to the Dhahran air base agreement and helped begin the modernization of the Saudi armed forces. President Dwight Eisenhower was determined to build a network of alliances around the Soviet Union and Communist China to contain the communist menace. "In American eyes the Dhahran facility was vital for regional defense."[10]

The rivalry between Saud and Faisal first came to a boil in July 1956 when seven of Saud's brothers signed a letter criticizing his stewardship of the Kingdom. They charged Saud with financial incompetence because of his spending, which risked bankrupting the Kingdom. The chief of the Royal Guard and Faisal were among the signers. A month later, Saud sacked the head of the Royal Guards and asked for American training for the guards.[11]

In November 1956 the British, French, and Israelis—operating in secret collusion—attacked Egypt. All felt threatened by the growing influence and power of Egypt's charismatic revolutionary leader Gamal Abd al Nasser. He had been a key player in the coup that overthrew the British-backed Egyptian monarchy and had thrown the British out of Egypt and the Suez Canal. Saudi Arabia broke diplomatic relations with both London and Paris as a consequence of the Suez crisis. Eisenhower also opposed the conspiracy against Cairo, fearing that it threatened to turn all the newly independent states of Africa and Asia against the West. If the old imperial powers behaved as colonial predators,

Eisenhower reasoned, only the Soviets would benefit. As a consequence of Ike's firm stand against the British, French, and Israeli conspiracy, his popularity in the Kingdom grew substantially.

Both King Saud and Crown Prince Faisal traveled to Washington the next year, 1957, to see Eisenhower, and both had extensive conversations with him.[12] During this official state visit to the United States, King Saud signed a five-year renewal of the Dhahran air base agreement. This would prove to be the final extension, and the base would revert to the Saudis in early 1962. While in the United States Faisal had two operations to remove his gallbladder and a small tumor.

At the start of 1958 the Arab Cold War between Nasser and the monarchies escalated. On March 5, 1958, Nasser accused Saudi Arabia of plotting to assassinate him and called, in turn, for the overthrow of the House of Saud.[13] This precipitated a wave of propaganda across the Arab world as the revolutionaries sought to bring down the monarchs and unite the Arab states into a single state. The Soviets enthusiastically backed the revolutionaries.

Against this background, the internal struggle in Riyadh came to a head. On March 24, 1958, Prince Fahd bin Abdul Aziz al Saud, a future king, along with eleven other senior princes, confronted Saud directly in the palace and demanded that Saud turn power over to Faisal. Within an hour a royal decree was published stripping Saud of political power and making Faisal regent. But Faisal did not demand Saud's abdication. With executive power now in his hands, Faisal quickly moved to cut government spending, end the purchase of luxury cars and other items for the princes, restore financial health to the Kingdom, and reduce corruption.

Later that year a revolutionary coup in Baghdad that overthrew the Hashemite monarchy in Iraq seemed to herald a decisive turn in the Arab world toward the nationalist forces. Nasser created the United Arab Republic, unifying Egypt and Syria. To forestall further coups, the United States sent U.S. Marines to Lebanon to shore up its pro-Western Christian government, and the United Kingdom sent paratroopers to Jordan to save the last Hashemite monarchy led by King Hussein bin Talal. But the nationalist forces were deeply divided; for example, Nasser did not control the revolutionary government in Baghdad. The wave of revolutions seemed to ebb for the moment.

Another major threat to the Kingdom came in 1961 when the revolutionary regime in Baghdad threatened to attack and occupy Kuwait. Kuwait had offered the Saud family asylum seventy years earlier and had hosted Ibn Saud for a decade. The House of Saud felt a bond of loyalty to the Kuwaiti al Sabah family. When two Iraqi divisions threatened to invade Kuwait in July 1961 the British send a battalion of Royal Marines to deter them, with full support from the United States.[14] Saudi Arabia also sent a small paratroop battalion to assist the Royal Marines. Only Jordan's King Hussein backed the Iraqi claims to Kuwait, because they dated back to the old Hashemite monarchy in Iraq. By the end of July the British were withdrawing and the Saudis took command of a joint Arab League force, including 1,500 Saudi troops, to defend the emirate. It was a harbinger of a future crisis that would test the Saudi-American alliance in 1990.[15]

At home Saud mounted a countermove against Faisal in December 1960, working with the so called Free Princes—a small number of more liberal Saudi royals who were attracted to Nasser's Arabist posture. Saud regained control of the executive powers from Faisal in this struggle. The leader of the Free Princes, Prince Talal, called for the closing of the United States Air Force base in Dhahran, leading to the nonrenewal of the U.S. lease. Saud's return to power was short-lived, however, as his health deteriorated and he had to travel to America for medical attention. Faisal was again made de facto regent and acting prime minister in November 1961.

Yemen, Kennedy, and Faisal

In 1961 America had a new president, John F. Kennedy, who would have a complex and uneasy relationship with Faisal and the Kingdom. Kennedy came into office determined to do better than Eisenhower at managing the Cold War. He wanted to avoid Eisenhower's black-and-white approach to third world nationalism. Kennedy appreciated that many of the newly independent states in Africa and Asia did not want to join either camp in the Cold War and, instead, wanted to be independent and aligned with neither great power. Leaders of these states also were determined to end colonialism and free any remaining colonies.

Kennedy had recognized the importance of appealing to the nationalist current in the so called Third World. In a major speech delivered in July 1957 titled "Imperialism—the Enemy of Freedom," Kennedy called on the Eisenhower administration to cease supporting France in its war to keep Algeria as a colony. Despite France's historic support for the United States, Kennedy argued that Paris's determination to hold on to Algeria only served Soviet interests by alienating Arabs and Africans from the free world. He cited Algeria's war for independence as a cause consistent with American principles. Kennedy also argued that the Algerian case was symptomatic of a broader imperative: the need to align America with nationalist forces and movements across what was then known as the Third World.[16]

In the Middle East this approach dictated an effort to reach out to Nasser's Egypt to see if Cairo could be a partner in stabilizing the region, not an opponent. A dialogue with Nasser would also keep Egypt from drifting further into the Soviet's orbit, Kennedy and his advisers believed. They had doubts that the traditional American allies in the region—the monarchies of Saudi Arabia, Iran, Libya, Yemen, and Jordan—could survive. There seemed a significant risk those monarchs would be toppled as had the kings of Egypt and Iraq. The ongoing power struggle in Riyadh between Saud and Faisal seemed to suggest the Kingdom was dangerously unstable and in urgent need of reform. If that were the case, Kennedy felt it would be wise to have a dialogue with the progressive nationalist forces in the Arab world. Not surprisingly, this approach "badly startled America's traditional Arab friends, especially Saudi Arabia."[17]

For the first two years of his administration Kennedy engaged in a delicate courtship of Nasser, with the two exchanging letters and emissaries to see if they could reach an accommodation. Riyadh followed the dialogue with great unease. The process came to a moment of truth in the fall of 1962, when a nationalist coup toppled the monarchy that ruled Yemen, the most backward country in Arabia. Egypt swiftly came to the aid of the nationalist forces with a massive troop deployment facilitated by the Soviet Union. Saudi Arabia, the United Kingdom, and Israel backed the royalists. Kennedy tried to find a middle ground but, ultimately, backed the Saudis. In the course of the Yemen crisis the power struggle between Faisal and Saud was also resolved, finally, in Faisal's favor.

The autumn of 1962 was an extraordinarily tense moment in the Cold War. The Soviets were introducing intermediate-range ballistic missiles and nuclear weapons into Cuba, deploying some 50,000 Russian troops to the Caribbean island. The Cuban missile crisis dominated world attention for most of October. At the same time China invaded India and defeated the Indian army in a border war in the Himalayas. Kennedy began an urgent airlift to resupply the Indians and stiffen their defenses.

Concurrently, Egypt and Russia intervened in Yemen. On September 19, 1962, the king of Yemen, Imam Ahmad bin Yahya, died. British prime minister Harold Macmillan later described his rule as "notorious for cruelty and despotism on a truly oriental scale . . . a combination of medieval squalor and obedience."[18] His thirty-six-year-old son, Muhammad al Badr, took the throne, but within a week the army mounted a coup. The Royal Palace was surrounded by tanks and demolished, but the young monarch escaped and fled to the northern mountains along the border with Saudi Arabia and joined his uncle, Prince Hassan, who was already mounting a tribal rebellion against the new republican government that set itself up in Sana'a and the other major cities.

The Egyptians were widely believed to be behind the coup and quickly moved to support the new government led by Abdallah al Sallal. The revolutionaries made clear from the beginning that their ambitions extended beyond Yemen. They openly called for revolution both in Saudi Arabia and in southern Yemen, which was then still a British colony centered around the port of Aden. In the view of both Riyadh and London, the coup was an existential threat. Prime Minister Macmillan, while noting the notoriety of the Yemeni royalists, told Kennedy from the beginning of the crisis that Nasser's goal was Saudi Arabia, "a great prize," and Aden the linchpin of British security in the Arab world.[19]

The royalists quickly rallied many of the Zaydi Shia tribes of northern Yemen to their side. The republicans controlled the cities and coastal lowlands. As early as October 2, 1962, the Central Intelligence Agency told Kennedy in his daily briefing that a "civil war is shaping up with direct backing from the United Arab Republic (Egypt) for one faction and from Saudi Arabia for the other." The agency reported the Saudis were arming and financing the royalists while Egypt and Russia backed the republic.[20] On October 4, 1962, the CIA told Kennedy two Saudi army battalions were actively assisting the royalists along with "a small Jordanian detachment."[21]

Nasser sent a battalion of Egyptian paratroopers to Sana'a in northern Yemen to strengthen the coup almost immediately. Within weeks the Egyptian deployment grew to 25,000 troops. The Egyptians did not have sufficient transport aircraft to lift them to Yemen and resupply them, so Cairo asked Moscow for help. The Soviets gave Egypt fifteen AN-12 transports (similar to the American C-130) with Russian crews to create an air bridge carrying the Egyptian army into Arabia. The CIA told Kennedy on October 16, 1962, that the Egyptians were receiving the AN-12s, the pilots were mostly Russians but also some Czechs, and the operation was tricky given the primitive nature of Yemen's airfields.[22] The planes had Egyptian markings on them, and by 1965 Egyptian pilots were trained to fly them, but for all intents and purposes they were Russian transport aircraft with Russian pilots under Egyptian command for most of two years.[23] The AN-12s were doing five to seven sorties a day to supplement ship deliveries from Egypt to the Yemeni port at Hudaydah. By March 1963, 30,000 Egyptian troops were in Yemen, later reaching 70,000, one-third of the Egyptian army.

Moscow also provided Nasser with long-range heavy bombers to strike the royalists. Two squadrons of TU-16 bombers were deployed in Egypt with Russian crews to fly combat missions in Yemen in support of the Egyptian and republican Yemeni ground forces. The Soviets built a military airfield outside Sana'a for smaller fighter aircraft and transports; some 500 Soviet combat engineers supervised its construction. The Russian bombers attacked targets across the border in Saudi Arabia, where the Saudis were assisting the royalists.[24] The Royal Saudi Air Force was unprepared and unequipped to respond; even worse, several of its pilots defected with their aircraft to Egypt. The Jordanians sent six Hawker Hunter jet fighters to Taif in Saudi Arabia to help deter air attacks by the Egyptians and Russians.[25] To the enormous embarrassment of King Hussein, the Jordanian squadron commander and two of the pilots defected to Egypt. The Jordanian deployment did help Faisal and Hussein tone down significantly the historic Saudi-Hashemite rivalry.[26]

The Kennedy administration monitored the rapidly deteriorating situation in Yemen even as it was coping with the Cuban missile crisis and the Chinese invasion of India. The Kennedy team still wanted to see if dialogue with Nasser could resolve the crisis. They also had grave doubts about the stability of the remaining Arab monarchies. Kennedy's top aide on the Middle East in the National Security Council was Robert W. Komer, a CIA officer with a "sharp pen, keen wit, abrasive spirit and ceaseless energy." Komer argued for trying to engage Nasser, as did the State Department. In time Kennedy would refer to the struggle in Yemen as "Komer's war."[27] The immediate question was whether to recognize the new republican government as the legitimate Yemeni government. London, Riyadh, and Amman all urged Washington to stall and not give this symbol of approval to Nasser and Sallal.

Faisal's Response

Faisal responded to the crisis in Yemen with determination and clarity. His response can be broken into three components. Most immediately, he backed building a coalition of states to support the royalists in Yemen. He wanted Kennedy to join this coalition but was also prepared to accept American security support for Saudi Arabia if he could not get active American help for the royalists. Second, he embarked upon building an Islamic alternative to Nasser's Arab nationalist movement. This would be manifested in Saudi support for Islamic institutions around the world, like the mosque in Brussels, and in the creation of an Islamic conference of states led by Saudi Arabia to act as a global representative of the Islamic world and to convene periodic Islamic summits. Finally, at home, he consolidated his power and, ultimately, ousted Saud and replaced him as king.

When the Yemen crisis began Faisal was in New York to attend the annual meeting of the United Nations General Assembly. He met with Secretary of State Dean Rusk at the Waldorf Astoria hotel. Faisal portrayed the coup and the Egyptian and Russian intervention as a threat to the Kingdom. He asked for a meeting with the president and urged the United States not to recognize the republican government.

Kennedy and Faisal met at the White House on October 5, 1962. Kennedy had met Saud a year before and was unimpressed. Faisal was a much more impressive figure. The two leaders began with a working lunch with their aides. Faisal said the Abdallah al Sallal regime was getting military aid "not only from the United Arab Republic but also from the Soviet Union." This was a major challenge to the stability of the entire Arabian Peninsula. Faisal noted

that Sallal in his first communiqué had called for the overthrow of all the monarchies in the Arabian Peninsula and the creation of a single republic. If the
royalists were not supported firmly, the Kingdom, Aden, and the Gulf states
would be at risk.[28]

After lunch Faisal and the president went upstairs in the White House to
the family quarters to continue their discussion in a more private and intimate
setting. In the family living room Kennedy pressed Faisal to make reforms in
the Kingdom. He suggested that the Kingdom's most serious threat came from
the same internal problems that had destroyed the monarchies in Yemen, Iraq,
and Egypt. He pressed the crown prince to consider allowing Jews to visit the
Kingdom in a gesture of tolerance.[29] Kennedy also assured the prince that "the
United States would consider its pledge of general support for the Kingdom to
apply to threats activated from without and from within." This was a crucial
expansion of America's commitment to Saudi security.[30]

Kennedy's pressure also represented a highly unusual direct American in-
trusion into Saudi internal affairs, reflecting the president's deep concern
about the sustainability of the monarchy. None of Kennedy's predecessors and
few of his successors would be so direct in suggesting the Kingdom needed to
change for its own good.

Faisal responded positively. "Then and there he promised Kennedy that he
would abolish slavery, institute basic civil rights and strive to eliminate corruption."[31] The Kingdom was one of the last countries in the world where
slavery was legal. Faisal said: "I concur with your ideas and I intend to implement precisely this kind of reform."[32]

Faisal kept his promise to Kennedy and in November 1962 made public a
reform program of ten points. The judiciary and the *mutawween* (religious
police) were reformed and the government promised to provide free medical
care and education. Slavery was made illegal, despite some objections from the
clerics. The Saudi government paid slave owners to encourage them to free
their slaves: $700 for a male slave and $1,000 for a female, until July 7, 1963,
after which all slaves were considered free and there was no further compen-
sation for owners.[33]

This was a unique example of an American president convincing a Saudi
leader to make major internal reforms in the Kingdom, with no president before or since having done so. Kennedy's timing was excellent. Faisal knew the

revolutionary tide was strong and that he needed to reform the Kingdom. The president also used discretion and tact; by making his case privately in the intimacy of the White House family quarters he spared Faisal any public embarrassment. Kennedy feared the royal family was heading toward collapse from internal and external pressures. In fact, the CIA told Kennedy after the White House sessions that Faisal was returning to a Saudi Arabia "heavily overshadowed by foreboding for its future."[34]

In addition to his reforms, on returning to Riyadh Faisal consolidated his position as chief executive. Saud's sons were removed from the council of ministers and replaced by Faisal loyalists. Prince Fahd became Interior Ministry, Prince Sultan took on the Defense Ministry, Prince Abdallah became commander of the Saudi National Guard, and Prince Salman became governor of Riyadh. All would hold those positions for the next half-century except Fahd, who would become king in 1982. Again, King Saud was not asked to abdicate but he was stripped of most of his power.

Faisal also appointed a commoner to be oil minister. Ahmed Zaki Yamani was only thirty-two in 1962, an Hejazi from Mecca whose father had been grand mufti in what is today Indonesia. Educated in Cairo, New York, and at Harvard Law School, Yamani was the king's protégé and would be his expert adviser on oil issues and international law and would serve as an effective diplomat for his monarch.[35]

The power struggle took place against a backdrop of unrest in the military. Between October 2 and 8, 1962, the crews of four Royal Saudi Air Force aircraft defected to Egypt with their planes. The entire RSAF was grounded in response. A month later, when the air force was allowed to fly again, seven more pilots defected with their planes to Egypt. The pilots had been part of a conspiracy to overthrow the king and establish a pro-Nasser republic. Again the RSAF was grounded, and Faisal strengthened the standing and power of the National Guard, which was more loyal than the regular military. Another coup plot by factions of the RSAF in 1969 prompted Faisal to ground the air force a third time.[36]

Faisal also moved to back royalists elsewhere. In January 1963 he broke relations with Cairo and restored relations with London. Saudi intelligence proposed to the British that they embark on a joint secret project to assist the royalists in Yemen. The British would provide a small number of former military specialists in guerilla warfare to advise and assist the royalists, which Saudi Arabia would fund. There would be no official British government role, but behind the scenes the United Kingdom would provide the expertise to help the royalists bog down Egypt and Russia in a quagmire. The entire operation would involve fewer than fifty experts and be run out of an office on Sloane Street in London.[37]

A third party joined the coalition. Israel also felt threatened by Nasser and was also eager to bog him down in Yemen. The royalists directly approached Israel for help. The Israeli intelligence service, Mossad, proposed that the Israeli Air Force would fly clandestine missions from southern Israel across the Red Sea to drop military supplies to the royalists. The British coordinated the supply missions with the royalists and the Saudis. Code-named Operation Rotev, *gravy* in Hebrew, the Israelis flew fourteen supply missions to Yemen in the next couple of years. Most of the weapons dropped to the royalists were Russian-made equipment captured by Israel from Egypt in the 1956 war, intended to ensure there was no obvious connection to Israel.[38] The arms appeared to be captured from Egypt in Yemen; this allowed Israel to maintain plausible deniability of any involvement in the war. A future head of the Mossad, Nahum Admoni, ran the operation, which was authorized by Prime Minister David Ben-Gurion.[39]

The Saudis avoided direct meetings with the Israelis, using the British as intermediaries. The Saudi operation in Yemen was run by Kamal Adham, head of Saudi intelligence, a graduate of Cambridge University and a brother of Faisal's wife. The one time the British tried to arrange a direct meeting at the Dorchester Hotel in London, Adham was very nervous.[40] Nonetheless, it was a remarkable example of Saudi realpolitik in action and Faisal's willingness to go to any partner to stymie Egypt in the early 1960s.

The United States did not join the coalition backing the royalists. In part this reflected Kennedy's continued strong preference for dialogue with Nasser. He and his key aides, including Komer, still wanted to find common ground with Egypt. As a result, after some delay, the United States gave official recognition to the new republican government in Sana'a, against the advice of Riyadh and London. Kennedy's reluctance to embrace the royalists probably also stemmed from their reactionary history. In a piece published after the death of Imam Ahmed in September 1962, the CIA characterized him as a ruthless monarch who ruled Yemen's 5 million people by keeping tribal leaders' sons as hostages, conducting mass beheadings of dissidents, and even publicly executing his own brother. The heir, Mohammad Badr, was described as eager "to drag Yemen out of the eleventh century but certainly not into the twentieth."[41]

Instead of backing the royalists, Kennedy proposed a compromise. Egypt would withdraw its army from Yemen while Saudi Arabia would cease providing arms to the royalists. Yemenis would then decide their own future without foreign interference. The devil, of course, was in the details. Who would go first, who would monitor the arrangements—and could either side be trusted?

In March 1963 Kennedy dispatched Ellsworth Bunker, a senior State Department diplomat, to the region to try to sell a deal. Bunker met with Faisal and offered to send a squadron of American fighter aircraft to the Kingdom to symbolize American security support as part of a mediated solution to the crisis.[42] Faisal was frustrated by the American mediation and had hoped for a more assertive line against Nasser. But he needed American support and agreed to Bunker's plan. He doubtless expected Nasser to fail to withdraw his troops and, thus, scuttle the initiative.

The Kennedy initiative never produced success. Although both Faisal and Nasser paid lip service to it, neither was prepared to retreat from Yemen. For the Saudis it was a matter of survival, and they had no qualms about the royalists. For Egypt the Yemen intervention was a chance to defeat the Saudis and British and consolidate Egyptian hegemony in the Arab world.

The United States did send jet fighters to Saudi Arabia after repeated Egyptian air attacks on Saudi border towns. Over the objections of United States Air Force Commander Curtis Lemay, who thought it a diversion from more important missions, eight F100D jet fighters, six KB-50 air-to-air refueling tankers, and more than 500 U.S. military personnel were deployed in mid-1963 to Dhahran and Jidda to fly combat patrols over the border. Operation Hard Surface was the only deployment of American troops into the Middle East on Kennedy's watch.[43] The mission lasted only six months, and the planes left Saudi Arabia in January 1964.[44]

After Kennedy's assassination in November 1963, President Lyndon Johnson continued the dialogue with Nasser but with much less conviction. In April 1964 Nasser made his only visit to Yemen during the war and gave a bellicose speech calling for revolution in Aden. That was the last straw for Johnson; the dialogue with Nasser petered out.

Before Nasser's visit to Sana'a, the power struggle in Saudi Arabia had reached its finale. In March 1964 Faisal persuaded the Wahhabi *ulema* to issue a formal call for Saud's abdication. Saud resisted and surrounded the royal palace with his Royal Guards. Faisal mobilized the regular army under Prince Sultan and the National Guard led by Prince Abdallah to surround the Royal Guards. A tense standoff ensued, but Saud was completely outnumbered on the ground and outmaneuvered by the clerics' alliance with Faisal. No blood was shed, but "the threat of force was necessary to depose the King."[45] He reluctantly abdicated and went into exile in Switzerland, Egypt, and Greece until his death in 1969.[46] During his exile in Egypt, Saud made pro-Egyptian radio broadcasts on Radio Cairo against his brother, but these ceased when Egypt was defeated by Israel in the 1967 war and Nasser needed desperately to make peace with Faisal.[47]

To solidify the Saudi family grip on power, Faisal developed a clear line of succession for the future. His brother Khalid was made crown prince in 1965, removing any suspicion that Faisal's sons might inherit the throne. In 1967 Prince Fahd, the interior minister, was made deputy prime minister, in effect, third in line to the throne. This ensured the line of succession for the next two kings and created a precedent for Faisal's successors.

Faisal created the modern Saudi political system. His choice of his brothers Khalid, Fahd, Abdallah, Sultan, and Salman for key positions in the council of ministers created bureaucracies run by powerful princes that could provide patronage and jobs to loyal retainers. The system gave the Kingdom its first modern government and worked effectively for over half a century. In time other senior princes would gain positions, for example, Prince Nayef as Fahd's successor as interior minister. With the infusion of oil money as Saudi production increased, the Kingdom became much more stable. Faisal had inherited a kingdom in disarray, still desperately poor, under siege from Nasser and beset with royal family intrigue. He would leave to Khalid a much more stable and secure kingdom. Another key to that transformation was the propagation of Saudi Islam.

Faisal's Islamic Mobilization

King Faisal was a true believer in the Islam practiced since Muhammad Ibn 'Abd al Wahhab. He was brought up in the family of Wahhab, the al Shaykhs. Despite his extensive exposure to the outside world, unique for a Saudi of his age and time, he remained a believer. As king he intended to use Islam as a practical force to strengthen Saudi Arabia's foreign policy and create an alternative to the secular world of Arab nationalists like Nasser. In the process he would begin the large-scale export of Saudi Islamic values and teaching to the *umma* across the world.

In May 1962 Faisal created the Muslim World League as a nongovernmental organization dedicated to propagation of Islam and Islamic values. The league became a mechanism for the creation of mosques and religious schools propagating Saudi Islam; that is, Wahhabism.

Faisal wanted to do more; he sought the creation of an organization of Islamic states to be a global player akin to the United Nations.[48] The cold war with Egypt and the hot war in Yemen made this difficult. Nasser could rally a substantial number of nationalist regimes against Faisal. Consequently it required time and extensive travels for the king to build support for his pan-Islamist dream. In December 1965 he went to Tehran and secured the backing of the shah of Iran. Additional trips followed to Morocco, Jordan, Pakistan, Turkey, Sudan, Guinea, Mali, and Tunisia in 1966.

The Saudi and Jordanian partnership in Yemen helped to reduce the rivalry between the two great families of the Arab world, the Saudis and Hashemites, and Faisal and Hussein became friends and confidants. This helped the nascent Islamic movement to grow. In 1965 the two kings signed a new border treaty that expanded Jordan's access to the Gulf of Aqaba, Jordan's only seaport and only access to the outside world.

The key turning point was the Arab-Israeli war in June 1967. Egypt was defeated in six days by the Israelis and lost the Sinai Peninsula. Jordan lost the West Bank and East Jerusalem, while Syria lost the Golan Heights. The Suez Canal was closed. It was a catastrophe for Nasser. At an Arab League summit in Khartoum, Faisal and Nasser reconciled. Egypt committed to withdrawing its army from Yemen; in return Saudi Arabia provided significant economic assistance to Egypt and Jordan. The Arab Cold War that had dominated the region from the 1950s ended.

In December 1967 Faisal created the Popular Committee for Aiding Martyrs, Families, and Mujahedin in Palestine. It was an organization dedicated to raising funds to support the Palestinians fighting Israel. Faisal turned to his half-brother Prince Salman, already the governor of Riyadh, to head the committee. He still heads it today. It began soliciting funds from Saudi citizens for the Palestinian cause and also received contributions from the state. It had a modest $5 million budget in 1968, which doubled to $10 million by 1978 and grew to $45 million in 1982 during the Lebanon war.[49] It was the first time the Kingdom, backed by the *ulema*, enthusiastically initiated fundraising for a political cause abroad and explicitly for fighting a jihad with mujahedin. Prince Salman, now king, was a central figure in the funding of the Afghan mujahidin in the 1980s, as we will see later. He plays a key role in funding the Palestinians today. In the second intifada in 2000 his Popular Committee raised funds for the families of martyrs killed by the Israelis. He personally wrote a check for $100,000 to the family of Muhammad al Durrah, a Palestinian teenager whose death in 2000 was caught on camera and became a symbol of Palestinian resistance.[50]

In September 1969 the first Islamic summit was convened in Rabat, Morocco. The summit created the Organization of Islamic Cooperation, which has its headquarters in Saudi Arabia. This became another instrument for promoting Islam. At its second summit in February 1974 in Lahore, Pakistan, it created the Islamic Solidarity Fund, another mechanism for promoting mosques and religious institutions of education.

At home Faisal also promoted religious education and created the modern Saudi educational system. In 1952 there were only 316 schools in the Kingdom, with fewer than 40,000 students, all boys. By 1973 there were 6,595 primary and secondary schools with over 700,000 students, many of them girls. Several universities were established. All these schools had a significant amount of the curriculum devoted to Islamic studies. Nonetheless, securing clerical support for girls' education was a challenge for Faisal. His wife, Queen Iffat, was a strong supporter of education for girls and the king and queen made an example by sending their daughters to school.[51]

Faisal needed teachers and professors to fill the new academic community he created. Far too few capable Saudis were available for the jobs needed. So the king turned to Egypt, especially the opposition Muslim Brotherhood. Nasser had outlawed the Brotherhood as a danger to his secular regime, depriving hundreds of Muslim Brotherhood professionals of their jobs. Now Saudi Arabia hired them to teach its children. Naturally they brought their own strict form of Islam with them, but that was acceptable to the Wahhabi clergy. As one Saudi intellectual later said, "The Muslim Brotherhood literally built the Saudi state and most Saudi institutions," especially in education, thanks to Faisal.[52]

Johnson and Faisal

Lyndon Johnson met with Faisal only once, on June 21, 1966, when Faisal came to Washington on an official visit. Johnson was told before the meeting by his staff that behind "this bearded robed desert king" is a man "a lot more modern than he looks. Under those robes you will find a sharp mind and deep devotion to educational and social progress." The king was looking for assurance that "we will not let Nasser swallow up Saudi Arabia." LBJ was reminded: "Our largest single overseas private enterprise is the Arabian-American Oil Company's $1.2 billion investment in Saudi Arabia."[53]

Johnson met privately with Faisal in the Oval Office for one hour and twenty minutes after the formal welcome to the White House. The two leaders spent a good deal of time discussing education in the Kingdom. Faisal described the progress the Kingdom had made on his watch, noting it was a "smooth evolutionary development" that accepted Saudi Arabia's "built-in peculiarities and checks." President Johnson was effusive in his praise for the king's efforts, likening them to his own efforts to build a great society in America. On Nasser and the Soviet threat, the two were in agreement; Johnson made clear he had given up trying to work with Cairo. The two leaders came away from the meeting in complete harmony.[54]

Washington was increasingly confident that Faisal had transformed the Kingdom from an unstable regime ripe for revolution into a stable and reliable ally. "Faysal's domestic position is strong. Mounting oil revenues will bring continued prosperity and economic advance" was the conclusion of a National Intelligence Estimate on the prospects for the Kingdom prepared by the CIA in December 1966.[55]

The short war between Israel and its Arab neighbors a year later, in June 1967, transformed the Middle East and profoundly changed the American-Saudi relationship. Faisal no longer saw Egypt as his top security challenge; the defeated and humiliated Nasser was now a threat to no one. Instead, Israel became Faisal's top concern, and he spent the rest of his life trying to undo the results of the June war.

It was deeply ironic that Egypt's swift defeat by Israel owed so much to Faisal's successful campaign to bog down the Egyptians in Yemen. The best of Egypt's military was still in Yemen when the 1967 crisis erupted in May. The CIA told LBJ that Israel had overwhelming military superiority over its Arab neighbors, and the Egyptian quagmire in Yemen only added to Israel's advantage.[56] Saudi Arabia sent an infantry brigade to help Jordan in the war but it arrived too late to see any fighting.[57]

Nasser blamed his defeat on the United States and the United Kingdom, claiming their air forces had assisted Israel. This false claim put enormous pressure on the other Arab states to take action against Washington and London. Iraq immediately cut off oil exports to the two countries on June 6, 1967. Arab oil ministers met in Beirut, Lebanon, later in June and passed resolutions calling for an embargo on oil sales. The Saudis were reluctant participants in the embargo because they recognized it would hurt their economy; Faisal was told by his economic advisers the embargo was damaging Saudi finances. At the Khartoum Arab summit where Faisal and Nasser had their public reconciliation, the Arabs agreed to end the embargo at Saudi initiative.[58]

The brief oil embargo in 1967 had little impact on the American economy because the United States did not import much oil at the time. The impact on the United Kingdom was much more significant because it imported almost all of its oil from the Persian Gulf. The closure of the Suez Canal due to the Israeli occupation on the east bank of the canal further damaged the UK's economy. The CIA, on June 7, 1967, predicted that a prolonged oil embargo would create a "severe economic depression" in Britain.[59] The embargo's economic impact played a key role in the subsequent decision of the British government to announce in January 1968 the withdrawal of British military forces from "east of Suez" by 1971, a decision that ended Britain's role as the preeminent outside power in the Gulf.[60] It would fall to Johnson's successor, Richard Nixon, to deal with the ramifications of the 1967 war and the British decision to quit the gulf.

Nixon, Kissinger, and Faisal

President Nixon and his national security adviser, Henry Kissinger, were not focused on the Arab world when they came into office in 1969. Vietnam was their first concern, and reordering America's relationship with Russia and China was their big objective. The Arab-Israeli conflict seemed frozen, with Israel the dominant power in the area. The White House followed Arab-Israeli events through the prism of the Cold War; the Soviets favored the Arabs and America backed Israel. Since Israel was the preeminent military power, the United States held the winning hand. The oil weapon was regarded in Washington (but not in London) as proven ineffectual by the 1967 case.

However, the withdrawal of the British forced some rethinking of American security policy for the Persian Gulf. Instead of reliance on the United Kingdom Nixon chose to rely on what was called a "twin pillars" strategy. Saudi Arabia and Iran would be the two regional powers armed and backed by the United States and responsible for maintaining order and stability.

In practice, Nixon and Kissinger regarded the shah of Iran as the main pillar of their strategy in the Gulf. When Nixon visited the region in May 1972, he stopped in Tehran and met with the shah, Mohammad Reza Pahlavi, but he did not visit Saudi Arabia.[61] Nixon was a long-time admirer of the shah. As vice president, he had first visited Iran in 1953 after the coup that ousted the leftist prime minister, Mohammad Mossadegh. The shah visited the White House three times during the Nixon administration. In contrast, Nixon never visited Saudi Arabia until the last days of his administration.

The shah was eager to modernize his country and project power in the region. He sent an expeditionary force to Oman to help the sultan of Oman defeat a communist insurgency based in South Yemen. He built a large army, air force, and navy to deter any regional or Soviet aggression. The shah backed Kurdish rebels in Iraq to keep the leftist government in Baghdad off balance. He also occupied several small islands in the Persian Gulf claimed by the United Arab Emirates when the British pulled out to enhance Iran's dominance of the region.

Faisal was more focused on the Arab-Israel conflict. He now was in the midst of his Islamic mobilization. The first Islamic summit took place on Rabat in 1969 and was called to action by Israel's annexation of East Jerusalem.

Faisal was deeply committed to the goal of returning Jerusalem to Arab and Muslim control. For him the loss of Jerusalem in 1967 was a great injustice. He had hoped the Johnson administration would behave like Eisenhower in 1956 and press for an early Israel withdrawal from captured territory. By 1969 the king realized that was not in the cards, and he began mobilizing an Islamic and Arab coalition to fight.

The king signaled his unease early to President Nixon. Just days after Nixon took office in 1969 Faisal met with the American ambassador and urged the new administration to take a "more balanced" approach to the Arab-Israeli conflict. Faisal bemoaned the spread of pro-Soviet governments in the Arab world, arguing Saudi Arabia was the only bulwark against the entire region becoming clients of Moscow. The Israeli victory in 1967 had enraged the Arab world, pushed many Arab leaders toward the Soviets, and weakened America's position in the region. He argued that Zionism was a partner with communism, pointing to the famous book, *The Protocols of the Elders of Zion*, as evidence. When the ambassador noted that *Protocols* was a forgery created by the Russian czar's secret police in 1905, Faisal not only rejected the allegation of forgery, he admitted the Kingdom was printing copies of the book in numerous languages to broaden its circulation.

The Saudi leader indicated his top priority was to end the Israeli occupation of Jerusalem. He signaled he was prepared to agree to give Israel "secure and recognized boundaries" that might differ from the 1948 cease-fire lines. Saudi Arabia would encourage other Arab states to accept such a settlement, Faisal said, but "the Israelis must leave old Jerusalem," meaning East Jerusalem, which they had occupied in June 1967. The Kingdom would never accept any agreement that failed to return East Jerusalem to Arab and Islamic control.[62] Faisal also summoned the American executives in the oil company Aramco and urged them to tell Nixon the status quo of Israeli occupation was unacceptable and unsustainable.

By the time the Middle East erupted again in the October 1973 war, which caught both Israeli and American intelligence napping, Nixon was immersed in the Watergate scandal and fighting to save his presidency. He was focused on his own political survival and left most of the foreign policy management to Kissinger. Nixon's vice president, Spiro Agnew, resigned from office during the first week of the war after corruption charges led to his indictment. "Nixon's drinking to excess became routine," one biographer has written, and Kissinger no longer "trusted Nixon to deal with the Middle East" crisis.[63]

In the months leading up to the war, Faisal began warning Nixon and Kissinger that he would use the oil weapon, cutting off oil exports, if the United States did not take action to resolve the Arab Israeli conflict and compel Israel to withdraw from the territories occupied in 1967. In April 1973 he sent his son Saud al Faisal and his oil minister, Ahmed Zaki Yamani, to Washington; for the first time they linked the future of oil production and exports to American policy on Israel. Without a change in the U.S. policy of supporting Israel, Saudi oil policies would be used to punish the United States. The Nixon administration dismissed their message as bluster.[64]

King Faisal went public with the message himself in the summer of 1973, telling *Newsweek* that "Saudi Arabia would use its oil as a political weapon if the United States continued to support Israel's policy of aggression against the Arab world."[65] Egypt's president, Anwar Sadat—who had succeeded Nasser after his death in 1970—and Syria's president, Hafez Assad, visited Riyadh in August 1973. The two leaders were well advanced in planning a joint attack on Israel, and they wanted to ensure that Faisal would support their war and use the oil weapon if the United States backed Israel.[66] Faisal agreed to use the oil weapon, asking Sadat to ensure the war lasted long enough for this weapon to be credible.[67] Sadat later praised Faisal in his memoirs as "always a rational and stable character and, above all, a real friend."[68]

Within days of the outbreak of conflict the United States initiated a massive airlift of supplies to Israel in response to a massive Soviet airlift and sealift of supplies to Egypt and Syria. On October 17, 1973, the oil ministers of the Organization of Arab Petroleum Exporting Countries (OAPEC) met in Kuwait and announced a 5 percent cut in oil production and exports to punish the United States for the airlift, promising that every thirty days that went by without a change in American policy would produce another 5 percent cut. The Saudis cut production 10 percent immediately. Ironically, Iraq, which had led the oil embargo in 1967, refused to participate in the 1973 cutback, arguing that it was too weak a gesture. Saddam Hussein, Iraq's dictator, actually increased oil production to take advantage of the Arab embargo.

On October 19 Nixon announced a $2.2 billion emergency military aid package for Israel. The next day Saudi Arabia cut all oil exports to the United

States, the Netherlands, Portugal, South Africa, and Rhodesia for helping Israel.[69] In December 1973 another OAPEC meeting in Kuwait cut oil production by 25 percent. Oil prices quadrupled, causing severe disruption in the United States and long lines at gas stations.[70] Yamani was the public face of Saudi oil policy but Faisal was the decisionmaker. The impact on the American economy was devastating. American gross domestic product fell 6 percent due to the Arab embargo between 1973 and 1975 and unemployment doubled to 9 percent; later in the 1970s, inflation soared well into the double digits, prolonging the economic impact of the embargo long after it had ended.

Faisal understood that a fundamental shift had occurred in the global oil markets. Ever since the end of the Second World War the world market had an excess of supply, largely due to the fast expansion in oil exports from the Middle East. The United States, moreover, had large oil resources of its own, and for many years had been only a marginal importer. That situation changed dramatically in the early 1970s. According to Daniel Yergin, the author of the best book on the oil market, U.S. oil imports grew from 3.2 million barrels per day (mbd) in 1970 to 6.2mbd in 1973. Saudi Arabia filled the demand. Its oil exports grew from 5.4mbd in 1972 to 8.4mbd in 1973, a staggering rise.

As Yergin puts it, Saudi Arabia replaced Texas as the global swing producer of oil, meaning it was the oil producer with sufficient excess oil production capability to meet global demand.[71] The Arab reduction in oil exports cut Arab oil exports from 20.8mbd on October 1, 1973, to 15.8mbd by December 15, 1973. Although Iran and Iraq increased production by 600,000 barrels per day, they could not fill the gap, and the global market lost 5mbd, or 10 percent, of global production. Unlike in 1967 America was no longer invulnerable. Oil prices soared from $2.90 a gallon in July 1973 to $11.65 in December.[72] The shah of Iran was the biggest price hawk despite not participating in the embargo and quietly shipping Iranian oil to Israel.

Kissinger visited Riyadh in November 1973, his first trip to the Kingdom and his first meeting with Faisal. It was also the first visit to the Kingdom by an American secretary of state since John Foster Dulles visited during the Eisenhower administration.[73] The king repeated his familiar remarks on the communist and Zionist collusion, the importance of Jerusalem, and the need for a comprehensive settlement to the Arab-Israeli conflict. On Nixon's instructions, Kissinger invited the king to Washington for a summit with the president. Nixon, although preoccupied with Watergate, realized the American public was focused on the oil crisis and desperately hoped that if he could engineer an end to the oil embargo it would benefit his flagging domestic position. Faisal turned down Kissinger and lectured him on the twin evils of Zionism and communism.[74] Nixon made another bid to end the oil embargo in January, asking Faisal to let him announce in the annual State of the Union address to Congress that the oil embargo would end; again Faisal rebuffed his request and demanded an end to the occupation of Syrian territory captured by Israel in the 1973 war. Nixon told Kissinger the oil embargo is "the only thing the country is interested in."[75]

The conclusion of a Kissinger-brokered Syrian-Israeli disengagement agreement—returning a token piece of Syrian territory occupied in 1967 and all the territory seized in 1973—finally led to an end of the embargo in the spring of 1974. Faisal had imposed a serious price on the American economy for American support for Israel. The global oil market had been radically transformed, oil was now in short supply, and prices were four times higher than before the war. An enormous transfer of wealth began from the oil-importing countries to the oil exporters, especially Saudi Arabia. The Saudis were the key to global oil economics.

Nixon traveled to the Middle East in June 1974 trying to build on Kissinger's success in disengaging the Syrians and Israelis on the Golan and the Egyptians and Israelis in the Sinai to boost his standing with the American public. Nixon became the first American president to visit the Saudi Kingdom; indeed, his three immediate successors had not visited the Kingdom in their presidencies. The reception in Jidda was subdued at best. At the state dinner on June 14, 1974, Nixon paid tribute to Faisal's extraordinary career in diplomacy from 1919 onward. He praised the king's wisdom and vision. He acknowledged the United States needed Saudi oil but stressed he wanted Saudi support on a wide variety of issues.[76]

In his remarks Faisal was direct. "Mr. President, the injustice and aggression which were wrought upon the Arabs of Palestine are unprecedented in history, for not even in the darkest ages had a whole population of a country been driven out of their homes to be replaced by aliens," the king argued. While thanking the president for the disengagement agreements, he went on to say, "We believe that there will never be a real and lasting peace in the area

unless Jerusalem is liberated and returned to Arab sovereignty, unless liberation of all the occupied Arab territories is achieved, and unless Arab people of
Palestine regain their rights to return to their homes and be given the right to
self-determination."[77] Faisal was confident the oil weapon gave him leverage
for the first time to achieve these goals.

Faisal's Assassination

Nixon resigned in disgrace two months later. His successor, Gerald Ford, kept
Kissinger on as secretary of state. On February 14, 1975, propitiously the
thirtieth anniversary of FDR's meeting with Ibn Saud, Faisal and Kissinger
had their last meeting together. By this time Faisal had come to distrust Kissinger who, the king believed, was interested in arranging a separate peace
between Egypt and Israel rather than a comprehensive settlement of the
Arab-Israeli conflict. Kissinger, in the king's mind, did not want to resolve
the Palestinian issue or restore Arab rule in East Jerusalem but, instead, wanted
to defuse the conflict by a separate Egyptian-Israeli agreement that would
significantly reduce the Arab states' strength and their capacity to make war.
The Riyadh meeting went poorly.[78]

The king also suspected Kissinger was behind press articles proposing an
American invasion of Saudi Arabia to grab its oil. In January 1975 *Commen-
tary*, a right-wing journal, had published an article suggesting the United
States should invade and occupy Kuwait, the Eastern Province, Bahrain, and
Qatar. Two months later, in March 1975, *Harper's* published "Seizing Arab
Oil," which advocated an American seizure of the Eastern Province in collu-
sion with Iran taking Kuwait. The royal family saw these articles as inspired
by Kissinger. Prince Fahd was especially worried.[79]

The Saudis were also unhappy with Kissinger's continued preference for
Iran as the chief pillar of stability in the Gulf. Their deep-seated aversion to
Persia was reinforced by America's tilt to the shah. Saudi oil minister Yamani
told the American ambassador in Riyadh in 1975 that all the rhetoric about
close American-Iranian ties "was nauseating to him and other Saudis." Yamani said the shah was a "megalomaniac" and predicted, "if the Shah departs
from the stage, we could have a violent anti-American regime in Tehran."[80]

On March 25, 1975, on the anniversary of the Prophet Muhammad's birthday, King Faisal was assassinated. In many Islamic countries the prophet's birthday is a holiday but in the Kingdom, keeping with its strict Wahhabi faith, it is celebrated only with special prayers. After his prayers the king went to a meeting with Yamani and a visiting Kuwaiti oil delegation. Among those in the audience chamber was one of his nephews, twenty-seven-year-old Prince Faisal bin Musa'id Abdul Aziz al Saud. When the two met, the prince pulled a revolver from his robes and shot the king three times, fatally.

The assassin had been educated in the United States, first at San Francisco State College, then at the University of Colorado, and finally at the University of California, Berkeley. This led to speculation that he was hired by the CIA on Kissinger's orders to kill Faisal in retaliation for the oil embargo. But the truth was more local. His brother had been killed in 1965 when Saudi police opened fire on a demonstration protesting the introduction of television into the Kingdom, which the protesters believed was an un-Islamic invention that would corrupt the values of the country. After a trial by religious authorities, the assassin who had sought revenge for his brother was beheaded in front of the Great Mosque in Riyadh.

With the assassination of Faisal, his brother Khalid bin Abdul Aziz al Saud became king. Vice President Nelson Rockefeller represented the United States at the funeral, becoming the first vice president to visit the Kingdom.[81]

Faisal's Legacy

King Faisal transformed Saudi Arabia. He inherited from his father a kingdom that had reached its historic borders dominating the Arabian Peninsula. But it was a backwater, desperately poor and almost entirely illiterate. His brother Saud had taken the kingdom to the edge of disaster by spending recklessly. The military was rife with coup plots, the Royal Saudi Air Force useless due to nationalist cabals and plots. Meanwhile, Egypt's Nasser seemed poised to bring down another monarchy.

By the time Faisal died, the Kingdom was truly transformed. The monarchy was solidly in place, the economy booming, and the country had become a world player. Faisal appointed his half-brothers to positions of authority, which they would hold for the next half-century, including four who would go on to be kings: Khalid, Fahd, Abdallah, and Salman. He created the modern ministerial system that runs the kingdom to this day. The military became a loyal institution of the state. Schools opened for millions of young Saudis, including women, and others enjoyed the opportunity to study abroad.

The oil boom of the 1970s accelerated all of Faisal's programs. The Saudi economy became an engine of growth, transforming the country with airports, shipping ports, and superhighways. At home and abroad huge sums were poured into building mosques and other religious institutions. Faisal made the country the leader of the Islamic world, giving the Kingdom enormous influence, what is now called "soft power."

Faisal was also the architect of the special relationship with America. His trip to Washington in 1943 set the stage for his father's famous meeting with FDR. Faisal negotiated the Dhahran air base deal. At President Kennedy's urging, he began reforms inside the Kingdom that would help stabilize the monarchy and solidify its hold on power. He oversaw the clandestine operations that bogged Egypt down in a Yemeni quagmire that left Egypt vulnerable to catastrophic defeat by Israel in 1967.

After 1967 Faisal tried to urge Washington to accommodate Arab interests, but neither Johnson nor Nixon listened to him. In 1973 he used the oil weapon against the United States, imposing a major penalty on the American economy and forcing Washington to alter its policies toward Israel and the Arabs.[82] The man who had created the uneasy alliance in many ways was also prepared to use the economics of energy to make America pay greater attention to Saudi interests.

Chapter Three

KHALID AND CARTER, 1975 TO 1982

K ing Khalid bin Abdul Aziz ruled the Kingdom of Saudi Arabia for seven
of its most critical and eventful years. He was confronted by two major
events in the first half of his reign: the fall of the shah's monarchy in Iran and
the separate Egyptian peace with Israel, both of which reached their climax in
early 1979. These two events dramatically shook Saudi relations with the
United States. Then in November 1979 the Grand Mosque in Mecca was seized
by a group of religious fanatics, and the king had to authorize the use of deadly
force to regain control of the holiest site in Islam. Almost immediately after
the crisis in Mecca, the Soviet Union invaded Afghanistan in December 1979,
and nine months later Iraq invaded Iran. The latter two crises pushed the
Kingdom closer to America.

Khalid was born on February 13, 1913, in Riyadh. He was Ibn Saud's fifth
son. In 1932 he was appointed viceroy of the Hejaz and served with the Saudi
army in the war with Yemen, and later helped negotiate the treaty that ended
the war. Ibn Saud then made him minister of the interior. He accompanied his
older brother Faisal to London in 1939 for talks on the future of Palestine, and

he accompanied Faisal again when they visited Washington in 1943 to lay the groundwork for the American-Saudi alliance.

The king had a history of heart trouble, and he had a serious heart incident in 1970, which led to heart surgery in Cleveland in 1972. As king he would return to Cleveland for more surgery in October 1978. Illness impacted his ability to rule, and Khalid delegated most of the day-to-day administration of the Kingdom to his younger brother, Crown Prince Fahd, giving him a major role in governing the Kingdom. Khalid remained the ultimate decisionmaker, however, and confronted alone the most serious challenge of his reign, the Mecca uprising, as Fahd was attending an Arab summit in Tunisia.

A CIA assessment prepared for the incoming administration of Jimmy Carter provides an American intelligence estimate of Khalid and his kingdom at the start of his turbulent reign. The assessment noted Fahd's day-to-day governance but said the king retained "the final authority." The CIA believed the "regime faces no threats of any consequence" at home. The Kingdom was stable although it would face daunting challenges as oil money led to rapid modernization of infrastructure and education. The CIA judged Khalid's top priority was a comprehensive settlement of the Arab-Israeli conflict, especially the Jerusalem issue. That would stabilize the region and reduce the dangers of war and terrorism. The king and crown prince believed "the U.S. is the key to a solution of the Arab Israeli problem because of its influence over Israel." The Saudis hoped President Carter would be their partner in peacemaking.[1]

John West, the new American ambassador to the Kingdom and friend of Carter, sent in his impressions of the royal family a few months later. He characterized Saudi Arabia as "presently undergoing an almost fantasy like experience similar to 'A Thousand and One Nights'—the whole country is changing overnight as though someone had rubbed Aladdin's lamp and said, 'Take this place into the Twentieth Century.'" He forecast this rapid change would "create tensions and frictions at all levels." The family was broadly divided between "liberals" led by Fahd and "conservatives" led by Prince Abdallah, third in line to the throne and a half-brother of Khalid and Fahd. He was more pious than most of his generation. Both factions were pro-American but the conservatives were more suspicious of Washington and worried that the pace of change was too fast. West warned Carter that "a failure of the Arab

Israeli peace negotiations coupled with continued U.S. support for Israel" was the most likely event to "cause real problems in U.S.-SAG [Saudi Arabia government] relations."[2] Carter read the report and wrote on it "superb report."

Twin Shocks Shake the Alliance

The Saudis were eager to get off to a good start with Carter after the bitterness of dealing with Henry Kissinger. In December 1976, at an Organization of Petroleum Exporting Countries (OPEC) summit in Doha, Qatar, the Kingdom refused to go along with Iran's push to raise oil prices again. Except for the United Arab Emirates, the rest of OPEC backed the shah. Saudi Arabia not only refused to increase its prices, it flooded the market by pumping more oil than ever before. The price remained constant, Iran was humiliated, and King Khalid and Oil Minister Ahmed Zaki Yamani had demonstrated who was really in charge of the global energy picture. Yamani publicly linked the oil decision to Saudi Arabia's hopes that Carter would take serious and decisive action to promote a comprehensive Arab-Israeli peace agreement. They were privately also pleased to see Iran lose clout.[3]

For his part, Jimmy Carter came into office in 1977 committed to achieving a comprehensive peace agreement to resolve the Palestinian issue. Carter was critical of Kissinger's diplomacy in general and his step-by-step approach in the Middle East in particular. He sought to convene jointly with the Soviet Union a peace conference in Geneva with all the Arab states and Israel to conclude a comprehensive peace. In May 1977 Crown Prince Fahd came to Washington to see Carter and engage in discussions on how to secure peace. The Saudis were prepared to live with Israel if the territories that Israel had occupied in 1967 were returned to the Arabs with minor border rectifications. Riyadh wanted the Palestinians to have their own independent state. Carter wrote in his diary that Fahd was very friendly and eager to find a settlement. He noted that the Saudis are "more interested in the Palestinian question than all the other problems" in the Middle East.[4]

On November 19, 1977, Egyptian president Anwar Sadat traveled to Jerusalem to meet directly with Israel's leaders and to address the Knesset. Sadat was frustrated by the slow movement of the Geneva process, which he felt gave too much leverage to the Soviets and Syrians. No Arab leader had ever met publicly with Israeli leaders before, especially not in Jerusalem. His unprecedented trip split the Arab world. Syria, Iraq, Algeria, Libya, and South Yemen accused him of seeking a separate peace with Israel that would return the Sinai Peninsula to Egypt, end the credible threat of an Arab military option against Israel, and leave the other Arab states abandoned to deal with a strengthened Israel. The Saudis, by contrast, were extremely reluctant to break with Sadat; they believed Egypt was central to the peace process. Sadat assured Khalid he did not want a separate peace. The Saudis cautiously waited to see what Sadat and Carter would do. Fahd told Secretary of State Cyrus Vance after Sadat's trip that it "was an impulsive act" but also an "important step."[5]

Carter traveled to the Middle East at the end of 1977. His Middle East trip began in Iran where he was received by the shah. On New Year's Eve Carter famously gave a toast declaring, "Iran, because of the great leadership of the Shah, is an island of stability in one of the most troubled parts of the world." His words, as he later wrote, "understandably, were derided when the Shah was overthrown thirteen months later."[6] In Iran, Carter met also with King Hussein of Jordan. Both the shah and the king urged Carter to pursue a comprehensive peace agreement.

After visiting India, Carter arrived in Riyadh on January 3, 1978, the second American president to visit the Kingdom. Carter was "pleasantly surprised at the vigor and involvement of King Khalid. Each day he has open court, so any citizen of his country can come and visit with him." Carter was especially impressed that Khalid ate with "common people" and "each evening when he goes back to his home palace he permits women to come in to meet with him."[7]

The detailed discussion of the region's problems was left to Crown Prince Fahd. Carter and Fahd reviewed Soviet activities in the region, oil policy, and bilateral relations. The Saudis were eager to get new American fighter aircraft, sixty F15s, for the Royal Saudi Air Force. They had raised this request at the beginning of the administration when Secretary of State Cyrus Vance met with Fahd in February 1977.[8]

The F15 sale was a political problem for Carter because it was opposed by the pro-Israel lobby in Congress. Israel was offered fifteen F15s (it already had sixty) and seventy-five F16s for itself and, after a bruising fight on the Hill, Carter was able to get the sale through the Congress by May 1978. The battle for the F15s was also Prince Bandar bin Sultan's maiden voyage into American politics. He had been training in Texas as an RSAF pilot when his father, Defense Minister Sultan bin Abdul Aziz al Saud, sent him to Washington to assist the lobbying campaign for the sale of the F15s. Bandar was good at working the Congress. Carter later recalled, "He was urbane, he was westernized adequately, he was eloquent, and he obviously had direct ties to the highest level of the royal family."[9] To reassure the Israelis, the prince conveyed an assurance via Washington that the RSAF would not deploy its F15s to Tabuk, its major air base near the Israeli state.[10]

But the major issue for Carter in Riyadh was the Arab-Israeli conflict. The Saudis pressed for Carter to commit to seeking a comprehensive agreement, not just an Egyptian peace treaty. Carter promised he would do so. Carter noted that the Saudis were "the only leaders I've met who want to see an independent Palestinian nation formed. Others [Arab states] only pay lip service to this, because of their reluctance to antagonize the Saudis." Carter said he was "very frank about this point. We [the United States] saw a real danger in an independent Palestinian state." Fahd told Carter the Kingdom wanted Sadat to succeed and was "eager to accommodate us on almost anything I request."[11]

Meanwhile, internal unrest began to snowball inside Iran. The Pahlavi dynasty faced many of the same socioeconomic frictions as the Saudis in modernizing rapidly. But Iran was also a more complex society with a much older history as a united nation. In Carter's diary the descent of the shah's regime can be traced over the course of 1978. Looking back later, Carter dates the beginning of the shah's downfall to the demonstrations that accompanied the monarch's visit to Washington in November 1977, which was marred by dramatic demonstrations across the street from the White House. In the summer of 1978 unrest became more frequent and violent. In October 1978 Carter noted the shah had broken all relations with Israel to appease the opposition, but this had no impact on the situation. On November 4, 1978, Carter notes in his diary that the shah was a weak and indecisive leader. On November 20 the president wrote, "We are concerned about the Shah's courage and forcefulness, and he seems to be excessively isolated." Carter found the Iranian situation to be a "quandary," but he was determined to give the shah as "much support as possible."[12]

The Saudis were shocked at what was developing across the Gulf in Iran. They were no fans of the shah, whom they regarded as arrogant and abrasive. His Pahlavi dynasty was founded by his father after World War I and had little legitimacy despite its pretensions to be the heirs of 4,000 years of Persian empires. The shah had seized several islands in the Gulf claimed by the United Arab Emirates when the British withdrew in 1972, an action that all the Arab states found threatening. His government had longstanding claims to Bahrain. Iran was also a close ally of Israel. Oil Minister Yamani once speculated that if there were another Arab-Israeli war, "Israel would occupy Tabuk in northern Saudi Arabia and Iran would occupy the Eastern Province and the small Gulf States." He told James Atkins, a previous American ambassador to Saudi Arabia, that the shah was "highly unstable mentally."[13]

Nonetheless, the unrest threatened a key U.S. ally against the Soviet Union and its radical Arab allies, like Iraq. Worse, the protests were a genuine national uprising against a monarch, orchestrated by the clerical establishment led by long-exiled Ayatollah Ruhollah Khomeini. The parallels to the Saudis' own position were all too obvious, although the Saudis argued they were fundamentally different situations. The Saudis were also convinced the Soviets were the real source of the opposition to the shah, somehow manipulating the situation behind the scenes to weaken an American ally and gain control of Iran. They were especially appalled that America seemed unable to smash the opposition and keep the shah, or at least a military government, in power. The Saudis had no formula for how to accomplish these goals, however.

The fall of 1978 proved to be a turning point for the Middle East. First, Carter hosted Sadat and Israeli prime minister Menachem Begin for a summit at the president's retreat at Camp David in Maryland. The result was a "framework" for an Egyptian-Israeli peace treaty and a much more vague agreement calling for autonomy for the Palestinians living in the West Bank and Gaza Strip. King Hussein of Jordan was to be the major interlocutor for negotiating autonomy, although he had not been invited to Camp David or informed about the negotiations as they were under way. Not surprising, he refused to take part in the Egyptian-Israeli autonomy talks. While the Camp David agreement was widely acclaimed in the United States and much of the world, it was almost universally seen in the Arab world as a betrayal by Sadat of the Palestinian cause and of Arab solidarity against Israel.

An Arab summit was convened in Baghdad on November 2, 1978, to discuss the Camp David agreement. Fahd attended for the Kingdom. The Baghdad summit agreed the Camp David agreements harmed the Palestinian cause, and the Arab leaders urged Sadat not to sign the peace treaty with Israel, freezing Egypt's position in the Arab League. For the Saudis it was an agonizing choice between Arab unity and the Palestinian cause on the one side and breaking with Egypt and the United States on the other. The king chose the Palestinian cause.

As the fall continued, the unrest in Iran escalated rapidly. By November massive demonstrations were sweeping Iranian cities, the oil industry was closed due to labor strikes, and the shah was isolated and confused. On the Shia holy day of Ashura that month, the day that commemorates the martyrdom of Ali's son Husayn in 680, millions of Iranians marched in massive demonstrations calling for the shah to abdicate or be overthrown. He went into exile in Egypt on January 16, 1979. The Saudis were stunned to see a monarchy collapse so quickly across the Gulf. By the end of February the monarchy was abolished and replaced by an Islamic Republic led by Ayatollah Khomeini, who promised publicly to overthrow the other monarchs in the region. The CIA told the White House that "Saudi reaction to Iranian developments is heavily colored by the conviction that the USSR is successfully engaged in a strategic effort to encircle Saudi Arabia," and the Saudis believed that Washington "does not appreciate the urgency of the situation."[14] The analysis argued a "conservative tide" was moving the ruling family away from close ties to the United States because of Camp David and the fall of the shah.

The Carter team tried to reassure the Saudis that America was still a reliable ally. Secretary of Defense Harold Brown traveled to Riyadh in February 1979 to propose closer military ties. A squadron of American F15 jets carried out a training mission in the kingdom, but to avoid raising tensions it was not armed with its usual complement of missiles. By the middle of 1979, the embarrassment of sending unarmed jets to defend the Kingdom, the U.S. support for Sadat's go-it-alone strategy, and the deteriorating situation in the Gulf had created "the most serious juncture in U.S.-Saudi relations since the 1973 Middle East War and oil embargo. Ties between the two appear to be marked by deepening frustration, conflicting goals and misunderstandings," reported the *Washington Post*.[15]

Sadat signed the formal peace treaty with Israel in Washington in March 1979. On March 31, 1979, the Arab summit in Baghdad was reconvened. Just before the Arab summit the two most hardline Arab states, Syria and Iraq, negotiated an end to their long-simmering feud over leadership of the Baath Party (a pan-Arab party with different factions ruling in Damascus and Baghdad). The temporary unity between Syria and Iraq greatly strengthened the anti-Sadat camp. As one expert notes, the Syria-Iraq rapprochement "forced the Saudis, privately reluctant to censure Egypt or antagonize Washington, to fall into line behind them."[16] Egypt's membership in the Arab League was suspended, and almost all the Arab states, including Saudi Arabia, withdrew diplomatic recognition from Egypt and closed their embassies in Cairo.

Crown Prince Fahd's standing in the Kingdom suffered seriously as a consequence of the twin setbacks. Fahd was rightly seen as the foremost advocate of close ties with both Carter and Sadat. He took an extended vacation in Europe from the end of March until the end of May 1979. This is a typical Saudi approach to the problem of being associated with an unpopular or unsuccessful policy gambit: escape the fallout by taking time out in your palace in Spain or elsewhere. Fahd's protégé, the head of royal intelligence, Kamal Adham, was relieved of his job, and Prince Turki bin Faisal became head of the General Intelligence Directorate.[17]

Khalid's decision to break with Cairo and Washington was consistent with Saudi policy toward the Arab-Israeli conflict. Since Ibn Saud's meeting with FDR in 1945, Saudi policy had been to support the Palestinians. In 1978 and 1979 Khalid was undoubtedly influenced by the legacy of his older brother Faisal. Given Faisal's actions during his own life, there is every reason to believe that if Faisal had been alive in the late 1970s he would have broken with Sadat and Carter over Camp David. Khalid, Abdallah, and a more reluctant Fahd were only doing what they expected Faisal would have done.

Officials in the Carter White House were highly critical of the Saudi decision to break with Sadat and not support Camp David. Gary Sick, Carter's National Security Council staff director for the Middle East, wrote a memo to the president characterizing Fahd's performance at the first Baghdad summit as "indecisive" and indicative of "a deeper malaise currently afflicting the

Saudi Royal Family." Khalid's well-known health issues kept him from day-to-day business, and now those problems reportedly were getting worse. "He has become very difficult to wake up in the morning and his concentration is said to be poor," Sick wrote. Faced with dramatic developments in the region, the Saudi leadership "is ill, indecisive and distracted by the succession struggle." The NSC experts recognized that Saudi Arabia was not Iran, but they raised concerns about the stability of the Kingdom and doubts about the CIA's ability to track unrest there.[18]

The perception that Saudi Arabia was ripe to follow Iran as the next monarchy to collapse into revolution was widespread in the United States in the wake of the shah's demise. A public opinion poll taken in early 1980 asked Americans about the chances of the Kingdom of Saudi Arabia being taken over by enemies of the United States in the new few years. Forty-three percent of those surveyed thought it was almost certain or somewhat likely, 29 percent thought it possible but not likely, and only 12 percent thought it not likely at all (17 percent answered "don't know").[19] Scholars at think tanks and universities wrote papers about the Kingdom's future, and many were bleak.

The White House convened a meeting of the national security team on April 27, 1979, to review ties with the Kingdom. The summary of the meeting's conclusions noted "a general consensus that the U.S. relationship with Saudi Arabia is undergoing a period of severe strain."[20] So with the U.S.-Saudi relationship in turmoil due to differences on the peace process and the collapse of the shah, an unprecedented domestic incident was about to shake the Kingdom. Washington would be almost entirely a bystander—a very worried bystander—in the next chapter in Khalid's reign.

The Assault on Mecca

The Grand Mosque in Mecca is Islam's holiest site, because at its center is the *Kaaba*, believed to be the first house of worship, built by Abraham. Muslims pray toward Mecca and the mosque five times a day and are buried with their heads pointing toward it. Only Muslims are allowed inside the city; it is a crime for non-Muslims to enter the city or its environs. For the House of Saud no role is more important than their responsibilities as custodians of the holy mosques. The Saudi conquest of Mecca from the Hashemites consolidated the modern Kingdom's hold on the Arabian Peninsula and made it a major power in the Arab and Islamic worlds. Between 1955 and 1973 the Saudis engaged in a major expansion of the mosque to increase its size and remove most of the vestiges of Ottoman or older architecture. Since 1979 the Saudis have engaged in three additional large-scale projects to expand the mosque's capacity.

On November 20, 1979, several hundred extreme fanatics entered the holy mosque. They secretly brought in weapons, ammunition, and food in coffins and other hiding places. Some of the local police and security guards were bribed into allowing in more weapons and supplies by back gates. There are no reliable numbers on how many extremists were involved in the assault (300 is a good guess), but they definitely took the security forces by complete surprise and had much more advanced small arms than the poorly trained and poorly armed police.[21] At dawn they brought their weapons out of hiding, quickly subdued the police, and took control of the mosque and several thousand hostages who had been worshiping that morning.

Our knowledge of the mosque's seizure and subsequent recapture by the Saudi authorities owes a great deal to Yaroslav Trofimov, an enterprising investigative journalist who published *The Siege of Mecca* in 2007 based on years of interviews inside the Kingdom, France, and the United States. He obtained access to the American ambassador's diary, a critical source for understanding the U.S. perception of the crisis from John West's pivotal position. Trofimov also secured considerable assistance from the then head of Saudi intelligence, Prince Turki bin Faisal, who was present at the battle and was a key interlocutor in securing help from the French for the final assault on the rebels.[22]

I was the Saudi analyst in 1979 in the CIA's office responsible for political analysis so I had a direct view of what the American intelligence community knew—and didn't know—about what was going on in the Kingdom. Some of that information recently has been declassified by the State Department. It was an extraordinary period. On November 4, just two weeks before the takeover of the mosque in Mecca, the American embassy in Tehran was seized by Iranian radicals, who would hold most of our diplomats hostage for the next 444 days. Shortly after the seizure of the mosque in Mecca, Iranian leader Ayatollah Khomeini accused the United States and Israel of responsibility for the attack. U.S. diplomatic posts across the Islamic world were the target of demonstrations and, often, violence. The embassy in Islamabad was sacked by a mob on November 21, and the embassy in Tripoli attacked by another mob on December 2.

When the mosque was seized, the first question asked by everyone was: who are these guys? An employee of the Haj Research Center in Mecca, Ziauddin Sardar, who was in Mecca that morning, later wrote:

> Saudi Arabia is a police state and bad news is buried quickly and permanently. There was a total blackout and no one had any idea what was happening. Mecca was under attack by Zionist and American imperialist plotters, said some. The Sacred Mosque had been taken over by renegade Shia from Ayatollah Khomeini's Iran, others speculated. A third theory postulated a split in the royal family, with Crown Prince Fahd's men trying to overthrow King Khalid.[23]

The Saudi authorities cut all communications to the Kingdom from the outside world. The mosque and the city were surrounded by concentric rings of security forces from the Saudi Ministry of the Interior run by Prince Nayef, the Saudi Arabian National Guard run by Prince Abdallah, and troops from the regular army run by Prince Sultan.

The rebels soon identified themselves to the authorities. They were Islamic radicals who believed the Mahdi had arrived. In Islamic eschatology, the Mahdi is a prophesied redeemer who will rid the world of evil and set the stage for the Final Day of Judgment. The Mahdi is not specifically referred to in the Quran, but there are many references to a Mahdi in the hadiths, the accounts of the Prophet Mohammad's life that are studied by Islamic theologians and scholars for insights into the religion. Not surprisingly, Sunni and Shia Muslims have very different visions of the Mahdi.

The insurgents in the Grand Mosque were led by two men. One was Juhayman al Utaybi, a former soldier in the Saudi National Guard who was the mastermind of the attack. The other was the self-proclaimed Mahdi, Muhammad Abdallah Qahtani, Juhayman's twenty-seven-year-old brother-in-law. Most of the rebels were Saudis, primarily from the Utaybi tribe, but others were followers of Juhayman from across the Islamic world. He had a particularly strong following in Kuwait. They freed most of the worshippers in the mosque after a few hours of trying to convince them of the legitimacy of their religious claims.

Juhayman had written a series of letters after he left the National Guard in which he attacked the House of Saud for its close ties to America and for widespread corruption, citing Wahhabi scholars to justify his arguments. His focus was on the concept of the Mahdi. Juhayman said it was revealed to him in a dream in late 1978 that his brother-in-law was the Mahdi because he had the right family heritage to be the redeemer and his physical appearance was as foretold in the hadiths. Juhayman's letters were published and circulated widely in the Kingdom and in Kuwait.[24]

It quickly emerged in the royal court that members of the Saudi religious clergy were well aware of Juhayman and his group. In fact, the top cleric in the Kingdom was their patron and protector: the blind shaykh Abdul Aziz bin Baz, who was a very conservative leader of the Wahhabi clergy. Baz was notorious for believing the world was flat and that high heels were evil. He intervened with Prince Nayef to keep Juhayman's followers out of prison at least once before 1979—not because he believed the Mahdi was coming imminently but because he believed Juhayman's followers were pious Muslims. Born in 1910, bin Baz had been chancellor of the Islamic University of Medina and the chairman of the Scientific Research and Religious Edicts group that issues edicts for the Kingdom. In 1992 he became grand mufti of Saudi Arabia. Bin Baz had been a patron of dozens of what one observer in Mecca then called "irrational zealots."[25] Bin Baz was not aware of Juhayman's plans to attack the mosque or to use force, but he knew exactly who Juhayman was.[26]

The mosque was a natural fortress that had been built and rebuilt over the centuries. Six large minarets, 292 feet high, provided excellent observation points and positions for snipers and machine gunners to control the inside and outside of the mosque. Under the surface is a series of tunnels and rooms called the *Qaboo* that made for an excellent hiding area and an almost impenetrable bunker to fight from, especially for fanatics ready to die for their Mahdi. In the early hours after the takeover, with no architectural plans for the site, the Saudi authorities were able to get the assistance of the bin Laden construction company, which was in charge of the mosque's expansion and had detailed plans for the mosque and the Qaboo. The Hajj Research Centre in

Mecca also provided detailed plans that could be used for the recapture of the mosque.[27]

King Khalid was in Riyadh when the attack occurred. It was the first day of Muharram in the Islamic year 1400—the Islamic New Year and the start of the fifteenth century for Muslims. Khalid was home alone, to a certain extent. Crown Prince Fahd was in Tunisia at another Arab summit to condemn Sadat; with him were Foreign Minister Prince Saud al Faisal and the intelligence chief, Prince Turki al Faisal. Deputy Crown Prince and National Guard Commander Abdallah was in Morocco on vacation. Khalid quickly convened the available senior princes: Prince Sultan and Prince Nayef, as well as Mecca governor Prince Fawwaz.

The royal family was relieved to learn there were no other uprisings in the Kingdom. The Sunni majority was quiet. The other holy city, Medina, was calm. Later, unrelated violence would break out in the Shia towns in the Eastern Province, but they were not believers in the Mahdi. On November 25 large demonstrations in those towns protested Saudi discrimination against Shia. Three days later, the National Guard used massive force to break up Ashura commemorations in Qatif, the stronghold of Shia in the province, which had turned into anti-monarchy protests. The National Guard's suppression was brutal and effective. The historic center of the old city of Qatif was totally demolished and replaced with a parking lot and a large Sunni mosque. However, the Shia unrest did not affect the siege in Mecca.[28]

The royal family asked the clerical establishment, the *ulema* headed by bin Baz, for a religious edict authorizing the use of force to retake the mosque. It took several days to gather the clerics together and for them to debate. On November 23, 1979, they issued a document authorizing the Kingdom to use "all measures" necessary.[29] Even then the family refrained from use of the Royal Saudi Air Force or bombing.

The ground assault was hampered by multiple chains of command. The Interior Ministry forces were directed by Prince Nayef, the National Guard by Abdallah or his subordinates, and the regular army by Prince Sultan. It was a bloody and messy affair as none of the three services was trained in urban warfare or well equipped for the battle. The Saudis attempted to use tear gas against the rebels, some of it provided by the United States, but the troops were untrained in how to use the gas and were poorly equipped with gas masks to defend themselves from it. By the end of the first week of the siege, however, the surface level of the mosque was back in Saudi hands, the remaining rebels having been driven into the Qaboo.

It took another week, with help from the French, to reclaim the underground chambers and capture Juhayman and the rest of his followers. Prince Turki secured the help of the French intelligence community to defeat the holdouts. Both Prince Turki and Prince Nayef had close relations with their French counterparts. Khalid took their advice and appealed to Paris, discreetly, for help. French president Giscard d'Estaing sent three French commandoes along with the chemical agent dichlorobenzylidene-malononitrile, or CB. The French commandoes never went into the Grand Mosque but they trained Saudis in how to use the agent, and it worked. The Qaboo was secured and all the remaining rebels killed or captured by the end of the second week of the siege.[30]

The Saudis had specifically turned down an offer of assistance from Jordan. King Hussein visited Riyadh on November 28, 1979, while the Qaboo was still in Juhayman's hands and offered the use of his elite special forces. Khalid and Abdallah met with Hussein and politely refused his offer. The last thing the Saudis wanted was to have the Hashemites recover Mecca for them from religious zealots.[31]

On December 6, 1979, King Khalid visited the mosque and was shown on Saudi television walking safely inside the holy site. Prince Nayef announced that seventy-five rebels and sixty Saudi soldiers had died in the battle. Ambassador West later reported to Washington that the real fatality toll was closer to 1,000. The self-proclaimed Mahdi had died in the battle, but Juhayman was captured. On January 9, 1980, sixty-three rebels were executed publicly in eight Saudi cities. Forty-one were Saudis, ten were Egyptians, six were South Yemenis, three Kuwaitis, and one each came from North Yemen, Iraq, and Sudan. Juhayman's organization was destroyed in Saudi Arabia by a ruthless crackdown by the Interior Ministry. A remnant survived in Kuwait for a few years.[32]

The governor of Mecca, Prince Fawwaz bin Abdul Aziz, resigned his post in late December, serving as the scapegoat in the royal family for the failure to see what Juhayman was planning and for the botched initial attempts to stop the takeover. He was an easy scapegoat since he was a fairly liberal prince and had flirted with Egypt's Nasser in the 1960s. Juhayman had criticized him for drinking alcohol and gambling. Several military commanders were also fired, including, for no obvious reason, the commander of the Air Force.[33]

President Carter and his team in Washington were worried observers to the Mecca mosque siege. The Saudis provided critical information about events in the first few days of the attack, despite their embarrassment about losing control of the mosque. The U.S. Embassy in Jidda was able to get some firsthand accounts of the situation from an American helicopter pilot who worked for the Saudi civil defense system and was flying reconnaissance missions over the mosque. He privately briefed the embassy on what he had seen and learned. The petroleum minister, Shaykh Zaki Yamani, was the first Saudi government official to brief Ambassador West on the attack and revealed that the attackers were Sunni zealots led by a self-proclaimed Mahdi.[34]

The day after the attack began, November 21, 1979, the embassy in Jidda reported (in a recently declassified cable to Washington) that the twenty-six-year-old self-proclaimed Mahdi, Muhammad Abdallah, had seized the mosque with between 200 and 500 followers. The mission reported that "there is no repeat no direct relationship with Iran and Muhammad and his followers deny any Khomeini influence in their actions." According to a senior Saudi cabinet official (Yamani), the Saudi authorities did not see the mosque attack as a fundamental danger to the monarchy because the attackers "lacked sophisticated leadership sufficient to translate their religious principles into overthrow of a civil government." Aside from a few minor incidents in Medina, the rebels had no broader support, the embassy reported.[35] The embassy reporting provided the basis of the intelligence community's assessment for the White House.

Reacting to the events in Tehran, Mecca, and Islamabad, the Carter administration in late November sent a United States Navy carrier battle group, led by the nuclear carrier the USS *Kitty Hawk*, to the Persian Gulf as a show of force. In announcing the deployment, the administration press spokesman reported that "some kind of disturbance, apparently a seizure of a mosque by a group" had occurred in Mecca at the Grand Mosque. This was the first public statement by any government about the takeover, breaking the Saudi efforts to keep it a secret.[36] The Saudis were livid. Prince Nayef, the head of the Interior Ministry, said later that the American announcement helped trigger the wave of violence against American diplomats that followed. He even speculated "about the reason why the Americans announced the report the way they did." Nayef would not be a friend of the United States for many reasons as he rose in prominence in the royal family, and this was one of those reasons.[37]

There was much speculation in Washington that Iran must be behind the attack in Mecca given the heated atmosphere over the U.S. hostages in Tehran and the unrest among Shias in the Eastern Province. The CIA fairly quickly concluded the mosque takeover was not an Iranian provocation, however: "The attack appears to have been the isolated act of a small group of religious fanatics. The Saudis have had to quell uprisings by similar groups in the past, most notably in the 1920s and 1930s when dissident elements of the Ikhwan— the military arm of the Wahhabi religious movement—rose against the Saudi monarchy. In 1975 King Faysal was assassinated by a religious fanatic."[38] The embassy reports and the Saudis' own reporting all confirmed that no Iranian hands were involved.

Despite the huge shock of the Mecca attack, the rebels never posed an existential threat to the survival of the House of Saud. Juhayman and his band of about 300 (the CIA estimated "several hundred")[39] could not have over- thrown the monarchy. They got no assistance from others in the Kingdom. Their connections with clerics like bin Baz were covered up quickly, and the Wahhabi clergy not only condemned them but sentenced them to execution. As the CIA noted in its retrospective shortly after the mosque was recaptured, the rebels enjoyed no mass support in the Kingdom: "On the contrary, most Saudis appear to be outraged by the desecration of the mosque and there have been numerous calls, especially from the Saudi religious establishment, for quick punishment of the attackers."[40]

Nonetheless, the attack on the holy mosque had a profound impact on the royal family. It symbolized the reality that the danger to the family's hold on power no longer came from Egyptian-inspired leftist nationalists like in the 1960s but, rather, extremist Islamic zealots outraged by corruption and change. The rapid modernization of the country inevitably produced resistance from those who were attached to core Wahhabi principles. As one Saudi historian has written, "The mosque siege unveiled the tension between the state and its own religion."[41] Even if the clerical establishment reluctantly agreed to modernization, some dissidents were ready to use arms to fight change and resist the royal family. Senior family leaders concluded, therefore, that the best assurance against such dangers was to embrace the faith even more vigorously, slow down social changes, bring the clerics closer to the family, and find causes for Faisal's global Islamic movement to support and encourage.

Only weeks after King Khalid's triumphal walk through the Grand Mosque such an opportunity would present itself. The Soviet Union would invade its Muslim neighbor Afghanistan and set the stage for the final and decisive battle of the Cold War. The invasion would present the occasion for America and Saudi Arabia to work together to defeat Moscow and international communism. It would, of course, have other consequences as well.

The Saudis spent billions restoring the mosque after the battle in November 1979 and then vastly expanding its size and transforming the neighborhoods around it. After Khalid's death, King Fahd expanded the mosque with fourteen more gates and two more minarets. A million worshippers could be accommodated during the hajj season. New roads and tunnels were built to speed traffic into Mecca and make the hajj more orderly. A third massive expansion began in 1988 with Fahd building a royal palace overlooking the mosque.[42] The contract for the expansion was given to the Saudi Bin Laden Group, the huge construction company founded by Osama bin Laden's father, the largest construction company in the Middle East. One of the most recent projects built more than 300 retractable canopies to shelter worshippers from the sun. From 1979 to 2016 the Saudis spent $26.6 billion on the mosque.[43]

Some Muslims have been critical of the Saudi expansion projects, arguing they have destroyed many old Islamic architectural treasures that could have been preserved. Some argue that the many accidents that have plagued the hajj in the last quarter century are due in part to the hasty expansion and the creation of tunnels and overpasses that become death traps for tired, thirsty pilgrims, especially the elderly. One critic called the reconstruction a Saudi "nightmare vision of modernity, turning Mecca into Disneyland."[44]

Today the largest bell tower clock in the world looks down on the Grand Mosque. Built at a cost of $15 billion, the Makkah Royal Clock Tower, part of Abraj al-Bait, a development in the heart of Mecca, is the third-tallest building in the world. The bin Laden group was the contractor; an Ottoman fortress was demolished to build it. The clock is visible for miles and is illuminated at night. The structure includes a shopping mall and the Hotel Fairmont Mecca, a five-star, luxury 800-room hotel for Muslims only. It has 1.5 million square meters of floor space and two helicopter landing pads on the roof. A one-room studio apartment sells for $650,000.[45] The minarets of the Grand Mosque are now overlooked by a much taller skyscraper.

Afghanistan and Iraq

Events in late 1979 outside the Kingdom quickly and dramatically altered the picture for King Khalid. On December 24, the Soviet Union invaded Afghanistan. The Soviet air force launched a massive airlift of troops into Afghanistan's capital, Kabul, to overthrow a failing Marxist government and replace it with another entirely beholden to Moscow. The 105 Guards Airborne Division, one of Russia's most elite military units, led the assault. Some 300 transport flights delivered the division to Bagram air base outside the capital. The previous regime was deposed, its leader killed, and a new Soviet-backed government imposed. Soviet armored forces also crossed the border from Soviet Central Asia and occupied all of Afghanistan's main cities in a couple of days. Over the Christmas holiday, the Soviet Union's Fortieth Red Army invaded and occupied Afghanistan.

President Carter was caught by surprise. His private diary shows he was at Camp David to celebrate Christmas and was shocked by the Russian attack. The American intelligence community had carefully monitored the buildup of Soviet forces in the months preceding the invasion but assessed that a Soviet invasion was unlikely because it would lead to a prolonged insurgency like Vietnam. The CIA thought the Soviet leadership was too smart to fall into such a quagmire.[46]

Immediately after the Soviet invasion, the president of neighboring Pakistan, General Mohammad Zia ul Haq, called King Khalid to discuss the Soviet threat, then urgently sent his intelligence chief to Riyadh to meet with King Khalid and Prince Turki. Zia was convinced the Soviet invasion of Afghanistan was the first step in a larger plan of Russian aggression. Zia believed Pakistan or Iran would be next, giving Moscow a warm-water port on the Arabian Sea and the Straits of Hormuz, along with control over the Persian Gulf and its oil resources. His fears matched those of the Saudis. The king agreed immediately to support Pakistan and assist its efforts to arm and train an Afghan resistance, the mujahedin, to fight the Soviet occupation.[47]

Carter scheduled a National Security Council meeting at the White House for December 28. His national security adviser, Zbigniew Brzezinski, set the stage with a memo to the president the day before the meeting. In it he argued that whatever Moscow's immediate motives for the invasion, once they were in Afghanistan the Soviets' motives and ambitions might grow, given the instability in Iran and Pakistan. Moscow's advances "could produce a Soviet presence right down on the edge of the Arabian and Oman Gulfs." To stop the Russians it was essential to provide "money as well as arms shipments to the rebels" in Afghanistan in "concert with Islamic countries in a covert action campaign to help the rebels." The Saudis would be a crucial partner in the struggle, and China should be enlisted, as well as European allies like the United Kingdom and France. Aid to Pakistan, which had been suspended because of the country's work to acquire nuclear weapons, must be restored as well.[48]

As he wrote in his diary, the president and his team decided to regard the Soviet invasion as "a radical departure from the reticence which the Soviets had shown for the last ten years since they overthrew the government of Czechoslovakia" and "to make this action by the Soviets as politically costly as possible." Carter said he "sent on the Hot Line the sharpest message that I have ever sent to [Soviet leader Leonid] Brezhnev, telling him the invasion of Afghanistan would seriously and adversely affect the relationship between our two countries." The president decided to impose economic sanctions on Russia: interrupting grain sales and high technology sharing; canceling fishing rights; restricting negotiations on culture, trade, commerce, and other bilateral exchanges; canceling visits to the Soviet Union; and establishing differences in technology and trade transfers that would benefit Communist China at the Soviets' expense. These moves were announced in January.[49]

The president also decided to sign a secret "Presidential Finding" authorizing a new covert action by the CIA to supply lethal weapons to the mujahedin through the Pakistani government. Signed on December 29,[50] this document notified the Congress of the covert action so it would be able to conduct oversight of the program.[51]

The chief of the Near East Division in the CIA's Directorate of Operations at the time was Charles Cogan, a longtime veteran of the CIA with years of experience in clandestine activity. Cogan quickly turned the Presidential Finding into action. Cogan had just become head of the division the previous summer, and he would stay in that key post until 1984. His officers were ready to act. As he relates in his memoir, "The first arms—mainly .303 Enfield rifles—arrived in Pakistan on January 10, 1980, fourteen days after the Soviet invasion." The initial goal was "for the purpose of harassing the Soviet occupation forces in Afghanistan."[52]

The arms were carefully chosen so their origin could not be traced to the United States, thereby allowing the operation to remain secret and giving the president plausible deniability that a secret war was under way. Carter wanted to emphasize Soviet-origin weapons so they would appear to be simply weapons captured on the battlefield. The CIA's professional operators saw the same need to keep hidden the CIA role.

Pakistani cooperation was essential to Carter's plan to resist the Soviet takeover. Carter called General Zia after the December 28, 1979, NSC meeting to ask him to receive Deputy Secretary of State Warren Christopher with an urgent message. According to Carter's diary, Zia was "reluctant" to have Christopher come immediately as the situation was "delicate, tragic and sensitive" in Pakistan, but he made clear that he wanted American aid for Pakistan and the Afghan resistance. Zia told Carter that Pakistan now faced an "onslaught" by the Soviets, but that Pakistan was determined to resist. Zia also wanted plausible deniability of the role to be played by Pakistan's intelligence service—just as Carter did for the CIA. The basis of American-Pakistani covert cooperation was established in the call.[53]

The president wanted to build a large global alliance against the Soviets and supporting Pakistan. Moscow blocked any significant action in the United Nations Security Council with its veto, but the UN General Assembly was urgently convened. Pakistani foreign minister Agha Shahi led the campaign to condemn the Soviets in the General Assembly, with strong support from Saudi Arabia's Prince Saud al Faisal. The General Assembly voted 104 to eighteen, with fourteen abstentions, to condemn the Russian action. It was a stunning diplomatic defeat for Moscow, which got support only from fellow members of the Soviet bloc.

The president convened another high-level meeting at a White House breakfast on January 4, 1980, to review aid to Pakistan and the Afghan rebels. His preference, as he outlined in his diary, "was to send them the kind of weapons they could use in the mountains in a portable condition, primarily against tanks and armored personnel carriers. We need to get as many other nations as possible to join us in a consortium so that the Paks won't be directly seen as dependent on or subservient to us."[54] The Saudi Kingdom was the key to the consortium.

Pakistani foreign minister Shahi was invited to visit Washington after the UN vote. Carter and Zia spoke on the phone again on January 8, 1980, and Carter met with Shahi four days later in the Oval Office. Carter proposed a $400 million aid package in combined economic and military assistance over a two year period. Washington would also urge aid for Islamabad "from the Saudis, European allies, and Japan," Carter recounts in his diary.

In February 1980 Deputy Secretary of State Christopher and Brzezinski went to Islamabad and Riyadh. The two American envoys presented General Zia and then King Khalid with a broad overview of Washington's post-invasion thinking. Brzezinski later said that he found Zia very self-confident and assured despite the dangerous waters around Pakistan. The Saudis were deeply alarmed by the Soviet threat and, despite the disappointments over Camp David and Iran, eager to work with Washington.[55] In a meeting of the national security principals on February 6, 1980, Brzezinski and Christopher reported a "change of mood in Saudi Arabia from a year ago" due to the Soviet invasion of Afghanistan and renewed Soviet subversive actions elsewhere in Yemen and East Africa.[56]

The centerpiece of the strategy was covert aid to the mujahedin. The CIA and the Saudi intelligence service, led by Prince Turki, would give money to the Pakistani intelligence service, the Inter-Services Intelligence Directorate (known as the ISI), to arm and train the Afghan insurgents in camps inside Pakistan. The ISI would also assist the mujahedin in carrying out attacks inside Afghanistan against the Soviets. The CIA and Saudi intelligence would have no direct presence in Afghanistan. Instead, Washington and Riyadh would be the financiers and arms suppliers for the war.[57]

The Christopher and Brzezinski mission was a success in both Islamabad and Riyadh. The Saudis agreed to match American funding for the mujahedin, and the partnership among the three intelligence services was set in place. "Zbig reported privately to me that his trip to Pakistan and Saudi Arabia was successful," Carter wrote in his diary on February 6, 1980. Both Zia and the Saudis also wanted American "protection," but they wanted it kept private. In public they would be defended by "unanimity among the Muslim world," Carter wrote. The secret war would stay behind the scenes.[58]

The Saudis also asked Zia for help protecting the Kingdom at home. Beginning in 1982 Pakistan deployed a reinforced armored brigade to Saudi Arabia stationed in Tabuk. Its primary mission was to guard against an Israeli attack from the northwest, but it also served as a loyal Praetorian Guard force if the royal family needed assistance. The 12th Khalid bin Walid Independent Armored Brigade grew to 20,000 troops at its height. Saudi Arabia paid for all the costs of the Pakistani deployment, which lasted throughout the 1980s. It was a hedge just in case the Americans were not reliable.[59]

In his State of the Union address on January 23, 1980, Carter explained his strategy to the American people without discussing the covert operation. He said the Middle East was now threatened by "the Soviet troops in Afghanistan." They posed a direct threat to "more than two-thirds of the world's exportable oil. The Soviet effort to dominate Afghanistan has brought the Soviet military to within 300 miles of the Indian Ocean and close to the Straits of Hormuz, a waterway through which most of the world's oil must flow. The Soviet Union is now attempting to consolidate a strategic position, therefore, that poses a grave threat to the free movement of Middle East oil."

Carter announced that after careful thought and consultation with key allies in the region it was vital to "preserve the security of this crucial region." He said, "Let our position be absolutely clear: an attempt by any outside force to gain control of the Persian Gulf region will be regarded as an assault on the vital interests of the United States of America, and such an assault will be repelled by all means necessary, including military force." Carter did not specifically refer to the Kingdom of Saudi Arabia, but his speech was the clearest statement by any president to date that America would defend the Kingdom by force if it were threatened.[60]

The "Carter doctrine," as it was labeled immediately, was implemented by creating a new military command to rush American forces to the region in an emergency. This would become, in time, the Central Command with its headquarters in Tampa, Florida. Carter also announced the United States would boycott the 1980 Olympic Summer Games in Moscow; eventually sixty-five countries joined the boycott.

The Saudi response to the Soviet invasion was not limited to the official financing of the covert war. Saudis, both royals and commoners, were enthusiastic supporters of the mujahedin and the fight against communism. Khalid appointed his brother Salman to lead a private fundraising campaign to raise more money for the Afghan resistance. Prince Salman bin Abdul Aziz was born on December 31, 1935, and had been governor of Riyadh province since 1962. Since most royals lived in Riyadh, Salman was closely connected to the family, literally knowing all its secrets. When the Kingdom had begun in the early twentieth century, Riyadh had only 10,000 inhabitants. By 2017 it had 7 million, with most of the growth occurring on Salman's watch.

Salman's impressive skills as a top administrator led Khalid and Fahd to select him to establish a "private" committee to raise funds for the mujahedin from Saudi princes and the public. The head of the Saudi Wahhabi clerical establishment, Shaykh Abdul Aziz bin Baz, issued a religious order, or fatwa, charging Salman's committee to raise funds from across the Kingdom to fund the jihad in Afghanistan. As a result, the Kingdom would contribute both official money and private money to the war.[61]

The private Saudi funds were especially critical in the first years, when American support was small. As the head of the Pakistan intelligence service's Afghan cell has written, "It was largely Arab money that saved the system. By this I mean cash from rich individuals or private organizations in the Arab world, not Saudi government funds. Without these extra millions the flow of arms actually getting to the mujahedin would have been cut to a trickle" before 1983.[62] One American estimate is that private Saudi donations through Salman's committee averaged around $20 million to $25 million a month.[63]

The cleric bin Baz was also active in the propaganda side of the war in Afghanistan. He wrote the foreword to an influential book published in 1984 titled *The Defense of Muslim Lands*. The author was a Palestinian, Abdallah Azzam, who had lived and studied in the Kingdom before moving to Pakistan after the Soviet invasion. Azzam's book argued that the war in Afghanistan was a jihad, a holy war that should be supported by every Muslim as a holy obligation to defeat Russian aggression against a Muslim country. It was an enormously successful book read by Muslims around the world and remains a major ideological statement of the global jihad today. Bin Baz's endorsement of it was a major statement of the Wahhabi and Saudi commitment to the jihad in Afghanistan.[64]

Other Saudis also volunteered to help the Afghan cause. The most famous today is Osama bin Laden, a son of Mohammad bin Awad bin Laden, the wealthiest construction mogul in the Kingdom. Born in 1908 in Hadramut Province of Yemen, Muhammad had immigrated to the Kingdom and built a construction empire. He was the builder of Ibn Saud's palace in Riyadh, the airports and seaports of the Kingdom, its modern highways, and, most important, the expansion of the holy mosques in Mecca and Medina. He also was in charge of the restoration of the third-holiest mosque in Islam in Jerusalem in the early 1960s at the request of Jordan's King Hussein.

Muhammad bin Laden was a pious man who funded the improvements to the Dome of the Rock and the Noble Sanctuary—the Haram al Sharif in Jerusalem—from his own pocket and hosted many pilgrims visiting Mecca at his own home. Among those were prominent Afghans and Pakistanis like Burhanuddin Rabbani, the future president of Afghanistan, and Qazi Hussain Ahmed, the leader of Jamaat e Islami, Pakistan's leading Islamist party. These men were "common faces" to Osama bin Laden, well before the Soviet invasion, because he had met them with his father and during their visits to Mecca after his father's death.[65]

In December 1979 the young Osama bin Laden flew to Pakistan to help the fight against the Russians. He arrived in Peshawar, Pakistan, on the Afghan border even before the first arms from the CIA arrived in Karachi. Just twenty-two-years-old in 1979, Osama bin Laden met with the leadership of Jamaat e Islami immediately after arriving in Pakistan. He established a close working relationship with the Islamists, who were also close to Zia ul Haq.[66] At first bin Laden's principle work was in facilitating the flow of the private Saudi money from the Kingdom's donors to the Afghans in Pakistan. He was perfect for the job since he was so well connected, through his father's company, with the powerful and wealthy leadership in the Kingdom and, on the other end, with the Pakistani Islamists and Afghan party leaders. His contacts in the Kingdom included not just Prince Turki bin Faisal, the intelligence chief, but the very powerful minister of the interior, Prince Nayef bin Abdul Aziz, brother of both Fahd and Salman.[67]

Osama bin Laden was ambitious and eager to be more than a financier. By 1985 he had recruited other Saudis to help him in creating an Arab fighting force that would join with the mujahedin in fighting inside Afghanistan. With the help of the bin Laden construction empire, bin Laden assisted in the building of the Zhawar base camp, the largest base inside Afghanistan for the Pakistani intelligence service and mujahedin, as well as underground fortresses for the mujahedin. In late 1985 he built a fortress for his own band, which he called the Lions' Den. Like the Zahwar camp, it was in eastern Paktia province, adjacent to the border with Pakistan. On August 17, 1987, bin Laden's small band fought an intense firefight with Soviet troops at the camp, known as the battle of Jaji. It was his first combat experience.[68]

Bin Laden was joined by hundreds of other Saudis eager to wage jihad. Thousands of Muslims from other countries came, as well, many inspired by *The Defense of Muslim Lands.* The Afghan Arabs, as they became known, were a trivial part of the military campaign against the 40th Red Army. Perhaps 500 Arabs and other Muslims died in the war against the Russians in the 1980s, according to the estimate of a senior CIA analyst who worked on the war at the time.[69] Tens of thousands of Afghan mujahedin died in combat with the Russians and over a million Afghan civilians died as a result of the war. Ultimately, it was Saudi money, not Arab jihadists, who contributed most to the victory. We return to Osama bin Laden's remarkable story in the next chapter as the war in Afghanistan comes to its climax under President Ronald Reagan and King Fahd later in the 1980s.

As 1980 developed, the Carter administration was increasingly consumed with the Iran problem. A rescue mission to free the American hostages in Tehran failed disastrously on April 24, 1980, with eight American soldiers killed. The hostages were immediately removed from the embassy compound where they had been incarcerated since November 1979, and dispersed in small groups around Iran, making another rescue attempt impossible. The Iranians secretly brought them back to Tehran during the summer and put most of them in Komiteh prison, where they were held until their eventual release.[70]

That same summer the Soviets conducted a secret military exercise in preparation for a possible invasion of Iran. It was entirely a Moscow headquarters exercise; no troops were actually deployed to simulate an invasion, but it caused serious worry in Washington. It was unclear then whether this exercise indicated a new Soviet interest in a possible invasion or was simply a routine Russian military drill.[71]

A Special National Intelligence Estimate prepared in August 1980 concluded that "the Soviets are indeed developing plans for military contingencies in Iran." The exercise involved an invasion force of sixteen divisions and would include elements of the 40th Red Army in Afghanistan. Brzezinski pressed for an explicit warning to Moscow that "any Soviet military action in Iran would lead to a direct military confrontation with the United States."[72] Again, most analysts at the CIA thought an invasion unlikely, but the exercise and modest increases in the readiness status of Soviet forces in Turkmenistan and the Caucasus region were worrisome.[73]

Then in September 1980 a series of clashes began along the Iraq-Iran border. The CIA warned the White House on September 17, 1980, that major hostilities were imminent. This would further complicate the hostage situation, disrupt Iraqi and Iranian oil exports, and "would involve Iraq in costly and protracted struggle with Iran." Early Iraqi successes would not mean Iran's defeat. The agency warned, as well, that Iran "would probably step up its appeals to Shia in Iraq to revolt and might also urge the Shias in Saudi Arabia, Kuwait, Bahrain and other Gulf countries to attack Iraqi and U.S. interests."[74] Within days the Iraqi army invaded Iran, beginning what was to become the largest and longest conventional war anywhere in the world since Korea; it would last eight years and kill hundreds of thousands. The Carter administration was preoccupied for weeks with containing the war and keeping it from spreading throughout the Persian Gulf. The sultan of Oman seriously considered allowing Iraq to stage bombing raids from its territory into Iran, for example, and the Carter team had to persuade the sultan that such a move would only expand the war.[75]

Riyadh was friendly with neither Iran nor Iraq. Iran was a Shia theocracy dedicated to overthrowing all the monarchs in the Gulf, while Iraq was a radical Baathist republic also dedicated to overthrowing the monarchs. King Khalid told a family conclave in September 1980 to recall lines from an Arab poem: "maybe the snakes will die from the poisonous stings of the scorpion."[76] But from the perspective of the 1980s, Iran was the greater long-term threat, so the Carter administration almost immediately was asked by the Gulf states to tilt toward Iraq.[77]

Despite their ambivalence, the Saudis supported the Iraqi attack on Iran from the start. It is unclear if they had any prior notification from Saddam that the invasion was coming, but they clearly welcomed Saddam Hussein's attempt to destroy the Islamic Republic. By the fall of 1980 the Iranian regime was openly calling for the overthrow of the Saudi monarchy and training Saudi Shia dissidents at camps in Iran. Iranian radio stations and other propaganda mediums broadcast constant attacks on the king and the House of Saud. The Iranians directed much of their effort at encouraging unrest in the Eastern Province and nearby Bahrain.[78]

The CIA warned President Carter that Iran might escalate the war and strike oil targets in Saudi Arabia to force the United States and the Soviets to pressure Baghdad to end its offensive. CIA director Admiral Stansfield Turner told the National Security Council on September 27 that this was a "very real possibility." Carter agreed to send U.S. Air Force AWACs (airborne warning and control aircraft) to Riyadh to improve Saudi air defenses. The Saudis agreed not to share the data collected with the Iraqis. Saudi defense minister Prince Sultan and the Pentagon began contingency planning in case the war expanded.

At first Saudi support for Iraq was primarily diplomatic, including support at the United Nations. The Saudis also urged other Arab and Islamic states to break with Iran and sought to bring the Gulf monarchies closer together to combat Iranian subversion. In May 1981 Khalid convened a summit of the six Gulf states and announced the formation of the Gulf Cooperation Council, which then served as a forum for closer intelligence cooperation among the participants.

The Iraqi invasion soon bogged down. By early 1982 Iran had successfully evicted the Iraqis from its territory and threatened to invade Iraq. The Iranians appeared poised to defeat Iraq and dominate the region, an outcome that had seemed improbable only a couple years earlier.

On June 13, 1982, King Khalid finally succumbed to a heart attack in his palace in Taif. His body was immediately brought to Riyadh, and he was buried the same day. Crown Prince Fahd ascended to the throne and Prince Abdallah became the new crown prince. Khalid's relatively short but eventful reign was characterized by strong continuities with his predecessor Faisal. Both were eager to have good ties with America. Both had been present at the creation of the relationship in Washington in 1943, and both saw it as crucial to defending the Kingdom from foreign aggression, especially by the Soviet Union. Yet both found it difficult to reconcile their desire for security from the United States with their strong dedication to the Palestinian cause. Prince Abdallah told Ambassador West in June 1980, "Arabs all over the Mideast are now convinced your policies are set in Tel Aviv and Jerusalem." West commented to Carter that this Saudi perception of U.S. policy "strikes at the very heart of the bilateral relationship" and produced deep disillusionment within the royal family.[79] In 1973 and 1979 the American-Saudi relationship was battered by differences over Palestine in general and Jerusalem in particular. Of course, Ibn Saud and FDR had the same difficulty decades earlier.

Faisal and Khalid were also deeply committed to the defense of Islam and especially to the Saudi-Wahhabi vision of Islam. Khalid was shaken by the attack on Mecca but he recognized it was not an existential threat to his reign per se. The Mahdi was an imposter but also a symbol of the latent deep commitment of many Saudis to the faith of Ibn 'Abd al Wahhab. The Afghanistan war gave Khalid the perfect opportunity to channel his own deep commitment to the defense of Islam with that of his people. The Islamic revolution in Iran would pose a new challenge to the longstanding Saudi conflict with Shiism, a conflict that dates to Wahhab's time in Basra. The Saudi-Iranian, Arab-Persian, and Sunni-Shia conflict was rapidly becoming the Kingdom's most immediate challenge as Khalid passed away. Fahd would face a summer of clear, present, and immediate danger for the Kingdom.

Chapter Four

FAHD, REAGAN, AND BUSH,
1982 TO 1992

King Fahd bin Abdul Aziz al Saud ascended to the throne in a summer of extreme danger for the Middle East in general and Saudi Arabia in particular. The Israeli army was at the gates of Beirut seeking to destroy the Palestine Liberation Organization (PLO) and remake much of the Middle East. The Iranian army was at the gates of Basra seeking to destroy Saddam Hussein's Iraq and open the road to Jerusalem. Saudi Arabia's regional foes seemed on the cusp of establishing their primacy in the region to the detriment of Saudi interests. From Riyadh's perspective Washington was abetting Israel's actions and seemed powerless to stop Iran.

Fahd had been the Kingdom's day-to-day ruler for the last seven years under Khalid and was completely prepared to be king. Born March 16, 1921, in Riyadh, Fahd attended the signing of the United Nations Charter in San Francisco in 1945 with his brother Faisal. In 1953 Fahd led the Saudi delegation to attend the coronation of Queen Elizabeth II in London, and later that year he became minister of education. When Faisal became king in 1962 he appointed Fahd to the crucial position of minister of interior.

*President George H. W. Bush and King Fahd bin Abdul Aẓiẓ al Saud share a laugh
during bilateral meetings at the Royal Palace, Jeddah, Saudi Arabia, November 1990.
(George Bush Presidential Library and Museum)*

As a young prince, Fahd had a reputation for being a playboy. Tales of
huge losses in his gambling in London and Monte Carlo were widely believed
in the Kingdom. One story had him losing $8 million in one night in 1962.[1] His
expensive palace in Marbella on the Costa del Sol in Spain was opulent and
considered decadent by many. After becoming crown prince in 1975, and especially after the Mecca siege, Fahd sought to change his image to be more
pious and conservative. Fahd began using the title "Custodian of the Two
Holy Mosques" to convey his more religious image. A debilitating stroke in
1995 made him a recluse, but in 2002 Forbes estimated his personal wealth to
be $25 billion.[2]

Perhaps as a legacy of his youthful days of indiscretion, Fahd was a night
owl who preferred to work in the late evening and early morning. Even when
traveling abroad he was notoriously late for even the most formal occasions.
In May 1975 he showed up forty-five minutes late for a state dinner with
President Ford at the White House.[3] He especially preferred to meet foreign
visitors after midnight, and Americans often found this difficult. One senior
American official I accompanied to see Fahd spent his two hours in the waiting

room in the palace endlessly adjusting the chairs, tables, and pictures on the walls to pass the time. No doubt the Saudi protocol officials noticed this and told Fahd, who probably decided to let his guest wait a little longer.

Fahd and Reagan

The Saudis were convinced that Anwar Sadat's separate peace with Israel would encourage Israeli leaders to use their overwhelming military superiority to impose their will on Israel's Arab neighbors. Without Israel facing the danger of a war with Egypt, the Saudis expected Prime Minister Menachem Begin and his defense minister, Ariel Sharon, to try to destroy the PLO and impose peace agreements on Israel's weaker neighbors. The Saudis looked to Washington to restrain Begin.

The Israeli Air Force raid on June 7, 1981, on Iraq's nuclear reactor outside Baghdad reinforced Saudi concerns. The attack was carried out only days after a summit meeting between Sadat and Begin, underscoring how the Egyptians had been neutralized by the Camp David agreement. The eight F16s and six F15s overflew Saudi territory en route to attack the Iraqi reactor, underscoring Saudi vulnerability. Ronald Reagan's new administration issued a pro forma denunciation of the attack but made no serious move to restrain Begin and Sharon.

Reagan did agree to sell the Kingdom AWACs aircraft for the Royal Saudi Air Force to enhance and, ultimately, replace the U.S.-manned aircraft Carter had sent at the beginning of the Iran-Iraq war. Another difficult congressional battle ensued with the pro-Israel lobby. The arms deal won favor in the Senate by only a two-vote margin in October 1981; the key vote came from Maine Republican William Cohen, who switched his vote at the last moment. The deal also included air-to-air missiles for the F15s sold by Carter, along with Boeing 707 aerial refueling tankers. The total package came to $8.5 billion. Again, Prince Bandar bin Sultan, still a pilot in the Royal Saudi Air Force, played a role in the lobbying effort for the arms sale.[4]

By the spring of 1982 the Arabs expected Israel to launch a major military attack into Lebanon to destroy the PLO, defeat the Syrian army in Lebanon, and impose a peace treaty on Lebanon with the cooperation of the Maronite

Christian minority. The American intelligence community had reached the same conclusion and warned the Reagan team an attack was imminent.[5]

On June 3, 1982, the Israeli ambassador to the United Kingdom, Shlomo Argov, was badly wounded in an assassination attempt outside the Dorchester Hotel in London. The assailants were members of the Abu Nidal organization, an Iraqi-based Palestinian group that opposed the PLO. One assailant was an Iraqi intelligence officer.[6] The Iraqis wanted to retaliate for the nuclear reactor raid by killing Argov. They also sought to preempt an Iranian invasion of Iraq by creating an Arab-Israeli crisis that Saddam hoped would rally the Islamic world against Israel and persuade Tehran against invasion. It was a foolish and desperate gamble. The Begin government ignored its own intelligence community reporting about Iraq's role and blamed the PLO alone for the London attack. PLO Chairman Yasser Arafat flew from his base in Beirut to Riyadh on June 4, and Israel invaded Lebanon two days later.[7]

Fahd ascended to the throne one week after the invasion, and throughout the summer of 1982 he pressed the Reagan administration to restrain the Israelis. He had little initial success. Reagan's first secretary of state, Alexander Haig, supported the Israeli game plan and deflected Arab opposition to the war. Only after the Israeli army began to besiege the PLO in West Beirut in late June did Reagan fire Haig and start pressing Begin to accept a cease-fire and allow the PLO and Arafat (who had returned to Beirut) to evacuate the city and move to Tunis. The PLO evacuation was not completed until early September.

Prince Bandar played a role in the diplomacy between Fahd and Reagan. He was appointed defense attaché in Washington in early 1982. During the crisis in Beirut, Bandar delivered messages from Fahd to Reagan and Haig. His credibility as a protégé of Fahd who had the king's ear was established with the Reagan team.[8]

Under growing international pressure, President Reagan put forward his own plan for resolving the Palestinian issue on September 1, 1982, calling for Israeli withdrawal from the West Bank and Gaza Strip and the creation of a Palestinian confederation with Jordan. Israel, which had not expected Reagan's plan, immediately rejected it. Eight days later, King Fahd put forward a Saudi peace plan at the Arab summit in Fez, Morocco. The Fahd plan called for complete Israeli withdrawal from the West Bank and Gaza as well as East

Jerusalem and the creation of an independent Palestinian state with its capital in Jerusalem.[9] The Arab summit endorsed the Fahd plan.

The war in Lebanon consumed much of Fahd's attention during his first weeks in office, but it was overshadowed for Saudis by a greater danger closer to home in the Persian Gulf. The Iranians successfully evicted the Iraqi army from all the territory it had seized in 1980, capturing 30,000 to 40,000 Iraqi prisoners in the process. Saddam's army was collapsing as the Iranians advanced.[10]

In Washington and Riyadh there were dark predictions that Saddam's regime was about to fall. The CIA's National Intelligence Council warned the Reagan National Security Council on July 20, 1982, that Iran was seeking to replace Saddam with "a fundamentalist Islamic" government beholden to Tehran. The CIA warned that if the Iranians broke through at Basra in their next offensive, all of southern, Shia-dominated Iraq, including the holy cities of Kerbala and Najaf, would be occupied by Iran, threatening to arouse the Shia populations of Kuwait, Bahrain, and the Eastern Province of Saudi Arabia. The memo concluded Iran would, thus, achieve "dominance over the Persian Gulf Region and 35 percent of known world oil reserves."[11]

Reagan's national security adviser, William Clark, told the president that "an Iranian invasion will create shock waves throughout the Gulf and pose further dangers for US interests in the Middle East which are already threatened because of Lebanon." Based on the intelligence estimates from the CIA, Clark told the president "the Iranians are massing 100,000 troops opposite Basra." If Basra fell the "Iranians will sit astride Kuwait, leaving the Kuwaitis very vulnerable to direct or indirect Iranian threats. The Saudis, Jordanians and Gulf States can be expected to turn to us for protection." Clark judged it was "likely that Iran will succeed in accomplishing its military objectives."[12]

Under strong pressure from the Saudis and Jordanians, Reagan authorized CIA director Bill Casey to share intelligence with the Iraqis on the Iranian buildup. A senior CIA officer, Thomas Twetten, traveled to Baghdad on July 27, 1982, with "satellite imagery, maps, battle line imagery and analysis" to help the Iraqis stop the Iranian attack. As Twetten later described the Iraqi reaction, "It was clear that they hadn't seen anything like it before, the intelligence made a big difference."[13] To follow up, Reagan sent Donald Rumsfeld to Baghdad to assure Saddam of American support.

For their part the Saudis began bankrolling Saddam's war effort. With much of his equipment destroyed or abandoned inside Iran, Saddam needed to rebuild and vastly expand his army and air force. Over the war's eight years Saudi Arabia would provide Iraq with $60 billion in loans and grants. Kuwait provided another $18 billion. It was a staggering amount of money for two monarchies to provide a left-wing republic, but it was essential to keeping Iraq in the war and keeping Iran out of Basra.[14]

The Iraqi army held, just barely, in 1982. Iran had launched a series of offensives in late 1981—code-named Path to Jerusalem, Undeniable Victory, and Jerusalem—that drove the Iraqi army out of Iran, captured thousands of prisoners, and created the image of an unstoppable juggernaut. In late July 1982 Iran began Operation Blessed Ramadan to take Basra and open southern Iraq to Iranian occupation. The Iraqis rallied, buoyed by American intelligence, and finally stopped the Iranian advance. The war then fell into a stalemate that would last six more years.[15]

The two crises in 1982 pushed Fahd and Reagan closer together. Washington encouraged Israel to gradually withdraw from most of Lebanon in 1983 and provided diplomatic support and intelligence to Iraq to maintain the stalemate along the Iran-Iraq border. Fahd agreed to provide financial assistance to Reagan's global campaign to combat the Soviet Union. Reagan's director of the Central Intelligence Agency, Bill Casey, provided money and arms to various anti-communist groups fighting Soviet-backed regimes around the world. The largest such covert action program was the one in Afghanistan and Pakistan begun in the Carter administration. In the first four years of the Reagan administration, Washington and Riyadh gradually increased their financial commitment to the Afghan mujahedin. In the second term Reagan and Casey, with the enthusiastic support of King Fahd and his intelligence chief Prince Turki, significantly increased the campaign against the Soviet army in Afghanistan.

King Fahd visited Washington after Reagan's November 1984 reelection victory to coordinate strategy even more closely. The February 1985 summit included meetings with the president and his advisers and a breakfast between the two leaders. The principle public message from the king was that "the Palestinian question is the cause of instability and turmoil in the region and the United States has a responsibility to make use of its powerful influence and to make a strong effort for achieving peace through a just solution to the Palestinian question."[16] The two leaders did not reconcile the Fahd and Reagan plans for resolving the Palestinian question, however, and there was no movement toward a peace agreement.

In private, however, there was much agreement on ratcheting up the pressure on the Soviets. The main battlefield was Afghanistan. The king and the president "agreed to keep the pressure on the Soviet Union to remove its occupation troops from Afghanistan," according to a Saudi account.[17] Casey pressed for an increase in the CIA budget for supporting the mujahedin to $250 million annually, with a matching Saudi contribution. Fahd agreed. Casey's deputy, Robert Gates, later wrote that "the character of U.S. policy toward Afghanistan changed dramatically" as a result of these consultations. The goal went from harassing the Soviets and tying them down in a quagmire to winning the war and driving the Soviet 40th Red Army out of Afghanistan.[18]

Within a year the United States began providing the mujahedin with Stinger shoulder-fired antiaircraft missiles, thus tilting the war toward the resistance. Other sophisticated equipment followed. At the same time the flow of volunteers from Muslim countries, including Saudi Arabia, expanded significantly. The Saudi religious establishment was encouraged by Fahd and Prince Salman to promote the Jihad in Afghanistan as a religious obligation. Gates wrote later that the CIA "began to learn of a significant increase in the number of Arab nationals from other countries who had traveled to Afghanistan to fight in the Holy War against the Soviets in 1985." The CIA had little contact with the Arab fighters; that business was done by the Pakistanis.[19]

The war against the Russians in Afghanistan came to a conclusion in 1988 when Moscow withdrew its troops. While the war between the mujahedin and the communist regime in Kabul would continue for another three years, with the American-Saudi-Pakistani alliance backing the mujahedin and the Russians backing the communists, the defeat and retreat of the Soviet 40th Red Army was a dramatic and decisive victory for the allies. Within months of the defeat of the Russian army, the Berlin wall fell, the Warsaw Pact crumbled, and the Cold War ended.

The collapse of the Soviet occupation of Afghanistan amounted to a major propaganda victory for the Kingdom. King Fahd could rightly say that his government had played a crucial role in the defeat of communism and Soviet imperialism. The credibility of Saudi Arabia as a leader in the Islamic world was hugely advantaged by winning in Afghanistan. Without question the agreement between Fahd and Reagan at their 1985 summit to escalate the war in Afghanistan was the summit's most important and consequential decision.

Fahd wanted another arms deal with Reagan, but the administration was reluctant to engage in yet another bruising battle with Israel over arms to Saudi Arabia. Fahd turned, instead, to the United Kingdom. Prince Bandar later described the subsequent *al Yamamah* (dove of peace) deal as the easiest arms deal he ever arranged. Fahd dispatched Bandar to see British prime minister Margaret Thatcher while she was vacationing in Salzburg, Austria. The prince told her the king wanted to purchase advanced Tornado strike aircraft plus jet trainers and even the infrastructure to build air bases. The prime minister replied immediately, "You have a deal." It was done in twenty-five minutes. In time it became the largest military sale in British history, worth $86 billion, and included seventy-two jets, two air bases, and a host of service contracts.[20]

The Tornado deal also proved to be controversial. Allegations of kickbacks to Saudi defense minister Prince Sultan and to Bandar surfaced soon after the ink was dry. Ultimately, another British prime minister, Tony Blair, halted any investigation in the United Kingdom of the 1985 deal and various follow-up deals on the grounds that British relations with Saudi Arabia were too important strategically to be undermined by investigations of impropriety in arms deals.[21]

By turning to London for advanced aircraft, the king acquired jets with no limits on where they might be deployed. Unlike the F15s, which the United States sold with the proviso they would not be based at Tabuk air base in northwest Saudi Arabia near Israel, the Tornados could be deployed wherever the Saudi leadership wanted.

The Saudi quest for advanced weapons was rooted in the country's sense of vulnerability in the dangerous Middle East region. Events continued to underscore those dangers. On June 5, 1984, two Iranian F4 fighter jets penetrated Saudi air space on the Persian Gulf coast. Two Royal Saudi Air Force F15s shot the intruders down. Eleven more Iranian aircraft took off immediately from their base to respond, the Saudi Air Force scrambled more jets, and the Iranians then returned to base. Prince Bandar told the *New York Times* that "our sovereignty was violated and we are determined to defend our country."[22] Meanwhile, with the land war between Iran and Iraq still stalemated, the two countries began firing short-range missiles, known as Scuds, at each other's cities and attacking tankers in the Gulf carrying oil from each country.

The situation in the Levant also troubled Saudi security planners. On October 1, 1985, eight Israeli Air Force F15s attacked the headquarters in Tunis of the PLO leaders who had been evacuated three years earlier from Beirut. The attack demonstrated that Israel could project power 2,000 kilometers, or 1,280 miles, from its air bases. The Saudis saw the Tunis raid, like the earlier raid on Baghdad's nuclear reactor, as a vivid demonstration of their vulnerability to Israeli military operations.

King Fahd and Defense Minister Prince Sultan decided to seek a deterrent capability to discourage Iran and Israel from any military operations against the Kingdom. They were well aware the United States and Britain would not sell them an intermediate-range missile system that might be used against targets like Tehran or Tel Aviv. Prince Sultan turned to his sons, Prince Bandar, now the ambassador to the United States, and the head of Saudi air defenses General Prince Khalid bin Sultan, to find a solution. Their answer was China.

Bandar opened the initiative by approaching his Chinese counterpart in Washington, Ambassador Han Xu, and asking him privately if Beijing would sell missiles to the Kingdom. Riyadh did not have diplomatic relations with Beijing so this was an extraordinary request. The Chinese were eager to develop relations with Saudi Arabia and agreed in principle to consider the request. Bandar was invited to talk to more Chinese officials to pursue the idea. He stole a page from Henry Kissinger's playbook. When Kissinger secretly opened ties with China in 1970, he used Pakistan as an intermediary. Bandar flew to Pakistan for more conversations with Chinese officials who had the authority to discuss military sales. They agreed to sell missiles and invited the prince to visit Beijing secretly to work out details.[23]

In July 1985 Bandar made his first of three secret visits to Beijing to work the deal. The Chinese then sent a military delegation secretly to Riyadh to engage with the Saudi military on the details. Prince Khalid was their host. In December 1986 an agreement was reached on how to bring intermediate-range ballistic missiles, Chinese-made CSS2 missiles, code-named East Wind, to the Kingdom, install them, train Saudi crews to operate them, and do all of this without the American intelligence community discovering the plot. Khalid then made four trips to China to work out the details and coordinate everything. The missiles were delivered and installed in 1987.[24]

Prince Khalid later wrote that the purpose of the missiles "was to give us the capability to counterattack in the event of an attack on us by either Israel or Iran, both in their different ways hostile neighbors." Khalid cited the Israeli incursion in Lebanon in June 1982, the raid on Baghdad in 1981, and the raid on Tunis in 1985 as the reasons why the king "decided to seek Chinese weapons." The Iranian threat to Iraq and its neighbors, highlighted by the June 5, 1984, aerial combat, was the other reason.[25]

The CIA detected the CSS2 missile base in Saudi Arabia in early 1988. President Reagan was furious with Fahd and Bandar for the duplicity and the deal. Initially the United States pressed for the return of the missiles to China or for American monitors to be placed at their bases. Riyadh refused but did promise not to equip the missiles with nuclear warheads. The story quickly leaked to the press with a front-page article in the *Washington Post* on March 18, 1988.[26]

The Saudis were now worried that Israel would attack the missile sites. Bandar approached Reagan's national security adviser, General Colin Powell, asking him to tell Israel not to attack Saudi Arabia and explaining that the missiles were for defensive purposes only. According to Powell's recollection, the situation was very tense for a few days, with both the Israeli and Saudi air forces on high alert. Reagan made a public statement making it clear he was "totally opposed" to an Israeli attack. The Israelis did not attack and the Chinese missiles remain in Saudi Arabia to this day. To demonstrate his pique at the American reaction to the missile deal, Fahd asked that American ambassador Hume Horan be removed from his post. Since he would be unable to do his job against the king's wishes, Horan was brought home.[27]

The East Wind missile deal remains something of an enigma to this day. The missiles were designed by the Chinese to carry a nuclear warhead. When Khalid inspected them in China, they were equipped with nuclear warheads.[28] When armed with only conventional warheads the missiles' value as a deterrent was diminished significantly. Many observers have questioned whether the underlying Saudi plan was to get Pakistani nuclear warheads for the missiles in a crisis situation. No hard evidence of a Saudi-Pakistani agreement to provide such warheads has surfaced, even from the 1980s when King Fahd and General Zia were collaborating so closely in Afghanistan—or in the years since. Even so, the rumors of such a deal have not evaporated.

By 1988 the relationship between Reagan and Fahd had been deeply shaken by another secret deal, this time an American plot to sell arms to Iran in return for help in freeing American hostages in Lebanon held by the Iranian-sponsored terrorist group Hezbollah. The operation also funded aid to right-wing guerrillas fighting the leftist government of Nicaragua, aid that the Congress had banned. The secret dealings broke into the public domain in November 1986 when the Iranians leaked news about some aspects of them to a Lebanese magazine.

At first the president tried to deny any knowledge of the scheme, but he finally admitted some responsibility in a speech on March 4, 1987. In fact, Reagan was at the center of what came to be known as the Iran-Contra scandal. He drove the policy process toward a secret opening with Iran because he was obsessed with freeing American hostages taken by Iran's allies in Lebanon. It was Reagan's decisions, not some rogue operation run by the CIA's Bill Casey, that led to America selling arms to Iran in return for promises, never fulfilled, to free the hostages. Despite his later denials, Vice President George Bush was also deeply involved in the policy process and kept fully informed on the efforts to free the hostages. Casey and Reagan believed they had a valuable Iranian partner (arms dealer Manucher Ghorbanifar) in a man who failed catastrophically every lie detector test he took. Casey's senior advisers all told him the Iranian was a liar; he ignored their judgment and went ahead recklessly. Casey's deputy at one point cabled his boss, who was traveling, that "everyone at headquarters advises against this operation not only because the principal involved is a liar and has a record of deceit. But secondly we would be aiding and abetting the wrong people." Nonetheless, despite "our counsel to the contrary," the operation proceeded as the White House and Casey ordered.[29]

Behind the scenes Reagan had a crucial and enthusiastic partner in Israel. Israeli leaders, including Prime Minister Shimon Peres, desperately wanted to restore the cozy relationship Israel had with Iran under the shah, when the two

states were aligned in a secret entente. The Israelis urged Reagan to try an
opening with Iran. Peres and his colleagues refused to believe the ayatollahs
would not sooner or later come back to partnering with Israel, even though
their professional intelligence officers told them this was a fantasy. Instead,
Israel became Iran's critical arms supplier during the Iran-Iraq war and en-
ticed America into joining it in the madness. American diplomats were told to
turn a blind eye to Israeli arms shipments to Iran even before Reagan got into
his own arms deals. Israel helped the Ayatollah Khomeini survive the Iraqi
war and persuaded Reagan to arm the Iranian regime.[30]

The Saudis and leaders of the other Gulf states were shocked by the Iran-
Contra scandal. They had believed the United States was on their side in the
confrontation with Iran, but now they discovered Washington was secretly
dealing with Tehran. To add insult to injury, for the Arabs, Israel was the
moving force behind the subterfuge. The longtime Saudi conviction that Israel manipulated American foreign policy was reinforced. The scandal produced a crisis in Saudi confidence in the Reagan administration.

Gulf War Escalates

The war in the Gulf also escalated. With the battle on the ground stalemated,
the Iraqis and Iranians each began attacking oil tankers exporting its rival's
oil in the Persian Gulf. With the Iran-Contra scandal damaging American
credibility, the Reagan administration determined again to assist the Iraqi
war effort. Kuwait asked Washington to protect tankers delivering oil from
its facilities, and Reagan agreed to do so. The U.S. Navy became an active
belligerent in the war during the spring of 1987 by defending oil traffic going
to and from Kuwait and attacking Iranian naval vessels threatening the export of Gulf oil to the outside world. As Secretary of Defense Casper Wein-
berger told National Security Adviser Colin Powell, "We should be seen as
supportive of Iraq. This is an opportunity to recoup some of our standing in
the region and regain credibility with the Arab states."[31]

Over the course of the next eighteen months the U.S. military engaged in
a series of operations to defend oil traffic to and from Kuwait, which had become Iraq's major access to the sea for its oil exports. Operations with code
names Earnest Will, Prime Chance, Nimble Archer, and Praying Mantis
gradually wore down the Iranian naval and air threat in the Gulf. Iranian oil-

rigs, frigates, and small ships were destroyed. At the same time Iraq began to gain the upper hand on the ground. Iraq launched a series of ground offensives, assisted by American intelligence support, which drove Iranian forces out of Iraq and began to destroy the Iranian ground forces.

As the war turned against it, Iran increased its support for subversion in Saudi Arabia. In late July 1987 Iranian pilgrims to the Hajj in Mecca staged political demonstrations that turned violent, and at least 275 Iranian pilgrims and eighty-five Saudi policemen died. The Saudi embassy in Tehran was attacked and Ayatollah Khomeini called for the overthrow of the Saudi monarchy. In August 1987 a new Iranian-supported terrorist group called Hezbollah al Hijaz attacked an oil facility in the Eastern Province. Hezbollah al Hijaz was composed of Saudi Shia trained by the Iranian Revolutionary Guards at camps in Lebanon, where they acquired battlefield experience by supporting the Lebanese Hezbollah fight against the Israeli army. The groups' military leader, Ahmad Ibrahim al Mughassil, was one of those trained in Lebanon fighting the Israelis. Mughassil traveled between Beirut, Tehran, and Damascus to organize operations. In Damascus Hezbollah al Hijaz operated from the Sayyida Zaynab mosque, which houses the tomb of Imam Ali's daughter Zaynab. The group called for an Islamic Republic in the Arabian Peninsula modeled on the Iranian example or the secession of the Eastern Province to form a Shia state aligned with Iran.[32]

More attacks on Saudi oil installations followed in 1988. An attempt was also made to attack the air base at Dhahran to destroy the AWACs aircraft stationed there. Hezbollah al Hijaz was also responsible for attacks on Saudi diplomats abroad in Ankara, Karachi, and Bangkok in 1988 and 1989. Several Saudi diplomats were killed and wounded in the attacks. In April 1988, in response to the attacks inside the Kingdom, the assassination attempts on Saudi diplomats, and the ratcheting up of the tanker war, Saudi Arabia broke diplomatic relations with Iran.[33]

The Saudis played a key role in the end game of the Iraq-Iran war. They were Saddam's bankers by this point. Saddam had built a million-man army and a military industrial complex that employed another million Iraqis. His army was flush with equipment purchased from Russia and China, his air force full of Russian and French aircraft. All this was expensive, and the Saudis and Kuwaitis had bankrolled all of it.

Saddam was now reluctant to end the war he was, at last, winning. The United States and other members of the United Nations Security Council were reluctant to stop him and had little leverage over Iraq even if they wanted to stop the war. Iran had no allies. On July 3, 1988, an American cruiser, the USS *Vincennes*, inadvertently shot down a civilian Iranian passenger jet, which the ship had misidentified as hostile Iranian military aircraft, killing 290 passengers and crew. By this point, Ayatollah Khomeini was finally ready for a ceasefire, and Iran used the shooting down of the airliner as justification for ending the war, citing aggression against it by "other countries," meaning the United States. Even so, Saddam was not yet ready.

UN Secretary General Javier Pérez de Cuéllar asked the Saudis to intervene. As his deputy, Giandomenico Picco, later recalled, the UN took its "cue from the Renaissance. Back then, in Florence, the great House of Medici resolved such disputes by applying a little financial pressure." Pérez de Cuéllar asked Prince Bandar and Foreign Minister Prince Saud al Faisal to use Riyadh's financial leverage to persuade Saddam. The Saudis were Iraq's banker and ally, but above all the Saudis wanted an end to a war that was escalating out of control. King Fahd called Saddam and then informed the secretary general that Iraq was ready to halt the war. Pérez de Cuéllar told Fahd he needed a call from Saddam himself. Within five minutes Saddam called the secretary general and said, "I would like you to know I concur with His Majesty."[34] Iran formally accepted an end to the war on July 18.

The Iran-Iraq war had cost a half-million lives, with another million wounded seriously. The economic cost was over a trillion dollars. The war also began the march of folly that would shortly lead to another war in the Gulf in 2003—the current American military engagement in Iraq. The Saudi decision to end the war with an ultimatum to Saddam was the right thing to do, but it would have grave consequences later as Saddam began to consider his next target.

Reagan's relations with Fahd had fluctuated wildly in the 1980s. After a difficult beginning due to the Lebanon war, the two became close partners in bringing the Cold War to a successful end by backing the mujahidin in Afghanistan, but the Iran-Contra affair badly damaged their relationship. Fahd felt betrayed by Reagan's foolish initiative with Iran, especially given its

Israeli inspiration. Fahd turned to London and Beijing for arms. Robust American military support for Iraq at the end of the war helped recoup some American credibility in Riyadh, but the Saudi distrust of Reagan never really diminished. It would be up to his successor, George H. W. Bush, to rebuild ties with King Fahd when the next great crisis came to the doorstep of the Kingdom, this one in Kuwait.

Desert Shield

The war for Kuwait in 1990–91 was a watershed moment for the American-Saudi alliance. Before the war the relationship was largely handled behind the scenes and was little known to most Americans and most Saudis. Diplomats, oilmen, and spies quietly ran the relationship for the most part. Only the oil embargo in 1973 had resonated with most Americans. The great collusion in Afghanistan was a covert project until some aspects of it became public knowledge in the late 1980s. The war for Kuwait finally brought the U.S.-Saudi partnership out of the closet and onto the front pages for everyone, Americans and Saudis. A half-million Americans, mostly soldiers, were deployed to the Kingdom by President Bush to first defend it from Iraqi aggression and then to liberate Kuwait. This marked the beginning of a decades-long American conflict in Iraq, and it marked the beginning of an increasingly violent blowback inside the Kingdom against the American alliance.

I had a ringside seat for the Kuwait war. At one in the morning on August 2, 1990, I was promoted from deputy division chief of the Persian Gulf Affairs Division at the CIA to deputy chief of the Persian Gulf Task Force. The task force was responsible for all intelligence analysis and production concerning the crisis and its implications for the agency. My good friend, colleague, and mentor, Winston Wiley, was the chief. Among my responsibilities was liaison with other intelligence services, including those in Saudi Arabia, whose de facto intelligence representative in Washington was Prince Bandar. When the fighting ended, I was promoted again to be the director of Persian Gulf and South Asian Affairs at the National Security Council for the remainder of the Bush term and the first year of Bill Clinton's administration. My bosses there included Brent Scowcroft, Bob Gates, Richard Haass, and

Martin Indyk, four good friends and fine colleagues. My daily interlocutor was Prince Bandar.

We are fortunate today to have a detailed account of the Persian Gulf crisis written by the Saudi commander Prince Khalid bin Sultan, along with a noted British expert on the region, Patrick Seale. Prince Khalid headed the Saudi Joint Force and had command over the regular Saudi military and the National Guard. Along with his American counterpart, General Norman Schwarzkopf, Prince Khalid commanded an international army with 750,000 troops from thirty-six countries.

Iraq ended its war with Iran deeply in debt. It owed billions of dollars to its creditors, especially Saudi Arabia, Kuwait, and the United Arab Emirates. But Saddam's enormous ambitions had not been reduced by the war. If anything, the Iraqi dictator emerged from eight years of conflict even more determined than he was in 1980, when he invaded Iran, planning to become the dominant player in the Middle East. He was still frustrated that the Saudis had reined in his army when it seemed to have Iran on the ropes in August 1988.

With Iraqi and Iranian oil back on the world market, the price of oil declined. Oil prices had been low throughout the 1980s, putting pressure on all the producers. With further decline in the wake of the war's end, Iraq was financially pressed even more. The creditor states, including the Saudis, did not press for immediate payment of Iraq's debts but did not want them forgotten or forgiven.

Saddam wanted to restore Iraq to the leadership position in the Arab world it had briefly enjoyed when it led the Arab opposition to Sadat's peace treaty with Israel. Ironically, Egypt's return to Arab politics from its isolation was facilitated by Iraq. Iraq had purchased large quantities of weapons from Egypt during the war with Iran. On February 16, 1990, Iraq, Egypt, Jordan, and Yemen formed an alliance called the Arab Cooperation Council, with Jordan's King Hussein as the principal mover. He backed Iraq enthusiastically in the war with Iran and had become close to Saddam. At the first summit of the council on February 24, 1990, Saddam gave a bellicose speech threatening Israel, and a few days later the CIA detected fixed launch sites were being developed in western Iraq within the range for Iraq to fire Scud missiles at Tel Aviv.[35]

None of the four partners told the Saudis their plan for the council. King Fahd had inklings that something was in the works but learned of the alliance only when it became public. From Riyadh's perspective the council looked like an alliance encircling the Kingdom, especially given Yemen's inclusion. Saudi-Yemeni relations were historically troubled. Fahd complained to Egypt's president Mubarak that the alliance looked to be anti-Saudi.[36]

Saddam paid a rare visit to Riyadh on March 17, 1990, to explain the council and to complain about low oil prices. Oil prices dropped from $22 per barrel in January to $16 in June. Saddam was especially angry with Kuwait for its high oil production, which contributed to the price decline. Inflation in Iraq rose to 45 percent as its economy came undone. In April Saddam called Fahd and asked him to send Prince Bandar to see him. Bandar met with Saddam in Mosul on April 5, 1990. Again, Saddam complained about Kuwait and oil prices, and Saddam asked Bandar to take a message to Washington and London that Iraq did not intend to attack Israel but was worried about an Israeli attack on Iraq.[37]

Against this backdrop of increasing tensions in the region, Saddam attacked Kuwait verbally at an Arab summit in late May 1990. He accused Kuwait of waging economic warfare against Iraq and colluding with the United States against Baghdad. In a private meeting with Fahd, Saddam called the Kuwaitis "rich, fat people" who came to Iraq to gamble, drink, and use prostitutes.[38] Saddam was right about Kuwait's wealth; the Kuwaitis had over $200 billion in reserves.

On the July 17 anniversary of the coup that had put him in power in 1968, Saddam publicly threatened Kuwait again. The American intelligence community quickly detected a massive buildup of Iraqi forces north of Kuwait. The elite of Iraq's army, the Republican Guard, dispatched an eight-division-strong force to the border with Kuwait.[39] The CIA warned the Bush administration an attack on Kuwait could come at any moment. Bush phoned key Arab leaders. All of them—King Fahd, King Hussein, and President Mubarak—assured the president that Saddam was just bluffing. They argued that at worse he might grab a couple of uninhabited mud islands in the Shatt al Arab waterway that belonged to Kuwait but blocked Iraq's access to the Persian Gulf. At Fahd and Mubarak's request, Iraq agreed to a meeting with the Kuwaitis in Jidda on August 1 to resolve the dispute. Instead, once they got to Jidda the Iraqis demanded that Kuwait forgive Iraq's war debts and provide Baghdad with $27 billion in reparations to help pay for the war's damage.[40] When Kuwait refused, the Iraqis left Jidda and returned to Baghdad.

The next week would be perhaps the most critical in the history of Saudi kings and American presidents. Shortly after midnight in the Persian Gulf on August 2, 1990, 120,000 Iraqi troops invaded Kuwait. The White House was surprised. Bush had relied too much on what the Arab leaders told him and too little on the intelligence that showed Saddam's buildup. Saddam was always a difficult person to read. He was impulsive, prone to bad decisions, and exercised poor judgment. The two wars he started were terrible mistakes. Some accounts, notably that of usually well-informed Egyptian journalist Mohamed Heikal, argue the final decision to seize all of Kuwait was made only two days in advance of the invasion.[41] Prince Khalid notes the invasion was poorly planned, as it did not provide for capturing the amir or rapidly controlling Kuwait's two air bases. It seemed hastily organized and not thought through carefully.[42] The CIA officer who debriefed Saddam after his capture in 2003, John Nixon, asked the Iraqi leader about this decision. Based on Saddam's statement, Nixon believes it was an impulsive decision. Saddam was broke, he needed money, and a very rich bank was next door. Certainly Saddam did not accurately assess the implications and reactions to his invasion.[43] It is difficult, if not impossible, to predict the moves of a leader who repeatedly makes such monumental mistakes.

President Bush convened a National Security Council principals meeting for August 3, 1990, but their discussion was inconclusive. The reality of what Saddam had done was not yet fully apparent. As Richard Haass later noted, it was too soon to be digested by the principals. The White House looked off-balance.

The next day, August 4, Bush convened his top aides again. At the start of the meeting, the director of central intelligence, William Webster, summarized a paper I had drafted for him. According to the recollection of General Colin Powell, by then the chair of the Joint Chiefs of Staff, "The CIA director gave us a bleak status report. The Iraqis," he said, "are within eight-tenths of a mile of the Saudi border. If Saddam stays where he is, he'll own twenty percent of the world's oil reserves. And a few miles away he can seize another twenty percent. He'll have easy access to the sea from Kuwait's ports. Jordan and Yemen will probably tilt toward him. Israel will be threatened. Saddam will be the preeminent figure in the Persian Gulf."[44] Brent Scowcroft, the president's closest confidant and national security adviser, remembered Webster saying that "this will fundamentally alter the Persian Gulf region. Saddam would command the second and third largest proven oil reserves with the fourth largest army in the world. His ego cannot be satisfied: his ambition is to have ever more influence."[45] Webster's opening brief put the issue clearly to the president and his team; they would be focused for the next few days on getting the Saudis to accept a massive American military expedition to save the Kingdom from a repeat of the Kuwaitis' mistakes of not taking Saddam seriously.

The Saudis had also been caught totally by surprise. At first, King Fahd did not believe the early reports from Kuwait. But then the Kuwaiti amir fled to the Kingdom in a rush, and Fahd was told by the Eastern Province governor, his son Prince Muhammad ibn Fahd, the complete truth about the invasion. Within weeks some 360,000 Kuwaitis flooded into the Kingdom seeking refuge. Prince Khalid was appointed to command Saudi forces on the border, where he found complete confusion. Only one brigade of the Saudi Arabian National Guard was deployed on the Saudi border facing Kuwait and Iraq. Some other Arab nations sent troops quickly, notably Morocco. Two more brigades from the Saudi army were rushed to the front from the borders with Jordan and Yemen, but even when they arrived the Saudis still would be outnumbered by more than twenty to one. "Our intelligence and our general military staff had paid little attention to Iraq, and no one had anticipated that a threat to the Kingdom would come from that direction," wrote Khalid.[46]

Prince Bandar was caught off guard by the invasion. On July 31, 1990, he left Washington for London to meet his wife Haifa and their children en route to what was planned to be a month-long vacation in China, Hong Kong, Singapore, and Thailand. He was confident the Jidda meeting would end the crisis. In London he learned of the Iraqi attack and turned back, rushed to the White House immediately, and began working to stop Saddam from invading his country.[47] Bandar's role would be critical in the crisis. Brent Scowcroft later said Bandar "became a de facto member of the National Security Council" during the crisis because of his unparalleled access to both Bush and Fahd.[48]

On August 5, 1990, the CIA detected that the Iraqis were moving the Republican Guard in force to the border. Logistics for an offensive were moving to south Kuwait, just north of the border with the Kingdom. Four more armored and mechanized divisions from the regular Iraqi army were moving into Kuwait. Bush convened the National Security Council again. I accompanied Webster to the meeting, briefing him on the latest information in the car as we drove down the George Washington Parkway from CIA headquarters in Langley, Virginia, to the White House. When he began the meeting, he again said the threat to Saudi Arabia was immediate and dangerous. The president dispatched Secretary of Defense Richard Cheney to Saudi Arabia that evening to press King Fahd to accept American military protection for the Kingdom.[49]

The royal family was initially divided on how to respond to Saddam's threat. Several senior princes, including Crown Prince Abdallah and governor of Riyadh Prince Salman, preferred an Arab solution that would be a diplomatic option to gain a mediated compromise. Other princes were more troubled. Prince Bandar, who had been briefed on the alarming intelligence by Powell in the Pentagon, believed Fahd needed to agree to invite American forces immediately.[50]

All week the Americans sensed Fahd was hesitating. Years later Bush told his preeminent biographer, Jon Meacham, that in his conversations by phone with Fahd and other Arab leaders after the invasion he detected an "openness to an accommodation with Saddam that would expand Iraq's power and reward Iraq's military strike." Cheney's trip, thus, in the American narrative, became crucial to influencing Fahd to take American military help and stand firm against Iraq.[51]

The Saudi version is different. According to Khalid bin Sultan's account, the king recognized immediately after the invasion the magnitude of Saddam's move. Once his son Prince Muhammad explained how the Iraqis had overrun Kuwait, Fahd was determined not to repeat the Kuwaiti errors. When Fahd asked the Iraqis on August 3, 1990, about Kuwait, they told him "the status of Kuwait has now been rectified. The clock cannot be turned back." It was clear that Iraq meant to annex Kuwait, which it now claimed as the nineteenth province of Iraq. Fahd had a "special feeling of consideration for Kuwait," because the Kuwaitis had provided a safe exile for his father, Ibn Saud, in the nineteenth century. But most important, he understood "the occupation of Kuwait was little different from the occupation of Riyadh itself and the disappearance of Kuwait would, sooner or later, pose a great threat to the security and identity of Saudi Arabia." Fahd also knew from his brother, Prince Sultan, minister of defense and aviation, and from Prince Khalid that even if all the Arabs sent troops to help Saudi Arabia, it would be too few to stop Iraq. In his memoirs Khalid lays out the numbers in detail. Even if Egypt sent its entire army to reinforce the Gulf states, Iraq would still have more troops, tanks, and aircraft.[52]

Bandar played a key role in convincing the king to get Bush's help. He pressed the Bush team to tell him what exactly they would send to defend the Kingdom. Bandar did not want a token American force. Bush told General Powell to brief Bandar, who was an old friend by now. Powell recalls that he told Bandar on August 3: "We'll start by bringing in the 1st Tactical Fighter Wing and the 82nd Airborne Division and a carrier. All told about one hundred thousand troops for starters." After the prince left, convinced he could tell the king that the Americans were serious about defending Saudi Arabia, Secretary of Defense Cheney told Powell he had exceeded his brief with such specific pledges, but by then it was too late.[53]

Operation Desert Shield commenced immediately after Fahd told Cheney on August 6 to send the troops Powell had promised Bandar. In his memoirs, President Bush noted, "In retrospect if Saddam had wanted to make a go for Saudi Arabia he probably made a mistake in that he did not do it in this brief window (early August); if he had he would have had a free run."[54] By the end of August, at the latest, Saddam had completely missed his window of opportunity. Enough American forces were on the ground in the Kingdom or offshore to destroy the Iraqis if they came south from Kuwait. President Bush and King Fahd had brought America and Saudi Arabia closer than ever. American popular attitudes toward Saudi Arabia shifted, as well. A Harris poll in January 1991 reported 33 percent of Americans thought the Kingdom was a "close ally" and another 44 percent saw it as "friendly." This 77 percent approval rating for Saudi Arabia as an American partner was unprecedented.[55]

There are no polls about Saudi popular opinion. The deployment of tens of thousands of foreign, presumably Christian, soldiers to the Kingdom and the resulting war with a neighboring Muslim country sent shock waves through Saudi Arabia. Saudis were stunned to discover that their country, which spent billions on arms every year, needed massive outside—American and European—military assistance to cope with the Iraqi threat. A few hoped the Western presence would bring reform and change. On November 6, 1990, forty-five women drove cars in a demonstration in downtown Riyadh. They were arrested and lost their jobs.[56]

The more significant reaction came from the dissidents in the religious community. In September 1990 the dean of the Islamic College at Umm al Qura University in Mecca, Safar al Hawali, publicly charged that the real enemy was not Iraq but, rather, America. Hawali then wrote an open letter to Shaykh Abdul Aziz bin Baz, the blind shaykh and the most senior cleric in the country, attacking the United States as "an evil greater than Saddam." Another cleric, Salman al Awadah at Imam Muhammad al Saud University in Riyadh, also called for the withdrawal of Western troops and warned their presence would be dangerous to Saudi moral values; he cited the women's driving protest as a sign of the country's disintegrating values.[57] Bin Baz and the top *ulema* had already endorsed Fahd's decision to invite the Americans into the Kingdom, so the criticism did not alter Fahd's position.

The protests did not end with the liberation of Kuwait. In the spring of 1991 open letters were sent to the king to undertake reforms. Some called for greater public participation in governance, but the most popular came from clerics Hawali and Awadah and called for a more Islamic society and the creation of an Islamic army to defend the Kingdom. It was openly critical of Fahd's pro-American foreign policies. The most senior clerical establishment did not endorse the letter but was reluctant to openly oppose it.[58]

Another voice of opposition was Osama bin Laden, who was back from Afghanistan by the summer of 1990. In Afghanistan and Pakistan, bin Laden had been the Saudis' most famous mujahedin supporter. He was famous at home, as well. He worked closely with the Saudi intelligence services, including with Interior Minister Prince Nayef and with Saudi general intelligence and Prince Turki. Turki's deputy later said, "He was our man." Nayef, the deputy noted, "liked" bin Laden.[59]

In July 1990 bin Laden proposed to Prince Turki, the head of Saudi intelligence, that he would organize a mujahedin-like insurgency to overthrow the pro-Moscow communist regime in South Yemen. Turki, who knew the Peoples Democratic Republic of Yemen, as it was called, was collapsing on its own, demurred and rejected bin Laden's advice. When Saddam invaded Kuwait, bin Laden again urged a mujahedin response to the royal court. The idea was rejected as too little to stop Saddam. Bin Laden was disappointed but he did not break with the House of Saud while the war with Iraq was under way.[60]

Operation Desert Storm

Saudi Arabia was safe by September 1990, but Kuwait was still occupied. Bush and Fahd had another momentous decision to make: how to liberate Kuwait. The Saudis were reluctant, at the beginning, to use force. As Prince Khalid noted, although the Saudis wanted Saddam overthrown at home, "we had no wish to see Iraq itself devastated. Despite our quarrel with its leader, Iraq was a brotherly country whom we had helped in its war with Iran, and whose regional role we valued as a counterweight to both Iran and Israel."[61] The Saudis worried about Iraq's efforts to acquire nuclear and chemical weapons, Khalid writes, but were troubled that Washington regarded "Israel's own nuclear bombs, chemical weapons and long range missiles in whose grim shadow the Arabs have had to live for decades as legitimate weapons of self defense whereas any Arab attempt, however feeble, to achieve a modicum of deterrence must be considered a threat to the 'civilized world.' "[62]

Saddam's refusal to leave Kuwait, the intense lobbying of the Kuwait royal family in exile in Taif, and pressure from Washington combined to persuade the king that force was the only option. When President Bush announced on November 8, 1990, a massive increase in the American force presence in the Kingdom, more than doubling the size of the American expeditionary army to a half-million, the king was in agreement that Kuwait could only be liberated by force of arms. Bush benefited from the counsel and insights of his fine ambassador in Riyadh, Chas Freeman, one of the best representatives Washington has ever sent to the Kingdom.

The Saudis in general and Bandar in particular were very worried that their traditional foes in the region, especially Yemen and the Hashemite Kingdom of Jordan, would take advantage of the Iraq-Kuwait crisis at the

Kingdom's expense. Jordan's King Hussein was close to Saddam and tried to persuade the Iraqi dictator to avoid war by leaving Kuwait. Saddam was very popular in Jordan, and King Hussein was reluctant to break with the Iraqi dictator. For the Saudis and President Bush this seemed a weak, vacillating approach. The Saudis feared King Hussein wanted to regain the Hejaz for the Hashemites. This was Saudi paranoia at work, but they believed their fears were real. Bandar wrote a scathing column for the *Washington Post* in which he took Hussein to task for arguing the Iraq-Kuwait border was a product of British colonialism. Bandar said: "Your majesty, you should be the last one to say that. Not only your border, but your whole country was created by the colonial British."[63]

Yemen worried the Saudis even more. King Fahd and his advisers feared that President Ali Abdullah Saleh nurtured ambitions to regain the territory lost in the 1930s to Saudi Arabia. Prince Khalid, Bandar's brother, worried that "there was a strong chance that other fronts might open up. The Yemenis might seize the opportunity to cross our frontier and attempt to seize our border province of Asir."[64] In September 1990 Riyadh broke relations with both Amman and Sana'a.[65] To counter the potential Yemeni threat, the Saudis deployed the Pakistani armored brigade away from Tabuk to the Yemeni border to back up the weak Saudi National Guard forces in the south. Later, when Saudi fears of Yemeni adventurism eased, the brigade was redeployed facing Iraq.[66]

The Pakistani task force, which had been in the Kingdom since after the Mecca siege in the early 1980s, was quickly joined by other Muslim units. Thousands of troops from Egypt, Morocco, and other Muslim states gave the emerging coalition an Islamic dimension. For the Saudis it was important that the coalition army in the Kingdom have as many Arabs and Muslims as possible, even if the core of the fighting force was American. Fahd, especially, sought support from Syria, a frontline state against Israel with a history of being at the forefront of Arab nationalism. Fahd urged President Hafez Assad to join the coalition, and eventually the Syrians sent a division to fight in Kuwait.

President Bush and First Lady Barbara Bush visited the Kingdom to see Fahd and meet the troops for Thanksgiving in late November. Fahd greeted them at the airport and they stayed in the King's marble guest palace. "The

King hosted a late state dinner for us—ten o'clock, which I was told was an early hour for him. It was an unbelievable meal. The only way to describe the amount of food was to say that if ever there was an occasion when tables groaned under a feast, this was it," Bush recalled later. But the dinner was kept short, only an hour, so that Bush and Fahd could talk past midnight about their plans for taking the offensive against Saddam.[67] Prince Khalid relates that after the Bush-Fahd summit the Saudis were brought into the intense American planning already under way for what would be called Operation Desert Storm.[68]

Khalid and General Norman Schwarzkopf, the top American commander, had occasional disagreements on strategy and protocol but generally worked smoothly together. A key disagreement centered on the Iraqi missile threat to the Kingdom and Israel. The Saudis felt more attention should be paid to preventing Saddam from using his Scud missiles to attack Riyadh than did the Americans. The Saudis also worried that Saddam would attack Tel Aviv with his Scuds to try to draw the Israelis into the war, which would turn a conflict among Arabs into an Arab-Israeli conflict and place Saudi Arabia on the side of Israel. Khalid pressed to make eliminating the Scuds the top priority of the air campaign at the start of Desert Storm. Schwarzkopf disagreed, arguing the Scuds were not a significant military weapon because they were so inaccurate and carried small warheads.[69]

When the war began on January 17, 1991, Prince Khalid was proven right. Iraq almost immediately began attacking Tel Aviv and Haifa in Israel, as well as Riyadh, with Scuds. By the time the war ended, Iraq had fired more than eighty missiles at Israel and Saudi Arabia. One hit a U.S. Army barracks in Dhahran and killed twenty-eight American soldiers. Fortunately, casualties from the other missiles were relatively light, with two Israelis killed and 230 injured in thirty-nine missile attacks, and one Saudi killed and seventy injured.[70] Belatedly, the United States deployed Patriot air defense missiles to Israel and Saudi Arabia to shoot down the Scuds; it turned out they were good for morale but had little success in defending against the Iraqi attacks.

Despite the low casualty rate, the Israelis were deeply alarmed by the Scud attacks, which brought their economy to a halt and created considerable anxiety. Prime Minister Yitzhak Shamir proposed sending one hundred Israeli aircraft through Saudi airspace to attack the Scud launching sites in western Iraq, or sending aircraft and paratroopers through Jordanian airspace to attack them. Bush firmly rejected both ideas and refused to give Israel the codes that would identify the Israeli aircraft as friendly; they would be regarded as enemy aircraft if they entered the battlespace. Bush did send more Patriot missiles to help defend Israel's cities.[71]

To underscore their concern, the Israelis moved their Jericho intermediate-range ballistic missiles from their bunkers into the open, knowing American intelligence satellites would see them. This was a way to rattle Israel's never-acknowledged nuclear option without going public. The Saudis were informed of the Israeli move.

For their part the Saudis considered using their Chinese-supplied CSS2 missiles to retaliate against Baghdad. Prince Khalid, who had been instrumental in acquiring the missiles from China, ordered them placed on alert when the Scuds fell on Riyadh. They were to be prepared for launch upon order from the king. "But after some anxious hours, King Fahd decided not to escalate the conflict. He made a rational decision to reserve the missiles as a weapon of last resort," Khalid later wrote.[72]

The ground campaign, which began on February 24, proved to be anti-climatic. The previous thirty-four days of air war had decimated the Iraqi army and smashed its morale. Prince Khalid commanded the forces that liberated Kuwait City; he made sure that contingents from every Arab army fighting in the war participated in the return to the capital. Kuwaiti forces restored law and order. After just a hundred hours of ground war, Bush announced a cease-fire.

The allies had planned carefully for all kinds of contingencies in the war but had given surprisingly little thought to the peace that would follow. No one discussed marching to Baghdad and overthrowing Saddam. As Prince Khalid later wrote, "Any suggestion of marching on Baghdad was out of the question for the Arab members of the coalition, and indeed would have been vigorously opposed by Saudi Arabia."[73] General Powell writes that "in none of the meetings on the war I attended was dismembering Iraq, conquering Baghdad or changing the Iraqi form of governance ever seriously considered. We hoped Saddam would not survive but his elimination was not a stated objective. Our practical intention was to leave Baghdad enough power to survive as a threat to Iran."[74]

The assumption in the White House was that Saddam would fall from power without any more pressure from the allies. Instead, he held on to power and ruthlessly suppressed uprisings by the Shia majority in the south and the Kurdish minority in the north. Meanwhile, the large foreign army in Saudi Arabia went home. Only an air wing remained in Dhahran. From the air base there, American, British, and French aircraft patrolled a no-fly zone, to protect Shias in southern Iraq, for the next twelve years.

In the war's aftermath, Bush did engage in a major diplomatic effort to resolve the Arab-Israeli conflict. He believed the war had opened new opportunities for conflict resolution. Such an effort would also make it easier for the Saudis and other Arabs to work closely with the United States to foster regional stability. After a marathon diplomatic campaign led by Secretary of State James Baker, a peace conference was convened in Madrid, Spain, on October 30, 1991. The parties agreed to establish bilateral talks between Israel and its neighbors along with multilateral talks on regional issues like the environment and arms control.

Prince Bandar attended the Madrid conference to represent the Kingdom, along with the secretary general of the Gulf Cooperation Council.[75] The Saudis and the other Gulf states participated in the multilateral talks, marking the first time the Kingdom got directly involved in the peace process with Israel. But the Madrid process soon bogged down and no progress emerged from the bilateral talks. It would take a secret Israeli-Palestinian dialogue in Oslo, Norway, to create a breakthrough on the watch of Bush's successor in 1993.

The Kuwait war illustrated more clearly than ever before the strong ties between Saudi Arabia and America, but it also vividly exposed the Kingdom's weakness and its dependence on American security to survive. If Saddam had attacked in early August 1990 after invading Kuwait, the Saudi Eastern Province and Bahrain would have fallen quickly. To liberate Kuwait the Kingdom needed a half-million American soldiers as well as British, French, and Arab troops. The Iran-Iraq war had already exposed Saudi military weakness; now the Kuwait war highlighted its vulnerability in a dangerous neighborhood. Iran had threatened the Kingdom in the 1980s, and Iraq stood on the precipice of invading it in 1990.

One consequence of this vulnerability was a renewed Saudi effort to build legitimacy by exporting its own brand of Islam to the world. Fahd expanded

Faisal's support for mosques and educational establishments across Europe, Africa, and Asia after the Kuwait war. This was one way to answer the domestic critics of his decision to turn to Bush for help in 1990.

After Bush lost his bid for reelection in November 1992 to Bill Clinton, he sent American military forces to Somalia to try to restore order and deliver humanitarian relief. On December 31, 1992, the president paid a visit to Riyadh en route to Somalia to see King Fahd. It was a poignant symbol of how close the king and president had become over the years and the importance the Kuwait war had in the Bush presidency. Fahd gave Bush an enormous replica of the fort in Riyadh that Ibn Saud had seized back at the start of the modern Saudi Kingdom to symbolize his affection for the president.

Chapter Five

ABDALLAH, CLINTON, AND BUSH, 1993 TO 2008

The palace of Abdallah Abd al Aziz al Saud in Jidda is intended to impress. In May 1998 Abdalluh, then the crown prince, was entertaining Vice President Al Gore for lunch. The luncheon was served in a room the size of six basketball courts, next to the palace's Olympic-size indoor swimming pool. The ceiling was painted blue with white stars to symbolize the desert sky in the evening. Behind the dining table was an enormous aquarium that extended from the floor to the ceiling and the length of the room. One guest at the luncheon estimated it was seventy-five feet long and thirty feet high. The glass wall was surrounded with pillars to appear as an ancient palace. The aquarium was filled with exotic fish swimming around what appeared to be ancient ruins. Several large sharks were among them.[1] I was accompanying the vice president as the National Security Council (NSC) representative. To me it was a scene right out of the first James Bond novel, *Doctor No*.

The lunch was an opportunity for Gore and Abdallah to get to know each other better. Much later Prince Turki, the Saudi intelligence chief, told the media that two of the 9/11 hijackers, Khalid al Mihdhar and Nawaf al Hazmi, were involved in a plot to attack Gore's party that day.[2] The Saudis captured anti-tank missiles the terrorists had smuggled in from Yemen to carry out the attack. This was months before al Qaida's first attacks on American targets: the U.S. embassies in Kenya and Tanzania in August 1998.

The Saudis did not tell the Americans about the plot until well after Gore had left the Kingdom. This was typical of the Saudi policy toward terrorism in the 1990s. The royal family was in denial about the fact that a significant infrastructure of terror had developed under the surface calm in the nation. Terrorist groups, especially al Qaeda but also Shia terrorists, had extensive underground networks inside the Kingdom. Saudi officials were convinced they knew how best to deal with any such problem, either through tough internal security measures, diplomacy abroad, or, if necessary, assassination. Above all, the Saudis did not want outsiders, especially Americans, dealing with the terror nexus in Saudi Arabia.

Abdallah Abd al Aziz al Saud was the tenth son of Ibn Saud. He was born in Riyadh; his date of birth is often cited as August 1, 1924, but it is not certain. His mother, Fahda bint Asi Al Shuraim, was from the rival al Rashid dynasty and the powerful Shammar tribe that dominates the northern Arabian Peninsula. She died when he was only six. He also suffered from a speech impediment. His half-brothers—Khalid, Fahd, Sultan, Nayef, Ahmed, and Salman—all had a different mother, Hussa bint Ahmed Al Sudairi, giving them the title of the Sudairis. The status of Abdallah's mother as an al Rashid made him somewhat of an outsider within the royal family.

But he overcame these issues early in life. In 1961 he was appointed mayor of Mecca, helping establish a lifelong reputation of piety. Unlike brothers Saud or Fahd, Abdallah was never considered a playboy. His image was of a pious Muslim with close connections to the tribal leadership. In 1962 Abdallah became commander of the Saudi Arabian National Guard, with the responsibility of regime protection. The National Guard is deployed in the holy cities, the capital, and the Eastern Province. The regular army is deployed on the frontiers. The National Guard was Abdallah's powerbase, and he kept command of it until 2010 when he passed control to his son Mutaib. The post gave Abdallah a special position in the family as the commander of what, in effect, was its Praetorian Guard and as the man most connected to the tribal elites. He, in turn, made sure the National Guard got the best training and best equipment needed to do its job. Most of that training and equipment has come from the United States or Canada.

King Khalid appointed Abdallah to be deputy crown prince in 1975 after Faisal was assassinated, and King Fahd made him crown prince in 1982 when Khalid died. For the next thirteen years Abdallah worked closely with Fahd. In 1995 Fahd suffered a massive, debilitating stroke, and for the next decade Abdallah ruled as de facto regent. On August 1, 2005, Abdallah ascended to the throne when Fahd passed away. He lived until January 23, 2015.

So for some twenty years Abdallah effectively ruled the Kingdom. While his half-brother Fahd was still alive he was careful to maintain the fiction that Fahd was in charge. When a senior American official like Gore visited the country, he went first to see Fahd in the royal palace. After picture taking and a few bland remarks, the official was dismissed and went on to see the crown prince. Abdallah always opened the substantive discussion that followed by asking how the visitor found Fahd's health. The correct protocol answer was that the king was in fine health.

Abdallah dealt with three American presidents: Bill Clinton, George W. Bush, and Barack Obama. Saudi-American relations during the Abdallah era began on the high note of the aftermath of Desert Storm in 1990–91. The 1990s represented almost a golden period of close cooperation on many issues, but underlying tensions would begin to emerge by 2000. Clinton's second ambassador to the Kingdom, Wyche Fowler, probably had the closest relationship to King Abdallah in the history of America's partnership with the Kingdom, in large part because the king liked Fowler, a former congressman from Georgia. In 2001 the storm broke when the towers collapsed with the 9/11 terrorist attack. For the remainder of the Abdallah era the relationship continued to be important and valuable to both sides but increasingly tense and contentious.

Clinton

It was inevitable that the successor to President George H. W. Bush would begin with a less intimate relationship with the Saudis. While Bush had saved the Kingdom via a war against Iraq, many of the Democrats elected with

Clinton in 1992 had voted against that war in the Senate. I was still the National Security Council's director for Gulf affairs, and my new bosses wanted a way to open a dialogue with the Kingdom and to begin to build relationships.

Prince Bandar bin Sultan bin Abdul Aziz, the Saudi ambassador, and I had an idea. Bill Clinton had graduated from Georgetown University in the same year that Prince Turki al Faisal, the Kingdom's intelligence chief, had attended the school. So Bandar and I worked to have a reunion of the two classmates to establish a bond. Turki visited the White House to meet with National Security Adviser Anthony Lake, and the president "dropped in" on the meeting to see his old classmate. It was a start to what became a strong working relationship between the Clinton White House and the House of Saud.

Bill Clinton pursued two major policy lines in the Middle East. First was enthusiastic and high profile support for negotiations to achieve a comprehensive and final peace settlement between Israel and all its Arab neighbors, including the Palestinians. Second was the dual containment of Iraq and Iran, which were judged threats to American vital interests and needed to be restrained from dangerous adventurism in the Middle East. The two policies were designed to reinforce each other. It would be easier to gather support among the Arabs to contain Iraq and Iran if the peace process involving Israel was vibrant and producing results. It would also be easier to get results in the peace process if two spoilers, Iraq and Iran, were successfully contained and marginalized in the region.

The Saudis were equally enthusiastic about the peace process although much less inclined to be as high profile in their efforts as Washington sometimes sought. They also agreed that Iraq and Iran were twin dangers but, worried that containment was unsustainable and costly, they preferred a coup that would remove Saddam and replace him with another Sunni strongman who would help rein in Iran. They had no capacity to affect such a coup, however, and neither did Washington.

The Clinton team inherited from Bush the Madrid peace process, which had become stalemated. Behind the scenes, however, Israel and the Palestine Liberation Organization (PLO) were engaged in secret diplomacy facilitated by Norway. The so called Oslo process achieved a breakthrough in mid-1993 when Israeli Prime Minister Yitzhak Rabin and PLO Chairman Yasser Arafat agreed to mutual recognition and the withdrawal of Israeli forces from most but not all of the Gaza Strip and the city of Jericho on the West Bank. The withdrawal from Gaza and Jericho was intended to initiate a process to end Israel's occupation of Gaza and the West Bank and produce a final peace treaty. The United States was not a party to the talks, but once briefed on the results, Clinton was eager to support the process and to host a signing ceremony at the White House.

As dean of the diplomatic corps in Washington (the longest-serving ambassador), Prince Bandar welcomed Arafat to Washington at Andrews Air Force Base in September 1993. Bandar attended the signing ceremony at the White House for the Oslo deal, representing the Kingdom. He also had the important, albeit somewhat unusual, job of persuading Arafat, behind the scenes, that he should not kiss the president or prime minister at the ceremony. Arafat had a fondness for embracing and kissing his interlocutors (I know from experience).[3]

The Saudis had long supported Arafat and funded the PLO. They were irritated at Arafat's tilt toward Iraq during the 1990–91 Kuwait crisis, but the Palestinian cause was deeply popular within the royal family, across the *ulema,* and among the Saudi public, so he was rehabilitated quickly after the war. Bandar hosted Arafat for every visit he made to Washington during Clinton's two terms in office, and the Palestinian leader called more often at the Clinton White House than any other foreign leader. Nonetheless, the Saudis were always distrustful of Arafat after 1990.

The Saudi preference was to be out of sight most of the time and keep a low profile, letting Arafat and his Syrian counterparts be in the public space. As one senior Clinton aide, Martin Indyk, later wrote, "The Saudis helped us quietly on the peace process, where they were willing to provide funding for Arafat's Palestinian Authority but were wary of engaging with Israel."[4]

Ironically the Israeli-Palestinian Oslo deal opened the door to an Israeli-Jordanian peace treaty. King Hussein was initially shocked at the Oslo agreements, from which he had also been excluded, but he saw in Oslo an opportunity to end Jordan's state of war with Israel and achieve a peace treaty. If the Palestinians had made a deal, so could Jordan. The critical negotiations were done secretly by the king and Efraim Halevy, the head of Mossad, the Israeli Secret Intelligence Service. Again, the Americans were largely excluded from the talks, but Clinton was invited to the signing ceremony. He insisted that he be the only witness, signatory, and guarantor of the treaty to underscore American centrality in the process.[5]

Clinton traveled to the region in October 1994 for the signing ceremony in Jordan. His itinerary included Egypt, Jordan, Syria, Israel, Kuwait, and Saudi Arabia. The Saudis still had not forgiven King Hussein for his tilt toward Iraq in 1990, but King Fahd welcomed Clinton to the Kingdom for a few hours in what would be the president's only visit to Saudi Arabia.[6] A year later Fahd suffered the debilitating stroke that removed him from managing the affairs of the Kingdom and placed Crown Prince Abdallah effectively in charge.

Abdallah continued Fahd's policy of quiet but effective support for the peace process. He was especially keen to secure a peace treaty between Syria and Israel. The Saudis believed such an agreement would take the Syrians out of their alliance with Iran and also permit Lebanon to sign a treaty with Israel, thus making the region more stable and weakening Tehran's influence. The election of former armed forces chief of staff General Ehud Barak to be Israeli prime minister in 1999 seemed to open the path to a deal with President Hafez Assad.

Clinton hosted Syrian and Israeli negotiators at the White House in late 1999. Bandar separately hosted the Syrian delegation at his Virginia home after the first day's talks. Syrian foreign minister Farouk Sharaa told the assembled representatives of the Arab states at Bandar's home that "they should inform their governments that Syria was about to make peace with Israel."[7] A deal seemed imminent, with the final negotiations to be hosted by Clinton at Shepherdstown, West Virginia.

Instead of a deal, Shepherdstown produced a "debacle."[8] The key problem was a disagreement on where to place the border between Syria and Israel on the northeast shore of the Sea of Galilee. Assad insisted it be on the lakeshore, where the Syrian army had been stationed on June 4, 1967, just before the Six-Day War. Barak insisted Israel control a narrow strip of territory along the shore, as had been the case when France and Britain had settled the border between their colonies in Syria and Palestine in 1919. Assad wanted to get access to the lake, but Barak was determined not to let his enemies' toes in the water at all. Clinton did not press Barak to give Assad the sliver of territory at stake. The talks ended in failure and damaged Clinton's credibility. In his memoirs Clinton wrote that "the Syrians came to Shepherdstown in a positive and flexible frame of mind, eager to make a deal." Barak was the obstacle, Clinton concluded.[9]

The Saudis played a central role in getting another chance at an Israel-Syria deal in March 2000 when Assad agreed to see Clinton in Geneva, Switzerland, at the end of Clinton's trip to India, Bangladesh, Pakistan, and Oman. Bandar traveled to Damascus to persuade Assad to go to Geneva. However, the small but crucial border problem scuttled the Geneva meeting, as well. When Assad saw the terms Barak was proposing, he said he was not going to agree. Clinton did not press Assad either, and it was all over in an hour. To add insult to injury, the president was suffering from the ill effects of food he had eaten in Islamabad the day before and was eager to get home to Washington.[10]

Assad died shortly after the Geneva summit. Prince Bandar hurried to Damascus to help Assad's son Bashar take power. Bandar used Saudi influence to persuade Syria's senior generals that Bashar was the best man for the job of replacing his father.

The Saudis were skeptical of Clinton's next major effort at peacemaking when, in July 2000, he convened another summit between Arafat and Barak, this time at Camp David, the presidential retreat in Maryland. As the president's special assistant for the Near East and South Asia, I was also skeptical that a deal was possible and advised both Clinton and National Security Adviser Samuel "Sandy" Berger about my skepticism. I was especially doubtful an agreement could be reached after the Assad failures—and particularly on the future of Jerusalem. Unfortunately, I was proven right and the Camp David summit failed. The two parties were far apart on all the issues going into the summit, and the gaps did not close significantly despite Clinton's sustained efforts. Almost immediately afterward the West Bank erupted into violence, marking the beginning of a Palestinian uprising, or intifada, in the occupied territories.

Clinton was not deterred from one last effort. In the closing days of his administration, he proposed his own "parameters" for a comprehensive Israeli-Palestinian peace agreement. Barak, facing a difficult election and under pressure because of the intifada, accepted them with considerable caveats. Bandar pushed Arafat to do the same when he came to the White

House in January 2001. Crown Prince Abdallah weighed in with Arafat, as well, according to Clinton's later account, but a deal simply was not possible at that point.[11] The Saudis were disappointed but hopeful that the newly elected president, George W. Bush, would continue the negotiating process his father had begun at Madrid. On this, Bandar and Abdallah were to be very disappointed.

Iraq

In the Persian Gulf, Iraq repeatedly challenged the cease-fire regime imposed at the end of the Kuwait war. The Iraqis were obligated by the United Nations Security Council resolutions following the armistice to destroy their weapons of mass destruction programs, under UN inspections and monitoring, and to agree to an official border demarcation with Kuwait. The sanctions imposed after the invasion in August 1990 were lifted only partially to allow Iraq to sell oil to purchase food and medicine for the Iraqi people.

Saddam Hussein interfered with the UN inspectors almost from the beginning, creating a series of mini-crises between Washington and Baghdad that began in the first Bush administration and continued through Clinton and into the next Bush administration. The Saudis were vital to American efforts to force Iraqi compliance with the UN resolutions since they hosted the largest American military air base in the region, at Dhahran. This meant U.S. forces remained in the Kingdom long after the liberation of Kuwait despite Bush's promises that American forces would leave once the war was over. It was an uncomfortable position for Fahd and Abdallah, but they backed both the United States and the UN.

Saudi support was particularly crucial for enforcing a no-fly zone in southern Iraq that Bush had established in 1992 to prevent Iraqi air strikes on Shia dissidents. American, British, and French aircraft patrolled southern Iraq to stymie such strikes. The no-fly zone also meant that the coalition partners controlled Iraqi air space bordering Saudi Arabia and Kuwait, thus making another Iraqi attempt at invasion of either country far more difficult and providing critical strategic depth for both. After losing his bid for reelection, Bush traveled to Kuwait in early 1993 to attend the second anniversary of the emirate's liberation. The Kuwaiti authorities discovered Iraq had smuggled a large car bomb into the country with the intent to kill the former president. They briefed the White House and, on June 26, 1993, Clinton ordered the launching of twenty-three Tomahawk cruise missiles to destroy the Baghdad headquarters of the Iraqi intelligence service that had plotted the assassination attempt.

Another major crisis came suddenly in October 1994 when Saddam sent two rebuilt and refurbished Republican Guard armored divisions to the Kuwaiti border, apparently threatening another invasion. By October 8, 1994, Iraq had 80,000 troops and hundreds of tanks just north of Kuwait. Clinton sent 350 aircraft to Saudi Arabia and Kuwait to deter Saddam and prepare to destroy the Iraqi tanks. He told the Saudis that if Saddam attacked, this time the United States would not stop the war until Saddam was finished. American ground forces, totaling over 50,000 people, were alerted to deploy to Kuwait and the Kingdom.[12] Iraq backed down and Saddam, in humiliation, formally accepted the UN-demarcated border with Kuwait.[13]

The most serious crisis between Clinton and Saddam came in the president's second term when I was his top Middle East adviser on the National Security Council staff and he was mired in the political scandal surrounding his relationship with Monica Lewinsky. Again, Saddam was interfering with UN weapons inspections. Sandy Berger and I urged the president to conduct a larger punitive air campaign to convince Saddam that the cost of these crises was serious. The main targets of the airstrikes would be those elements of the Iraqi regime that were Saddam's principal protectors: the Special Republican Guard and the intelligence services, both of which were also directly involved in thwarting the UN.[14]

Clinton agreed, and on December 16, 1998, after Clinton made a short trip to Jerusalem and Gaza, the United States and the United Kingdom began a four-day bombing attack from bases in Saudi Arabia and Kuwait, targeting eighteen command centers, eight Special Republican Guard barracks, six airfields, and nineteen intelligence sites in Iraq. Called Operation Desert Fox, this was the last major crisis between Iraq and the UN coalition in the Clinton era.[15]

The continuing danger posed by Iraq in the 1990s meant that Washington and Riyadh remained engaged in containing Saddam's regime. Crown Prince

Abdallah and Bandar were frustrated that Saddam survived in power, but they had no enthusiasm for another major war on Baghdad. Nor did Clinton and his team. That, too, would change under President George W. Bush.

Iran

Iran was the other half of Clinton's dual containment policy. The containment of Iran appealed to the Saudis' long-standing and deep concerns—dating to the shah's rule—about Iran's pursuit of regional hegemony in the Persian Gulf. But unlike Iraq, no United Nations resolutions limited Iranian ambitions and no sanctions kept Tehran under international controls. Indeed much of the world was eager to expand economic and trade relations with Iran and to sell products to Iran in exchange for oil.

Iran in the early 1990s was especially interested in buying a large number of civilian aircraft to replace aging civilian planes from the shah's time. The European consortium Airbus and the American company Boeing were the two suppliers most likely to make such a deal. Clinton did not want to block the Boeing company from a lucrative deal, and, thus, benefit its competitors, but he also did not want Iran's purchase of American jets to weaken his containment effort.

I proposed that Washington persuade Saudi Arabia to buy a large number of American civilian aircraft, to keep the airline business happy, while reaching a private understanding with the Saudis that we would then not compete for Iran's business. I raised the idea with Bandar, who was enthusiastic. So was the president, and several weeks later, in 1993, Clinton sent Secretary of Commerce Ron Brown and me to the Kingdom, where Fahd agreed, and the Saudis bought $6 billion worth of jets. The massive deal was formally announced (without mention of the Iran connection) in February 1994.[16]

On June 25, 1996, the most important U.S. military facility in the Middle East was attacked by terrorists. A large truck bomb (equivalent to 20,000 pounds of TNT) was detonated outside a barracks at the Dhahran air base, in a suburb called Khobar. The attack on the residence known as Khobar Towers killed nineteen United States Air Force personnel and wounded another 372. Several hundred Saudis and guest workers in the nearby town were also injured. Dhahran was a vital facility, home to the Operation Southern Watch aircraft that patrolled the no-fly zone in southern Iraq.

At the time I was deputy assistant secretary of defense for Near East and South Asia affairs and traveling in the region with Secretary of State Warren Christopher. We learned of the Khobar attack while we were in Jerusalem, and Christopher immediately decided to go to the scene of the attack. En route my boss, Secretary of Defense William Perry, instructed me to stay in Dhahran after Christopher left and wait for him to come to the region in a few days. I spent a week in Dhahran living in the consulate residence and working with the embassy and U.S. Air Force on the aftermath of the bombing.

Prince Bandar arrived on the scene shortly, as well. I met with him at the palace of the governor of the Eastern Province. Bandar said the Saudis were still developing information on the attack, but he clearly pointed a finger at Iran as responsible for the operation. When Perry arrived a few days later and met with the king, crown prince, and interior minister, they also suggested Iranian involvement but were quick to say the investigation was still in its early days.

It was not the first serious terrorist attack in the Kingdom against American targets. On November 13, 1995, a bomb detonated in the parking lot outside the headquarters of the Saudi Arabian National Guard training facility in Riyadh. Five Americans were killed and thirty wounded. The Americans were employed by the Vinnell Corporation, which had a $5.6 billion contract to train the National Guard. That attack apparently was the work of Sunni extremists who had fought in Afghanistan and were influenced by the speeches of Osama bin Laden. The Saudis captured four of the perpetrators and executed them after their confessions were aired on Saudi television. Minister of the Interior Prince Nayef bin Abdul Aziz refused to give the FBI access to the terrorists before their execution.[17]

Nayef resisted cooperation with the United States on the Khobar attack, as well. In part this was personal; Nayef was not a friend of the United States and he jealously guarded his prerogatives as interior minister. He did not want Americans involved in his investigation or in the Saudi judiciary process. But Nayef's reluctance was shared by the crown prince and other senior princes. Their concern was with what Washington would do with the results of the investigation. If an Iranian hand were involved, would Clinton attack Iran, as he had attacked Iraq for the Bush assassination plot? Would the situation escalate into another Gulf war with Saudi Arabia in the crosshairs of Iran's terrorist apparatus and missiles?[18]

The immediate shared requirement after the Khobar attack was to find a more secure base for U.S. Air Force operations in Saudi Arabia. Perry pressed Crown Prince Abdallah and Defense Minister Prince Sultan for a new location with better security than Dhahran. The Saudis provided the air force with Prince Sultan Air Base in the desert fifty miles southeast of Riyadh. That base was surrounded by miles of open desert, and it was enormous, eighty square miles. It also was isolated from Saudi civilians, and from a security perspective it had much better "stand off" distance than Khobar, which was right in the center of a busy metropolitan area.[19] The U.S., British, and French air forces all moved their aircraft and crews to the base before the end of 1996.

The Saudis gradually revealed that they had caught a Shia Saudi smuggling explosives into the Kingdom from Jordan a month before the Khobar attack; he said the terror group he was working for had surveilled the Khobar barracks. The group responsible was Saudi Hezbollah.

The Saudis, especially Nayef, were well acquainted with Saudi Hezbollah, or Hezbollah al Hijaz, from its terror attacks in the mid-1980s (see chapter 4). They knew the leader of the military wing of the group was Ahmed Ibrahim al Mughassil and that it was closely connected to the Iranian Revolutionary Guard Corps and its base in Syria. They determined that Mughassil was responsible for the Khobar attack and was in the truck bomb when it was parked outside the barracks.

The driver of the get-away car was another Saudi Shia, named Hani Abd Rahim al Sayegh, who had fled to Canada. The Canadian Security and Intelligence Service in March 1997 concluded that Sayegh was a "direct participant" in the attack and that Mughassil was the "mastermind." Sayegh admitted to having been provided with a false passport by the Iranian intelligence service and to having plotted in Syria and Iran with other members of Saudi Hezbollah.[20] Eventually Sayegh was extradited to the United States, but he refused to cooperate with the FBI and was, ultimately, sent back to the Kingdom.[21]

In February 1997 Defense Minister Sultan visited Washington. He was received by Perry's successor, former Maine senator William Cohen, and by other senior officials. He was given the rare privilege of a visit to the National Security Agency headquarters in Fort Meade, Maryland. Sultan was pressed to encourage more cooperation in the investigation.[22]

By the spring of 1997 the White House felt the evidence was sufficient to take some action against Iran. I had by then moved over to the National Security Council to become special assistant to the president and senior director for Near East and South Asia affairs. Richard Clarke, the senior director for counterterrorism, and I proposed that the United States take action against the Iranian intelligence service and the Iranian Revolutionary Guard Corps by disrupting their operations around the world. This would be a simple matter of "outing" their operatives around the world—letting them know that we knew who they were.[23]

Operation Sapphire, as it was called, was a big success. The Iranian intelligence chief in Saudi Arabia was among those "outed."[24] George Tenet, director of the Central Intelligence Agency, later wrote in his memoir that John Brennan (who would later become a CIA director) "handled the local Iranian intelligence chief in Riyadh himself. John walked up to his car, knocked on the window, and said, 'Hello, I'm from the U.S. Embassy and I've something to tell you.' The guy got out of the car, claimed Iran was a peace loving country, then jumped back in the car and sped away."[25]

Later that summer Ayatollah Mohammad Khatami was elected president of Iran. Khatami was a reformer who wanted to open Iran to outside influences and publicly called for better relations with the United States. Khatami attended the summit of the Organization of the Islamic Conference, which King Faisal had created, and argued for a revitalization of Islamic civil society and a reduction in tensions. Crown Prince Abdallah was present at the summit and was impressed. A Saudi-Iranian rapprochement followed, including signing of a security cooperation agreement. Former Iranian president Ayatollah Rafsanjani visited the Kingdom in 1998 and Khatami visited in 1999. In a very unusual gesture, the crown prince sent a Shia as ambassador to Iran.[26]

Khatami's election also changed the dynamics of U.S.-Iran relations. President Clinton wanted to engage Khatami, who clearly had no involvement in the Khobar attack himself and was the enemy of the hardliners in the Iranian Revolutionary Guard Corps. When Vice President Al Gore traveled to Saudi Arabia in May 1998, he carried an appeal from Clinton asking Crown Prince Abdallah to send a message to Khatami welcoming a change in American-Iranian relations and urging Iran to open a direct diplomatic channel to Washington.

Clinton continued to try to engage Khatami directly for the remainder of his presidency, but Khatami's domestic situation was too fragile to allow him to have a direct diplomatic opening to Washington. In June 1999 Assistant Secretary of State Martin Indyk and I traveled to France to see the sultan of Oman at his chateau outside Paris to give him a message to take to Khatami. Oman has long enjoyed good relations with both Riyadh and Tehran, so the sultan was an important intermediary.

The sultan has ruled his country since 1970, when the British engineered a coup against his father, who ruled almost as a medieval monarch, and put him on the throne. He is something of a recluse, only visiting Washington once in his reign. I've met him several times and always found him smart, insightful, and direct. On this occasion he immediately agreed to help Clinton.

At the meeting in Fontaine le Port I read a written message to the sultan and his foreign minister, Yusuf bin Alawi, that was focused on the Khobar attack. Subsequently declassified, the message said the United States government had acquired evidence that directly linked the Iranian guards to the attack. The United States sought a clear message from Khatami and the Iranian government that it would stop any further terrorist plots against American targets and bring to justice those involved in Khobar. Bin Alawi delivered the message to Khatami in Tehran on July 20, 1999, and explained that Clinton wanted good relations with Iran but needed assurance that Khobar would not be repeated. Khatami listened carefully to the foreign minister and said he was unaware of any Iranian involvement in the operation but would investigate.

The Iranians formally responded to the Omanis in September 1999. They categorically rejected the "allegations" of involvement as "inaccurate and unacceptable." But the message also assured that "there exists no threat from the Islamic Republic of Iran" to Americans, an implicit commitment that "there would be no additional Iranian terrorist attacks on American citizens," as

Indyk later wrote.[27] Until the American invasion of Iraq in 2003, that would be the case.

The president raised the Iran issue directly with Crown Prince Abdallah when he visited Washington on September 25, 1998. Unfortunately, that visit occurred in the midst of the Monica Lewinsky scandal. The crown prince spent the bulk of his meeting with the president assuring him of his personal support despite the scandal and suggesting that the Mossad was probably responsible for the affair.[28]

The Bush administration formally brought charges against Mughassil, his accomplices in Saudi Hezbollah, and Iran in June 2001. The Department of Justice issued an indictment that laid out the case against them. The Saudis were kept fully informed of the case, and Bandar quietly welcomed the formal indictment.[29]

Abdallah's close ties with Clinton had a price, helping exacerbate the tensions between extremists and the Kingdom. Osama bin Laden turned on the House of Saud as he embarked on his global jihad against America. In 1991 bin Laden left Saudi Arabia and went into exile in Khartoum, Sudan. He kept a low profile until 1994, although he was active privately in support of dissident critics inside the Kingdom.

In December 1994 bin Laden sent an open letter to Chief Mufti Shaykh al bin Baz of Saudi Arabia who had endorsed his work in Afghanistan a decade before. In this open letter, bin Laden's first public statement evoking his new jihad, he attacked bin Baz and the clerical establishment for endorsing the Oslo accords. The cleric had issued a statement endorsing the Oslo agreement and the Saudi support for the peace process. Bin Laden attacked this as "conferring legitimacy on the contracts of surrender to the Jews that were signed by traitorous and cowardly Arab tyrants," a reference to the House of Saud.[30] He repeated his earlier criticism of the Saudis for allowing American troops into the Kingdom in 1990, but he made clear that the breaking point with the royal family and their clerical allies was the peace process with Israel. As one expert wrote later, "The letter makes it plain that Palestine, far from being a late addition to bin Laden's agenda, was at the center of it from the start."[31]

Under pressure from Washington and Riyadh, the Sudanese government encouraged bin Laden to leave in 1996, and he moved to Afghanistan where he reconnected with his mujahedin friends from the past. On August 23, 1996, he issued a statement calling for the expulsion of "the polytheists from the Arabian Peninsula," meaning the American base in Saudi Arabia. This public document justified attacks, such as the Riyadh and Dhahran bombings, because of Israel's occupation of Palestine and Jerusalem and America's presence in the Kingdom and the two holy cities. While mentioning the two attacks in Riyadh and Dhahran, bin Laden did not take credit for them. This was his declaration of his coming jihad.[32]

It was another two years, however, before words became action. On August 7, 1998, bin Laden's al Qaeda attacked simultaneously the U.S. embassies in Kenya and Tanzania. Two hundred and fifty-seven people were killed, most of them locals but twelve of them Americans, and hundreds more were injured, mostly Africans. A plot to blow up the American embassy in Tirana, Albania, was foiled at the same time.[33] The CIA quickly told Clinton that al Qaeda was responsible. According to Clinton's recollection, "The CIA also had intelligence that bin Laden and his top staff were planning a meeting at one of his camps in Afghanistan on August 20 to assess the impact of their attacks and plan their next operations." Berger was instructed to plan a missile strike to "wipe out the al Qaida leadership."[34]

On August 15 the president told his wife Hillary and his daughter Chelsea that he had lied about his relationship with Monica Lewinsky, and two days later he told the nation he had misled it. Then the first family went on vacation in Martha's Vineyard in Massachusetts. From there he issued the executive orders for the missile strike designed to kill bin Laden. Several al Qaeda operatives were killed as well as "some Pakistani officers," but as Clinton recalls bin Laden had either left the camp early or was never there.[35]

From August 1998 Clinton put fighting al Qaeda at the top of his agenda. Berger organized an interagency effort to hunt down and fight al Qaeda around the world. The Saudis were skeptical that bin Laden was as dangerous as the Americans argued, but they did provide some support in the campaign. Prince Turki went to Pakistan to try to use Pakistan's leverage with the Afghan Taliban, bin Laden's host in Afghanistan, to have him extradited to Saudi Arabia. Instead, the Pakistanis let Turki deal directly with Taliban leader Mullah Omar, who rejected any move against bin Laden. Turki and Omar ended their meeting in a shouting match, Turki later told me.

The Saudis may have also tried to assassinate bin Laden. After the Clinton cruise missile attack failed, bin Laden claimed that his security detail had foiled a plot ordered by the Saudi governor of Riyadh, Prince Salman (the future king), to kill him. As governor of Riyadh, Salman was responsible for "policing" aberrant behavior in the royal family and its close allies like the bin Ladens, so the story is plausible.[36]

But for the most part the Saudis remained convinced they had no serious al Qaeda problem at home. They were in denial about the growing support for bin Laden among the Saudi population. In October 2000 al Qaeda struck again, attacking a U.S. Navy destroyer at the port in Aden, Yemen. Even after the Aden attack, one on the Arabian Peninsula itself, the Saudis were still reluctant to see the enormity of the threat posed by bin Laden and his organization. Unfortunately, as we will see, so was the incoming Bush team.

During the Clinton years Washington and Riyadh cooperated on a wide range of issues, from peace diplomacy to counterterrorism. A good example of this close and intimate cooperation involved Libya. The Libyans were responsible for placing a bomb on Pan Am flight 103 on December 21, 1988, which exploded over Lockerbie, Scotland, killing all 243 passengers and sixteen crew. The United Nations imposed sanctions on Libya and demanded Tripoli turn over two Libyans suspected of involvement in the attack.

After years of stalemate the Libyans decided in 1999 to approach the United States to seek to resolve the Lockerbie incident. They asked the Saudis to set up a dialogue with Washington, and Prince Bandar approached the White House. Ambassador Martin Indyk and I then held a series of meetings with a Libyan team to discuss Libyan compliance with the UN resolutions. The dialogue was conducted at Prince Sultan's home in Geneva, Switzerland, and Bandar's home in England. In the end, the two Libyans were put on trial in The Hague, and one was convicted in 2001 of responsibility for placing the bomb on the aircraft.

It was a good example of cooperation between Washington and Riyadh to achieve a common interest, the resolution of an outstanding dispute in accordance with UN resolutions. One of those killed on Pan Am 103 was a colleague of mine from the Central Intelligence Agency. The secret diplomacy with Bandar helped bring a measure of justice and closure for his family.[37]

Not surprising, Clinton and Saudi kings Fahd and Abdallah did not always agree. The Saudis were much more determined to press their case against
some of Saddam's friends from the Kuwait crisis than were the Americans.
Jordan was one such case; Riyadh never really reconciled with King Hussein.
Yemen was the other, and the Saudi leadership looked for every opportunity
to undermine President Ali Abdallah Saleh for his support for Saddam in
1990.

In 1994 the Saudis got their chance. South Yemen, which had merged with
the north only in 1990, seceded from the union. The Saudis gave their support to the southerners against Saleh, including purchasing military equipment for them. Washington was not eager to join the fray, suspecting it would
become either a long-term quagmire or an outright Saleh victory. Saleh, indeed, did quickly win the 1994 civil war, leaving the Saudis without any
influence in their neighbor.

The 1990s were an era of strong relations between Riyadh and Washington, perhaps the strongest ever. The Madrid and Oslo peace processes eased
the recurring tensions over Israel. Iran was contained and, under Khatami,
seemed less dangerous. Saddam was defeated in Kuwait and far less dangerous
than before 1991. He was mostly a threat to his own people.

But by the end of Bill Clinton's eight years in office, some serious strains
were under the surface in the Saudi-American relationship. The failures of
Clinton's peace diplomacy in 2000 undermined the Saudis' confidence that
America was truly serious about promoting final, just, and fair settlements.
Saudi worries about Israel's political influence in Washington, always just
below the surface, came back into play. In Riyadh, it seemed the Tel Aviv tail
wagged the Washington dog. On his last day in office, Clinton gathered his
NSC staff for a group picture. He turned to me and said, "You were right about
Arafat." The next day Clinton called incoming Secretary of State Collin Powell
and told him never to trust Arafat.

The terrorism issue was also undermining the U.S.-Saudi relationship.
Both on Khobar and al Qaeda, the Saudis were convinced they knew better
than America what to do and how to respond to terrorism involving Saudis.
They were reluctant to trust America with sensitive information. Prince Nayef
was the most reluctant, and his stonewalling against cooperation would only
get worse after Clinton.

Bush

The Saudis, especially Bandar, expected that George W. Bush would come to the presidency with many of the same views of the Middle East as his father George H. W. Bush. In particular they expected him to continue his father's efforts at reaching a comprehensive Arab-Israeli peace agreement. Bush did share his father's appreciation for the importance of the American-Saudi partnership, but he had little or no interest in promoting a peace agreement between Israel and the Palestinians. In part this was because of Clinton's spectacular failures the year before. If Clinton could not get a deal, why would Bush want to try? But Bush and his team also did not believe the Palestinian issue was as crucial to regional stability as Clinton and Bush's father did. The previous presidents' experiences had taught them its centrality; Bush did not have that experience. Early in his tenure Bush hosted a small dinner for Israeli president Moshe Katsav and told one of the guests, "The Saudis thought this Texas oil guy was going to go against Israel, and I've told them you have the wrong guy."[38]

Bush's national security adviser, Condoleezza Rice, and her deputy, Stephen Hadley, asked me to stay on at my job in the White House for the first year of the Bush presidency. Rice and Hadley were smart and experienced security experts, but they had little experience in the Middle East. Both are unfailingly polite and thoughtful, and I was honored to be asked; I agreed to one last year at the National Security Council.

The Palestinian intifada that had followed the failure of peace talks at Camp David was the critical Middle East problem early in the Bush presidency. As Rice later wrote in her memoirs, "The low intensity war between Palestinians and Israelis dominated our security agenda" for the first nine months of Bush's opening year at the White House.[39] The intifada produced endless violence, including horrific suicide bombing attacks in Israeli cities by the extremist Islamic group Hamas and bloody Israeli retaliation operations in the West Bank and Gaza. The cycle of violence only got worse.

The Bush team was divided on how to handle the low-intensity war. Secretary of State Colin Powell and director of the CIA George Tenet (who had been at Camp David with Clinton) favored a balanced approach that sought to work with both sides, including Arafat, to reduce tensions. They also believed

Bush needed to articulate his own vision of a just peace to provide some incentive to end the violence. White House officials, including Vice President Richard Cheney, were more inclined to just back Israel and its new right-wing prime minister, Ariel Sharon. As Rice noted later, this division hampered decisionmaking, especially given the "ultra hawkish" staff in the vice president's office.[40]

But Bush and his entire team were united on one thing. They urgently wanted to establish a good relationship with Saudi Arabia, and to do that they wanted a meeting with Crown Prince Abdallah. Bush, Cheney, Powell, Defense Secretary Donald H. Rumsfeld, and Rice all wanted to get Abdallah to Washington for a meeting with the president.

The invitation was sent through Bandar. The answer was a firm and unequivocal no. The crown prince would not see the president until Bush took action on Palestine. He wanted Bush to take dramatic action to halt the violence between Israel and the Palestinians; he wanted Bush to see Arafat; and he wanted the Israeli occupation of the West Bank and Gaza to end. He was already framing in his mind a peace proposal that he would put forward in February 2002.

To mark the tenth anniversary of Kuwait's liberation in March 2001 Powell traveled to the region for his first engagement as secretary of state with Middle East rulers. In Saudi Arabia he invited the crown prince to Washington; Abdallah again refused and urged the secretary to do more to ease the crisis in the West Bank and East Jerusalem.

Powell tried again on June 29, 2001, in Paris where the crown prince was visiting the French leadership. As in March, I accompanied the secretary, representing the NSC. The meeting took place in the magnificent George V Hotel. A large conference room had been transformed with oriental carpets and lush Louis XIV furniture into a Saudi *diwan* with the chairs all forming a giant rectangle with the crown prince at one end and all his princes attending to hear what transpired.

After some opening pleasantries, the crown prince passed a book of photographs to the secretary. It featured dramatic pictures of Palestinian children and women killed in the intifada. The imagery was disturbing and awful. Of course, both Israelis and Palestinians were dying in the conflict, but Abdallah was focused only on the Palestinians. He told the secretary that they died at the hands of American weapons provided to Israel, that America had a moral obligation to stop the carnage, and that since Powell was a military man by profession he had a special, personal responsibility for acting to save children. Powell and Abdallah got emotional. The two exchanged comments candidly and hotly. It was clear, once again, that Abdallah was not coming to Washington.[41]

George H. W. Bush tried to use his own relationship with the crown prince on his son's behalf. The father had stayed in close contact with Abdallah after 1992 and had traveled to Riyadh in November 1998 and in January 2000.[42] After the 2000 election Bush senior went to England to see Prince Bandar at his home outside London, and the two met again in Washington the night before Bush's son was inaugurated.[43] Now he called the crown prince to assure him that the president was committed to finding peace in the region. The Saudi was duly respectful of the former president but made clear he was not budging.[44]

Prince Turki, the intelligence chief, came to Washington in July to see me and other officials. He wanted to know why Bush junior was not acting like Bush senior.[45] I met with him at his hotel suite in Tyson's Corner near Washington. It was clear to me that Turki and Bandar were in some trouble with the crown prince for not anticipating better how George W. Bush would perform in office.

The Kingdom's two preeminent American experts had given their boss predictions about Bush that had not come to pass. That fall, when Turki was removed from his position as chief of intelligence, it was perceived in the White House that his removal was a sign of Abdallah's anger at Washington.[46] Turki went on to be Abdallah's ambassador to the United Kingdom and later replaced Bandar in Washington.

The crown prince next dropped a bombshell on the White House. In August 2001 Abdallah cancelled with no notice a high-level military visit to Washington. The Saudi armed forces chief of staff, who had arrived early for the meetings, was called home abruptly.[47]

Then the crown prince sent a momentous letter to Bush. The letter crystallized the depth of Saudi anger at Washington. It "rocked the White House," as one senior National Security Council official described it later. Another characterized it as "a Saudi threat of some kind of fundamental reevaluation of the relationship unless America committed to doing something serious to stop the violence."[48]

Bandar showed the letter to Marwan Muasher, the well-plugged-in Jordanian ambassador in Washington. Muasher recalls that the letter "pointedly said it had become clear to Saudi Arabia that the U.S. administration was working against Arab interests, and in a clear reference to oil prices, he [Abdallah] wrote that Saudi Arabia would reciprocate by pursuing its own interests without consideration for American interests."[49]

Just six months into the Bush administration, the relationship was in acute crisis. This was the darkest moment in American-Saudi relations since 1973, with the first explicit threat of the oil weapon since the spring of 1974. The military relationship forged in 1990–91 was at risk, as well. The situation moved to the top of Bush's agenda.

Rice and Powell instructed William Burns, the assistant secretary of state for the Near East, and me to draft a response to the crown prince. Our instructions were to find a way to heal the breach with Abdallah and get the relationship back on track. Our draft letter was reviewed by all the top players in the Bush administration and signed by the president. The key commitment was the president's promise that the goal of American policy in the Israeli-Palestinian dispute would be the creation of an independent Palestinian state. While Clinton had implicitly been working for a two-state solution after Oslo, Bush's letter was the first overt and formal American commitment to a Palestinian state. Bush promised in the letter to announce publicly his commitment at the United Nations General Assembly meeting in New York in September.[50]

In the first days of September 2001 Bandar was invited to the White House to receive the response letter directly from the president. Bandar was optimistic it would be persuasive. He flew to Riyadh immediately. Upon his return to the United States, on September 7, 2001, Bush, Cheney, Rice, Hadley, Bandar, and I met on the Truman Balcony of the White House in the early evening. Bandar reported that the letter and the Bush commitments had resolved the crisis with the crown prince. Bush was relieved and pleased. The White House official photographer recorded the moment.[51]

On Saturday, September 8, 2001, Bandar attended a wedding celebration party for my wife and me in Old Town Alexandria. He was beaming. He said, "I'm the happiest man in town." He and Director Tenet went out to a late dinner after the party, where Bandar told the director the royal family had never been angrier with Washington than that summer.[52]

The next day, Sunday, September 9, Ahmed Shah Massoud, the Tajik leader of the opposition to the Taliban and al Qaeda in Afghanistan, was assassinated at his base in northern Afghanistan. The two assassins, who had posed as journalists, were members of al Qaeda, and the assassination of the Taliban's top enemy was the essential precursor to the attack on America that soon followed. On Monday Ambassador Muasher delivered a letter from Jordan's King Abdallah II—who had succeeded his father in February 1999—calling on Bush to stop the violence and convene a final peace agreement conference.[53]

The next morning, Tuesday, September 11, I was in the White House Situation Room with Rice when the second hijacked aircraft smashed into the World Trade Center. The events of 9/11 seemed to change everything for the Bush White House, America, and the world. It was the bloodiest day in American history since the Civil War, and we are still grappling with the impact of the 9/11 attacks more than fifteen years later.

Richard Clarke, the administration's top terrorism adviser, who had held the same job for Clinton, would later testify to the 9/11 Commission that he believed Bush, Cheney, and Rice paid insufficient attention to the warnings of an impending al Qaeda attack in the spring and summer of 2001. George Tenet, the director of central intelligence, consistently warned that an attack was imminent and that it would be far more devastating than the African or Aden attacks. (Despite the fact that I was the special assistant to the president for Near East Affairs with responsibility for Saudi issues in particular, I was never asked to testify to the commission or any official investigation of the attack—probably because I would have seconded Clarke's point.)

Bandar and I spoke often on the phone on September 11, 2001. He rapidly communicated the Kingdom's horror at the attack and sympathies for the victims. Once it became clear that Osama bin Laden and al Qaeda were behind the attacks, Tenet arranged for Bandar to get a complete briefing on the plot. Crown Prince Abdallah supported Bush's decision to invade Afghanistan and topple the Taliban government. The Saudis had long ago soured on the Taliban, especially after its leader Mullah Omar refused to hand bin Laden over to Prince Turki in 1998.

*Foreign Minister Prince Saud bin Faisal meeting with President George W. Bush,
September 2001. Also attending are Prince Bandar, and on the right,
Secretary of State Colin Powell and the author. (Author's collection)*

Bandar had to devote much of his attention after 9/11 to the mounting
anger in the United States at Saudi Arabia. The media put much of the blame
for the rise of al Qaeda on the Saudis and their Wahhabi faith. Even Bandar
and his wife Haifa were accused of helping the hijackers.

The annual opening of the UN General Assembly was postponed until
November due to the disruption in New York City. On November 10, 2001,
Bush addressed the General Assembly and said the Taliban and al Qaeda "are
now virtually indistinguishable." He promised their swift defeat.

Bush also said, "The American government also stands by its commitment
to a just peace in the Middle East. We are working toward the day when two
states—Israel and Palestine—live peacefully together with secure and recognized borders as called for by the Security Council resolutions." Bush had
lived up to his commitment to Abdallah from September.[54]

Despite Bush's unprecedented public American commitment to support a
Palestinian state, the violence in the region got worse. Dozens of Israelis died
in horrific suicide bombings in Tel Aviv, Jerusalem, and other cities. Prime

Minister Sharon responded by sending Israeli forces back into cities that had been turned over to Palestinian hands as a result of the Oslo process. Arafat's headquarters in Ramallah on the West Bank was surrounded by the Israeli army and put under siege.

In an interview with *New York Times* columnist Tom Friedman, in February 2002, Crown Prince Abdallah revealed his own plan for a permanent peace agreement. An Arab summit in Beirut in March endorsed Abdallah's call for full Israeli withdrawal from the occupied territories, to be matched by full normalization of relations between Israel and all the Arab states. Abdallah called it "full withdrawal for full normalization."[55] Prime Minister Sharon promptly rejected the historic Saudi initiative.

Armed with Bush's General Assembly commitment and his own Arab summit-blessed peace plan, Crown Prince Abdallah made his long-awaited visit to see Bush in April. They met at Bush's home in Crawford, Texas, on April 25, 2002. The tête à-tête was almost a disaster. After listening to Bush explain why he could not stop Sharon's siege of Arafat in his office in Ramallah and argue that Saddam Hussein was the biggest threat to regional peace, Abdallah gathered his advisers to leave. They told the president's Arabic translator, Gamal Helal, that the crown prince had decided to leave the summit, break off the conversation with Bush, and hold a press conference on his way home. The crown prince would say his mission to end the siege and promote his peace plan had failed due to Bush's intransigence. As Bush wrote later, "America's pivotal relationship with Saudi Arabia was about to be seriously ruptured."[56] Rice later wrote that the Saudi walkout would have been a "disaster."[57]

In their accounts of what came next, Bush and Rice both emphasize the president's decision to take the crown prince on a ride around his farm. Bush tried to calm tensions by talking about farming, but he "wasn't making much headway" when a turkey was spotted by the side of the road. Then Abdallah grabbed Bush's hand and said it was an omen: "a sign from Allah." Tensions melted. Later Bush wrote, "I had never seen a hen turkey on that part of the property before, and I haven't seen one since."[58]

Although amusing, the turkey story is obviously misleading. Translator Helal, who was the only other person on the ride, says Bush made a clear and firm commitment to Abdallah to get the siege of Arafat's headquarters in

Ramallah lifted immediately.[59] As one of Bush's aides wrote later, "Within days, on April 28, the Israeli cabinet decided to move the tanks back and free Arafat; Abdallah presumably saw an American hand at work in that decision."[60] But the relief proved temporary, and the war between Israel and the Palestinians escalated throughout the remainder of the year.

In June 2002 Bush dramatically changed the dynamics of Palestinian relations with America when he gave a speech in the Rose Garden calling on "the Palestinian people to elect new leaders, leaders not compromised by terror." He said, "I call upon them to build a practicing democracy, based on tolerance and liberty." Rice played a key role in the formulation of the new American policy of calling for Arafat's removal and replacement by a functioning democracy in an Arab country.[61]

For the Saudis it was a difficult solution to the impasse. They had no particular affection for Arafat, who they had always distrusted. But they were no fans of democracy, either. Particularly disturbing for the Saudis was the idea that democracy could be more or less imposed on an Arab state by the United States. If Washington could dump one Arab autocrat for a democratic alternative, where would it end? If democracy is the only path to stability and peace in the Middle East, where does that leave a theocratic absolute monarchy? These questions were not muttered in public, but they certainly were pondered in the palaces of Saudi Arabia and other countries.

The near disaster at Crawford illustrated how damaged the American-Saudi relationship had become by mid-2002. The Palestinian issue was the main driver in the steady deterioration. The Saudis never trusted Bush's handling of the Israeli-Palestinian conflict after 2002 and distanced themselves from American diplomacy toward the conflict. Abdallah continued to push his peace plan.

Iraq

One issue that got little Saudi attention at Crawford was Iraq. In fact, the Bush administration had already decided to make Iraq the centerpiece of its Middle East policy. Bush told Abdallah that he was determined to do more about Saddam Hussein, but he and his team were not ready to discuss their plans in any detail.

The Kurds were the first leaders in the Middle East to learn of the president's decision to remove Saddam Hussein from power as the next step in his global war on terror. In 1991 after Desert Storm, President Bush senior had created a no-fly zone in northern Iraq to protect the Iraqi Kurdish minority from Saddam's repression; this mirrored the similar zone protecting Shias in southern Iraq. In the wake of the Iran-Iraq war in 1988, Saddam had murdered thousands of Kurds, some by using poison gas. After Desert Storm the Kurds rose up in rebellion and were again attacked by Saddam's weakened but still deadly forces. Bush created Operation Provide Comfort to defend the Kurds.

By 2002 Provide Comfort had helped create an all-but-independent Kurdish state in northern Iraq ruled by two competing Kurdish parties: Masoud Barzani's Kurdish Democratic Party and Jalal Talabani's Patriotic Union of Kurdistan. Both had long ties to the CIA, but bitter experience led them to doubt American promises of help. Nixon had abandoned a Kurdish rebellion backed by the CIA in 1974; Reagan had stood by passively when Saddam gassed the Kurds in 1988; and Bush senior had been slow to stop Saddam in 1991.

But if Washington wanted good intelligence on what was going on in Iraq in 2002, it badly needed the Kurds. Only in the north could American intelligence operate on Iraqi territory. So Bush authorized Tenet to tell the Kurdish leaders that he was seriously determined to oust Saddam. In March 2002 Tenet met with both Barzani and Talabani secretly in Washington to enlist their aid in the coming campaign to overthrow Saddam by military invasion. It marked the first decisive step toward war.[62]

Talabani returned to northern Iraq via London. By March 2002 I was a member of the Royal College of Defense Studies in London. I had known Talabani for over a decade, since I had first brought him to the White House in 1992 to meet with Brent Scowcroft. I had visited him in his home in Sulaymaniyah in 1994. Over lunch at a restaurant close to Harrods in London, Talabani told me Tenet had promised that if Bush made a final decision to go to war with Iraq the goal would be to remove Saddam from power. Talabani was ecstatic, thrilled to be planning his oppressor's end.

The White House held off briefing the Saudis, suspecting they would be less thrilled with the news. The Saudis did not get their formal briefing on Bush's plans until long after the de facto decision to invade Iraq had been made. They did notice the drumbeat of war much earlier, of course, for example on August 26, 2002, when Vice President Cheney gave a high-profile speech in Nashville, Tennessee, signaling U.S. intentions about Iraq. He said, "Simply stated, there is no doubt that Saddam Hussein now has weapons of mass destruction." It was the opening public salvo in what would be a rush to war.[63]

Prince Turki had taken up his new job as ambassador to the United Kingdom, and he asked me to dinner after the Cheney speech. He expressed grave concerns about a war to topple Saddam. What would replace Saddam? Would elections be held to create a new Iraq? That would lead inevitably to a Shia-dominated state, given that the Shia are the majority of the population in Iraq. And that would give Iraq to Iran, Turki warned, upsetting the balance of power in the Middle East in general and the Gulf in particular.

Turki said much the same in public. In a visit to Washington he told the *Washington Post* that the idea that the United States could solve its problems in the region through the use of military might in Iraq was wrongheaded and downright dangerous. "A military invasion with U.S. soldiers is not going to be welcome, not by the Iraqi people, not by other people in the region. We Saudis will have to live with the consequences."[64]

The official Saudi request for Bush to explain his Iraq policy came on November 15, 2002, when Bandar called on the president in the White House. Bandar had been out of town most of the weeks since the Crawford meeting. Officially, he was ill. It was an old Bandar tactic. When the Saudis were upset with the White House, Bandar played hard to get, literally. He did not want to be the messenger of bad news for the crown prince nor convey more bad news to Bush from Riyadh. So he simply stayed out of town for months. But by November he needed to ask Bush directly what his plans were.

Bush was still not ready to tell the Saudis. So Bandar, instead, gave Bush Riyadh's view. Any move to topple Saddam had to be linked to meaningful progress on the Israeli-Palestinian issue. That was the bargain Fahd and Bush senior had made in 1990–91, and the same bargain was essential in 2002.[65]

Bandar finally got his briefing on Bush's war plans on January 11, 2003. In a deliberate repetition of August 3, 1990, Cheney invited Bandar to his office (now in the White House, not the Pentagon as in 1990), where the vice president, Secretary of Defense Rumsfeld, and Chairman of the Joint Chiefs of

Staff General Richard Myers briefed Bandar on the war plan to oust Saddam. It was detailed and specific, with a clear goal of marching all the way to Baghdad. Bandar asked if Bush was really serious about going all the way. Cheney told him Saddam would be "toast" when the war was over. Two days later Bush met with Bandar directly and told him the same bottom line. He asked for Saudi support.[66]

Bandar flew immediately to Riyadh to convey the briefing from Bush to the crown prince. Abdallah told him to keep the message absolutely secret until he decided how to respond.[67] Abdallah and the senior princes were not eager for war. They wanted Saddam removed, certainly, but they were deeply concerned about the day after. The problems Turki had laid out with me and in his interview with the *Washington Post* were on their minds. What would replace Saddam? If elections were held, it would inevitably mean a Shia-dominated Iraq, anathema to the Saudis. On the other hand, the Saudis did not want to break publicly with Washington on such a major issue. The relationship with Washington was already on the ropes over Palestine; another public blow-up on Iraq would not help. The Saudis stayed on the sidelines as the war drums beat in Washington and London.

On March 15, 2003, Bandar called on Bush again in the White House. He had a message from the crown prince. The Saudis were still eager to avoid a war, Bandar said, but if it had to happen, do it quickly. Bandar deliberately stressed the urgency part of the message, not the appeal to avoid war. The president's team noted that the ambassador was "tired, nervous and excited . . . sweating profusely" and overweight. The strain of the job was showing clearly, and Bandar was not handling the pressure well.[68]

The Saudis agreed to provide very quiet assistance to the American war effort. The Prince Sultan air base was used to support the war, and American Special Forces operated from Saudi bases along the Iraq frontier. But the bulk of the American and British invasion force came out of Kuwait. As soon as the war ended, the American forces left the air base, which reverted to exclusive Saudi use in late April 2003. American military forces were no longer present in the Kingdom for the first time since August 1990.[69]

Bandar played a complicated game during the build-up and launch of the war. Of course, he knew the Kingdom was a reluctant partner in the conflict and that Abdallah shared the doubts expressed by Turki about the wisdom of

Bush's adventure in Iraq. He also knew Abdallah was much more concerned with the Palestinian issue. But he recognized the central importance of the war for Bush and his presidency. In public he was much more supportive of the war and its goal of eliminating Saddam than any other Saudi official. When the war succeeded in removing Saddam, Bandar openly praised the removal of "a great evil from the world" and lauded Bush for his leadership.[70] When the occupation of Iraq quickly spawned an insurgency against the American and British forces and developed into a political disaster for Bush, Bandar found himself increasingly in the doghouse in Riyadh. He was losing the confidence of the crown prince.

Terror at Home

The American focus on Iraq in the spring and summer of 2002 was also noted by Osama bin Laden and al Qaeda. The American intervention in Afghanistan had toppled the Taliban Islamic Emirate, but bin Laden and most of his top lieutenants got away, fleeing into Pakistan.[71]

Before September 11, bin Laden had been careful not to carry out violent operations in his own country. Although he endorsed the attacks on American military troops in Riyadh in 1995 and in Khobar in 1996, he made clear that he had no direct involvement in either operation, and no evidence suggests he did. Perhaps he did not want to open a campaign at home prematurely, before his cadres were strong enough—or perhaps he was just eager to keep a low profile inside the Kingdom so he could continue to raise money and find recruits there. The U.S. invasion of Afghanistan led to a change in bin Laden's posture. The unexpected swiftness of the invasion and its rapid toppling of the Taliban regime were partly responsible. In 2002, after the fall of Kabul, several hundred Saudi members of al Qaeda returned to the Kingdom and worked with sleeper cells that had been operating covertly there for several years at bin Laden's direction.

In February 2003, on the eve of the Iraq war, bin Laden issued an audio message directed at Iraqis. He said he was "following with intense interest and concern the Crusaders' preparations for war to occupy one of Islam's former capitals, loot Muslims' riches and install a stooge government to follow its masters in Washington and Tel Aviv to pave the way for the establishment of a Greater Israel." He called on all Muslims to be prepared to fight the American invasion and work together to sabotage it. Bin Laden had already dispatched a key aide, Abu Musaib al Zarqawi, to organize the resistance to the American invasion and occupation.[72]

But al Qaeda had even bigger ambitions than to turn Iraq into a quagmire for America. Bin Laden's goal was to overthrow the House of Saud itself. Bin Laden previewed the insurrection in the Kingdom in a major address to the Muslim world on February 14, 2003, coinciding with the eve of the U.S.-led invasion of Iraq. Delivered on the holy day of Eid al Adha, bin Laden's statement was the first and only in which he framed his argument in the form of a sermon. He wanted to give this message special importance. The address came just a few days after his "Letter to the Iraqi People," in which he urged Iraqis to get ready to fight the invaders. Bin Laden was evidently preparing for an epic battle on two fronts simultaneously.

Bin Laden accused the House of Saud of betraying the Ottoman Empire to the British in the First World War and opening the door to Western (Crusader) and Jewish (Zionist) domination of the Muslim world (the *ummah*). Moreover, he argued that the goal of the Crusaders was to divide the Saudi Kingdom into smaller states to make it easier to control and accused the Saudi family of complicity in this endeavor. The goal of the Crusader invasion of Iraq and of the Crusader military forces in the Arabian Peninsula, bin Laden said, is to consolidate Greater Israel, which will incorporate "large parts of Iraq and Egypt within its borders, as well as Syria, Lebanon, Jordan, the whole of Palestine and a large part of Saudi Arabia."[73]

Bin Laden then called for the overthrow of all the monarchies of the Arabian Peninsula (in Kuwait, Bahrain, Qatar, Saudi Arabia, and the others), which he said were nothing but traitors or "quislings," a reference to the Norwegian Nazi who betrayed his country to Adolf Hitler. The Saudis must be overthrown for many reasons, he claimed, but above all because they have betrayed the Palestinian cause to "Jews and Americans." Bin Laden railed against Crown Prince Abdallah for his proposal at the Beirut Arab summit in March 2002 suggesting a permanent peace agreement with Israel by all the Arabs if Israel withdrew to the 1967 lines, an act he said "betrayed the *ummah*."

Bin Laden admitted that overthrowing the monarchies would not be an easy task, given America's support for the Saudis, but he reminded his listeners that no one anticipated the fall of the Soviet Union in Afghanistan. America has been defeated before, he said, in Lebanon in 1982 and in Somalia in 1993. Most important, he recalled 9/11, which he pronounced a "brave and beautiful operation, the likes of which humanity has never seen before destroying the idols of America" and striking "the very heart of the Ministry of Defense and the American economy." That operation "in Manhattan was a result of the unjust policies of the American government on the Palestinian issue," he said. He concluded that "America is a super power . . . built on a foundation of straw."

Just prior to this public declaration of war on the House of Saud, bin Laden met secretly in Pakistan with the head of al Qaeda's infrastructure inside the Kingdom. Yusuf al Ayiri, known by his nicknamed "al battar" or "the Sabre," was reluctant to start an insurrection in the Kingdom because he feared the al Qaeda organization was not strong enough. Bin Laden insisted and the Sabre return to the Kingdom to start the war.[74]

The first major attack came on May 12, 2003, when al Qaeda terrorists simultaneously attacked three compounds in Riyadh where foreign workers were housed. One was used by employees of the Vinnell Corporation, which trains the National Guard. Twenty-seven people died in the attacks, nine of them Americans, and more than 160 were wounded. It was the worst act of terrorism in the capital's history.[75]

Central Intelligence Agency director George Tenet immediately traveled to Riyadh to see Crown Prince Abdallah. Tenet told the crown prince that the CIA believed "your family and the end of its rule is now the objective" of bin Laden. "Al Qaeda operatives are prepared to assassinate members of the royal family and to attack key economic targets," Tenet told Abdallah. The United States would provide all the assistance it could to help defeat al Qaeda in the Kingdom.[76]

Shaken by the bombings and Tenet's assessment of al Qaeda, Abdallah decided to give operational command of the counterterrorism battle to Muhammad bin Nayef, the son of Interior Minister Prince Nayef. Educated in the United States at Lewis and Clark College in Oregon, Prince Muhammad had extensive experience with the FBI and Scotland Yard. His father distrusted the

Americans and British and had badly underestimated al Qaeda (he had famously blamed the Mossad for the 9/11 attacks rather than al Qaeda). The crown prince decided he was not the right man for defending the Kingdom.[77] Prince Nayef kept the title of minister of the interior, but his son was now in charge.[78] Tenet later credited him with winning the war that lay ahead inside the Kingdom.[79]

For the next three years the Interior ministry, with help from the National Guard, engaged in a bloody and dangerous war with al Qaeda inside the Kingdom. It was by far the most serious internal challenge to the House of Saud since the founding of the modern Kingdom by Ibn Saud. Dozens of firefights occurred in every major Saudi city as the Interior ministry tracked down members of the terrorist underground. The Sabre was killed in a confrontation with the police on May 30, 2003, and was replaced by another bin Laden appointee.

Muhammad bin Nayef provided extensive assistance to two journalists who wrote an authoritative account of the war in 2014. Using materials captured by the Interior ministry in raids on al Qaeda safe houses and the interrogations of captured terrorists, their book, *The Path of Blood*, is the prince's insider look at the war.

In November 2003 an attack on another residential compound killed seventeen and wounded more than one hundred. The next month a Saudi major general was injured in an attack. On December 17, 2003, the American Embassy in Riyadh ordered nonessential staff to leave the country. The United States evacuated most of its diplomats from the Kingdom in April 2004 and urged Americans not to travel to Saudi Arabia due to "credible and specific intelligence" of imminent attacks.[80]

One of the worst series of attacks occurred in Khobar, the Saudi town where the Saudi Hezbollah had attacked the United States Air Force barracks in 1996. On May 29 and 30, 2004, an al Qaeda team calling themselves the Jerusalem Squadron killed twenty-five people in multiple attacks on Western targets. In June an American engineer was kidnapped and then beheaded by another al Qaeda team in Riyadh. Prince Muhammad's position was elevated to the level of minister to give him more authority to command the counterterrorist forces.[81]

The American consulate in Jidda was attacked on December 6, 2004. One American female diplomat, Monica Lemieux, narrowly escaped death in the attack, but four Saudi security personnel and five local employees of the embassy died. The attackers were killed or captured by Saudi security forces.[82] At the end of the year the Ministry of the Interior headquarters in Riyadh— an iconic building shaped like an inverted pyramid—was attacked by multiple car bombs.

Gradually the Interior ministry got the upper hand. The violence of the al Qaeda attacks dried up popular support for the terrorists among most Saudis. While many were sympathetic with the jihadists when they attacked abroad, attacking Saudi targets inside the Kingdom killed many innocents. The insurgency in neighboring Iraq also siphoned off many potential recruits for al Qaeda inside the Kingdom. Hundreds of young Saudis went to Iraq to fight the American and British occupation, which was unpopular in both Iraq and Saudi Arabia.[83] U.S. officials estimated that at least 45 percent of the foreigners in Iraq fighting the occupation were Saudi citizens.[84] Saudi sources said that 5,000 Saudis had joined the insurgency by October 2003, most of them joining Zarqawi's al Qaeda in Iraq.[85]

Most important, Prince Muhammad bin Nayef led a ferocious and ruthless campaign against the al Qaeda infrastructure. Lists of the most prominent terrorists were circulated among the population, and then those on the lists were systematically hunted down until killed or captured. The Sabre had been right: the Interior ministry was too strong for al Qaeda. In December 2004 bin Laden issued another appeal to Saudis to overthrow the monarchy, but by then the tide of battle was favoring Prince Nayef. This 2004 statement criticized Fahd for ruling the country despite a debilitating stroke, arguing that "the idea that the entire length and breadth of the land is ruled in the name of a king who for a decade has no longer known what is going on is incredible." He attacked the royal family for corruption and self-indulgence, noting the King's palace in Jidda occupies more land than the entire emirate of Bahrain. Prince Bandar was singled out for bin Laden's criticism for planning the invasion of Iraq with Bush and Cheney.[86]

The Saudi clerical establishment joined the royal family in the battle. The minister of Islamic affairs, Shaykh Salih Bin Abd al Aziz al Shaykh—a descendant of Muhammad Ibn 'Abd al Wahhab—organized the clerical establishment to condemn and castigate the terrorists as enemies of Islam and of the state. Working with the Interior ministry, the clerics set up rehabilitation centers to reeducate captured terrorists and persuade them to provide intelligence on the al Qaeda leadership.

In contrast, the clerics openly favored the insurgency in Iraq as a holy war against foreign and infidel occupation. A group of three dozen clerics issued a statement publicly in December 2006 supporting the struggle against the Crusader-Safavid occupation, alleging America and Iran were secretly colluding against Iraqi Sunni Arabs. The statement said, "It is clear that their goal is to take over Iraq as a partnership between the Crusaders and the Safavid, realizing their ambitions in the region which are protecting the Jewish occupiers in Palestine, removing Sunni influence, encircling the Sunni in the whole region and creating a Shia crescent" across Iraq and Syria.[87]

The official Saudi clerical position was announced by Minister Shaykh al Shaykh in October 2007. He said only the Saudi king had the right to send Saudis abroad to fight in jihad. Thus, al Qaeda was wrong to urge young Saudis to fight in Iraq without royal blessing. In practice, however, the minister's proclamation had little effect. In a more practical move, Nayef built a double-tracked barbed wire electric fence along the Saudi border with Iraq to discourage traffic across the frontier.

The last major al Qaeda attack in Saudi Arabia occurred on February 24, 2006, when terrorists struck the Abqaiq oil refinery in the Eastern Province, the country's single most important economic target. The operation was a failure, and within days the Saudi authorities killed all involved in the planning and execution of the attack. Gun fights between al Qaeda members and Interior ministry forces would continue for several more months, but the Abqaiq attack in retrospect was the final major operation of bin Laden's war on the House of Saud.[88]

The war with al Qaeda inside the Kingdom preoccupied the country's leadership for almost four years. King Fahd passed away on August 1, 2005, and Abdallah succeeded him. Bandar departed Washington a month later, ending his two decades as the king's man in America. Prince Turki took his place as the ambassador. It was a job he did not relish taking.

After his 2004 reelection, Bush had a second meeting with Abdallah in Crawford in April 2005, but it was little more than a photo opportunity. Bush had announced two years earlier that America was determined to build democracy in Iraq and that the American agenda in the Middle East would now feature the support of democratic reforms. Bush emphasized this campaign to bring democracy and freedom to the region in his January 2004 State of the Union address.

The Saudis were appalled. In August 2004 Egyptian president Hosni Mubarak, another autocrat, visited the Kingdom. Abdallah and Mubarak called for an end to the U.S. occupation of Iraq. America's two most important allies in the Arab world were, thus, publicly on record opposing the continued American presence in Iraq. Increasingly the Saudis criticized the Iraq war for empowering their rival Iran. Foreign Minister Prince Saud al Faisal visited Washington in September 2005 and warned the White House that Iraq was disintegrating into civil war and that Iran was the major beneficiary. Prince Saud told the press, "Iraq is finished forever. It will be dismembered which will bring so many conflicts in the region that it will bring the whole region into turmoil." Worse, Saud said, the Bush decision to invade Iraq "handed the whole country over to Iran without reason." Later he added a more colorful line: Bush had given Iraq to Iran on a "golden platter."[89]

In practice, the Bush rhetoric about promoting democracy was never turned into a serious policy initiative toward the region as a whole. The only practical manifestations were in Palestine and Iraq, where the calls for democracy were manifestations of broader policy goals. Riyadh was critical of both. Instead of supporting political reform in the Palestinian Authority after Arafat's death in 2004, the Saudis encouraged the two main Palestinian parties, Fatah and Hamas, to work together. King Abdallah summoned both to Mecca in February 2007 and pressed them to unite against the Israeli occupation. The unity deal they agreed to in Mecca did not last long, but it was a sign of further stress in the partnership with Washington.

At the Arab summit in March 2007, the Saudi king urged adoption of a joint statement labeling the American presence in Iraq "an illegal foreign occupation." Prince Turki said the promotion of democracy in Iraq by the United States was a disaster. Turki said: "Democracy turned to a hateful sectarianism, justice turned to oppression, the rule of law ended up being the rule of the militias and human rights became death warrants." The White House was furious with Turki, and Abdallah declined another invitation to visit the United States.[90]

By the end of the Bush administration, the American relationship with Saudi Arabia had soured immensely. Only in the counterterrorism business was the relationship healthy. Prince Muhammad bin Nayef and the king carefully kept that essential business undamaged by the disagreements on other issues. As a sign of the tension, Prince Turki left as ambassador after only eighteen months on the job. He had found the job even more difficult than he anticipated. Bandar had tried to keep the American portfolio in his own hands even after leaving Washington in 2005 and had a habit of coming to town without telling Turki. Bandar had little credibility with the Bush team, however, after his failed last years as ambassador. The Bush team disliked Turki for his frank and honest comments about Bush's policies. What had seemed, eight years earlier, to begin as a return to the good old days of George H. W. Bush had turned into a failed partnership. Bush's successor would have to try to get things back on track.

Chapter Six

OBAMA AND TRUMP,
ABDALLAH AND SALMAN,
2009 TO 2017

Prince Saud al Faisal inherited the dignity and grace of his father, King Faisal. A graduate of Princeton and fluent in seven languages, Prince Saud served as the Kingdom's foreign minister for forty years. He represented his country at countless international meetings, always impressing his counterparts with his eloquence and command of his brief. I knew him for more than three decades. Once he entertained a delegation headed by Madeleine Albright, America's first female secretary of state, at his home in Riyadh, where we had the pleasure of meeting his wife and daughters.

In August 2008, during a visit to Washington, Prince Saud asked the Obama presidential campaign for an informal meeting with a campaign foreign policy expert to discuss the state of Saudi-U.S. relations. I had joined the campaign in the spring of 2007 at the request of Anthony Lake, my former boss at the National Security Council in 1993 and the head of Obama's foreign policy advisory team. The campaign sent me to have lunch with the prince at his suite at the Hay-Adams Hotel near Lafayette Square and the White House.

Prince Saud characterized the relationship, after almost eight years of George W. Bush, as a "train wreck." He repeated his public line that the war in Iraq had given Baghdad to the Iranians on a "golden platter." The war in Lebanon in 2006 between Israel and the Iranian-backed Hezbollah had strengthened Iran's grip on Beirut, and the Arab-Israeli peace process was in shambles. A peace conference Bush had called in Annapolis, Maryland, in 2007 had not led to any breakthroughs. The so called "Freedom Agenda" Bush had announced was rejected by America's allies in the region, including the House of Saud. The dialogue between Riyadh and Washington was poisonous, Prince Saud said, and King Abdallah was very disappointed. Only on counterterrorism issues was there a productive conversation. He credited Prince Muhammad bin Nayef, the minister of interior, and Prince Muqrin, the chief of intelligence, with that success story.

The foreign minister hoped the next president, whether it was Senator Barack Obama or Senator John McCain, would work to put the relationship back on a stable and productive path. It was too important to both countries not to do so. He also urged Washington to look closely at King Abdallah's interfaith dialogue project, where the Saudi monarch was hosting discussions between religious leaders from all the world's faiths.

Abdallah

Barack Obama inherited a country in deep trouble. The financial markets had melted down in the fall of 2008, causing the worst recession in American history since the 1930s. Unemployment was soaring, and millions of people had lost their homes or much of their life savings; sometimes both. America was engaged in two major ground wars overseas. The war in Iraq had stabilized somewhat because of a large surge in American forces in 2007, but the insurgency had not been defeated and al Qaeda in Iraq remained a deadly foe. In Afghanistan the Taliban were resurgent, and next-door in Pakistan al Qaeda was thriving. The search for Osama bin Laden had gone cold.

Obama was determined to reset America's relationship with the Muslim world. With two large American armies occupying two large Islamic countries, it was imperative to reach out to the Islamic world and restore some measure of confidence in American leadership. Obama planned to make a major address to the Islamic world from Cairo, Egypt, in June 2009.

Before arriving in Cairo, Obama stopped first in Riyadh to meet King Abdallah; it was his first-ever visit to the Kingdom. The stop was a clear sign of the importance Obama placed on getting ties with the Kingdom back on track. Obama is the son of a Kenyan Muslim, and he spent part of his childhood in Indonesia, the world's most populous Muslim country. He billed his stop in Riyadh as a chance to come to where Islam started.

But Obama's meeting with the king went poorly. Obama had promised to shut down the notorious prison in Guantanamo Bay, Cuba, housing terrorism suspects, on the first day of his presidency. His homeland security adviser, John Brennan, had worked with the Saudi security services to persuade the Kingdom to take dozens of the Guantanamo prisoners from Yemen to Saudi Arabia to help empty the Cuban jail. Apparently the staff work on the Saudi side was incomplete; the king knew nothing about the deal and was surprised when Obama brought it up as an agreement. It was not agreed at all, the king said.[1]

Obama's main goal in Riyadh was to try to jump-start the stalled Israeli-Palestinian peace process, which had been stalemated since Bush's failed Annapolis summit. Obama was pressing Israeli prime minister Benjamin "Bibi" Netanyahu to halt all settlement activity in the occupied territories, including East Jerusalem, to set the stage for a resumed peace process with the Palestinians. Netanyahu vigorously opposed a freeze but had suggested that if Obama could deliver a major gesture from the Arab states—in particular a public meeting between Bibi and King Abdallah—he could accept a temporary freeze. When Obama made the case to the king, Abdallah turned him down. Abdallah said the Kingdom "will be the last to make peace with the Israelis" after all the other Arabs have been satisfied in their requirements.[2] It was unimaginable for a Saudi king to meet publicly with an Israeli prime minister until after a Palestinian state was created and full Israeli withdrawal was implemented. The royal family, the clerical establishment, and the general population would never have approved such a meeting. It was puzzling that Obama and his aides thought it was even possible.[3]

One reason the idea might have seemed plausible to them was the growing animosity in both Israel and Saudi Arabia toward Iran. Both Israelis and Saudis seemed more worried than ever about Iran's growing influence in the region, a byproduct of the Iraq war, and some observers suggested the Saudis might be willing to take a more flexible line on Israel to build a regional consensus against Iran, an argument strongly pressed by right-wing forces in Israel. It was in 2009, and remains today, a fantasy. The Saudis have long been willing to have discreet contacts with Israel, often via third parties, to contain regional threats. They did so in the 1960s against the meddling in Yemen by Egypt's Nasser. But they are not willing to compromise their policy toward the Israeli-Palestinian question or to meet publicly and officially with Israeli leaders. The notion of an Israel-Sunni Arab entente against Shia Iran, with the Kingdom at its center, is a mirage. The Saudis are not interested in an alliance with Israel.

The president's speech in Cairo was a public relations success that took attention away from the Riyadh disappointments. Obama acknowledged the "great tension between the United States and Muslims around the world" and called for "a new beginning based on mutual interest and mutual respect." He promised to close the Guantanamo prison, end torture of captured suspected al Qaeda prisoners, bring home all American troops from Iraq, and seek a two-state solution to the Palestinian question. He deliberately criticized Bush's push for democracy in the Arab world as discredited by its "connection to the war in Iraq," and promised America would not impose any system of government on other states. He did call for the promotion of human rights and greater tolerance in Islam, and he praised King Abdallah's "interfaith dialogue."[4]

Obama flew home from Cairo without stopping in Israel, a striking change from his predecessors, Democrats and Republicans. No president before Obama would have thought to make a formal state visit to Saudi Arabia or Egypt without a matching visit to Jerusalem.

Just as Obama arrived in the Middle East, Osama bin Laden and his Egyptian deputy, Ayman Zawahiri, each released messages from their hideouts in Pakistan. Eight years after 9/11, both were still alive and plotting more attacks. Both statements called on Muslims to shun Obama and predicted his policies would just be more of the same as his predecessor.[5] It was a stark reminder that Bush had not defeated al Qaeda and a preview of how Obama's administration would be grappling with al Qaeda and its offshoots for the next eight years.

Another dramatic illustration of al Qaeda's continued danger came in the summer of 2009. A Saudi al Qaeda operative named Abdallah al Asiri offered to defect to the Saudis and provide inside information on the al Qaeda organization in Yemen. Al Qaeda had reinvented its Saudi operation in the Arabian Peninsula in early 2009, after its defeat inside Saudi Arabia, by merging its Saudi and Yemeni wings together to create al Qaeda in the Arabian Peninsula. Asiri promised to give secret information on the merged network and induce further defections if he got a meeting with Prince Muhammad bin Nayef, the interior minister.

Prince Nayef agreed, despite having been the target of at least two previous al Qaeda assassination attempts. This turned out to be a third. Asiri's brother was a brilliant bomb maker and had hidden a bomb in al Asiri's rectum. Fortunately, when the bomb exploded, only the terrorist was killed. Prince Muhammad sustained some injury but survived. It was a close call.[6]

Obama tried hard to implement the promises he made in Cairo but with little tangible success. By November 2010 Secretary of State Hillary Clinton told a Brookings Institution forum that the president's peace initiative had broken down and would be replaced by American shuttling between the parties. Her successor, John Kerry, tried again in Obama's second term to restart negotiations and failed again. Guantanamo stayed open, albeit with fewer prisoners. Polls showed Muslim antipathy toward American policies in the region was as intense during the Obama years as in the Bush years.

Iran's pursuit of nuclear weapons and regional hegemony was a top Obama priority. In part, King Abdallah shared these concerns. The Saudis were not that worried by Iran's nuclear program per se but rather by its pursuit of regional dominance and its use of Shia subversion to accomplish that goal. Abdallah's efforts at rapprochement with Iran in the late 1990s had long since sputtered out. He was appalled that Bush's war in Iraq had strengthened Iranian influence. When Secretary of Defense Robert Gates visited Riyadh in the last year of the Bush administration, Abdallah pressed for an American military attack on Iran. Gates explained that the United States had its hands full in Iraq and Afghanistan and became irritated at the notion America should "send its sons and daughters into a war with Iran in order to protect Saudi interests as if we were mercenaries."[7] Abdallah backed off, impressed by Gates's candor, but he was still very concerned about Iran.

Obama wisely kept Gates on as secretary of defense. Both feared that if Iran got close to building a nuclear weapon, Israel would take military action to try to stop it, just as it had done to Iraq in 1981 and Syria in 2007. Gates later said, "Israel's leaders were itching to launch a military attack on Iran's nuclear infrastructure." An Israeli attack on Iran, Gates believed, would almost certainly require the United States "to be drawn in to finish the job or to deal with Iranian retaliatory attacks against Israel and our friends in the region," including the Saudis. This would provoke a regional war.[8]

Gates traveled to Riyadh again in March 2010 to see Abdallah. They met at the king's farm. Kansas-born Gates said it was like no farm he had seen before. "We had dinner inside a tent—with crystal chandeliers—that could have held the entire Ringling Brothers circus and then some." After dinner Gates and the king agreed on a massive new U.S. arms sale to the Kingdom, the largest ever. It would cost at least $60 billion and include the purchase of eighty-four new F15S fighter planes, upgrades for the seventy F15S jets the Saudis already owned, twenty-four Apache attack helicopters, and seventy-two Blackhawk helicopters. The enormous sale was intended to increase Saudi capabilities to defend against Iran, but Gates found "Abdallah was very cautious about any kind of overt military cooperation or planning with the United States that the Iranians might consider an act of war." Later, after intense discussions between Netanyahu and Gates, Israel agreed not to press its supporters in Congress to fight the sale to Riyadh, in return for a promise of twenty more F35 "stealth" aircraft from the United States.[9]

The Arab Spring

The outbreak of revolutions across the Arab world in 2010–11, which quickly became known as the Arab Spring, surprised everyone. Leon Panetta, then director of the Central Intelligence Agency, wrote later that CIA analysts for years had warned of "building pressures across the Middle East and North Africa—increasing numbers of young people unable to find work; rising income disparities; deepening anger at corruption; alienation from ossified regimes." The CIA, Panetta noted, identified the "sources of pressure long before they blew. At the same time, we did not anticipate the flash points or the speed with which events might unfold. We scrambled to keep up."[10] The CIA was not alone in being surprised and scrambling. Among the others was Saudi Arabia.

Protests and demonstrations began in Tunisia in late 2010, and President Zine al Abedine Ben Ali was toppled from power in only a few days. King Abdallah welcomed him to live in exile in Saudi Arabia immediately. (And he is still there.) The king also cut short a vacation in Morocco and returned home.

The unrest spread rapidly to Egypt, the Arab world's most populous country and a close Saudi ally since Hosni Mubarak replaced Sadat in 1981. On January 25, 2011, massive demonstrations took place in Cairo, and within three days the army was called into the streets to restore order. Mubarak's regime seemed vulnerable very quickly.

Inside the Obama administration there was a split on how to respond to the rapidly developing situation. According to Bob Gates's account, Gates, Clinton, Vice President Joe Biden, and National Security Adviser Tom Donilon counseled patience and caution. They wanted to work with Mubarak and the army to arrange a smooth transition of power over several months to a successor chosen by Mubarak, most likely intelligence chief Omar Sulaiman, who was well known in Washington. Obama's National Security Council senior advisers, Dennis McDonough and Ben Rhodes, homeland security chief John Brennan, and the vice president's top adviser, Tony Blinken, were more eager to support rapid change and press for Mubarak to go quickly.[11]

Mubarak had been a strong American ally for three decades, steadfastly maintaining the 1979 peace treaty with Israel. He had sent two divisions to help defend Saudi Arabia against Iraq in 1990. But the American message, both privately and publicly, to the Egyptian army was that American assistance to Egypt would be in danger if force and violence were used to keep Mubarak in power. The Pentagon reinforced that message directly to senior

Egyptian generals. On January 29 Mubarak fired his cabinet and made Sulaiman vice president.

Obama and Clinton then sent Frank Wisner, a former U.S. ambassador to Egypt, to Cairo in hopes of encouraging an "orderly transition" of power. Mubarak, however, refused to leave before his term in office expired in September. Obama responded publicly with a call for an orderly transition that "must begin now." Obama had sided with the activists in the White House; Mubarak had to go. The White House said: "When we said now, we meant yesterday."[12] On February 11 the Egyptian army forced Mubarak to resign, and army commander General Mohamed Hussein Tantawi took power as an interim leader pending elections.

Obama hailed the move as a sign that "the arc of history has bent toward justice once more." He likened the change in Egypt to the nonviolent movements led decades earlier by Mahatma Gandhi and Martin Luther King Jr. Obama also enthused that there is "something in our souls that cries out for freedom."[13]

King Abdallah and the other Gulf monarchs were outraged. America had just abandoned a friend and helped force him from office. If Obama could dispense with Mubarak so quickly, what future did they have if the revolutions spread to their countries?

The hypothetical became a pressing reality next door in Bahrain just as Mubarak was falling. The small island nation has a majority Shia population but a Sunni ruling family, the Khalifas. The population of the island is 1.3 million, with slightly less than 50 percent being Bahraini citizens (and 75 percent of them are Shia). The Shia majority periodically staged demonstrations and rock-throwing riots throughout the 1980s and 1990s, demanding political reforms and more development for Shia neighborhoods. Inspired by the events in Tunisia and Egypt, demonstrations quickly began in Bahrain. In February 2011 more than 100,000 people demonstrated in Manama's Pearl Circle, the city's center, demanding change.

The Khalifa rulers in Bahrain and the Saudis saw the demonstrators as pawns of Iran. Rather than accepting their legitimate demands for better treatment, they jointly determined to repress the demonstrations. For the Saudis, what happens in next-door Bahrain is an existential issue. If the Shia majority took power in Bahrain, that would inspire unrest in the Eastern Province, a longstanding area of Shia turbulence inside the Kingdom and the home of its oil wealth. In the worst case it would mean Iran acquired a foothold on the southern shore of the Persian Gulf.

King Abdallah was inclined to fear the worst case in 2011. As Secretary Clinton wrote later, the Saudis "saw the hidden hand of Iran. They worried that their large adversary across the water was fomenting unrest in order to weaken their government and improve its own strategic position."[14] Clinton called her Bahraini counterpart and urged patience and conciliation. The Bahraini crown prince began a dialogue with the protesters, aided by Clinton's diplomats.

On Friday March 4, 2011, the demonstrations grew to 200,000 people, equal to almost one-half of the country's citizens. They called for the overthrow of the king. Secretary Gates arrived in Manama a week later to try to calm the situation.

Bahrain has been an American ally for decades; the United States Navy has had an installation in Bahrain since 1947. By 2011 that base was the headquarters for the Fifth Fleet, which was responsible for operations in the Gulf and the Indian Ocean. The Navy, therefore, had a strong interest in keeping the Khalifas in power. But Gates was uneasy with America propping up indefinitely a minority government hated by so many of its people. He told King Hamad and Crown Prince Salman that "baby steps" toward reform were not enough. He predicted that if the unrest went on long enough Iran would take advantage of the situation.[15]

The Bahrainis briefed the Saudis on Gates's message. Feigning illness, King Abdallah told Gates not to come to Riyadh. He had already made his decision. He communicated to Obama that if the United States interfered in Bahrain it would provoke a rupture in Saudi-American relations. On Sunday, March 13, the demonstrators stormed Manama's financial district, taking control of the island's economy. The American defense attaché in Riyadh reported that the Saudis were preparing to use force to quell the unrest by sending troops over the causeway linking the island to the Eastern Province (the Saudis had built it with sufficiently wide lanes to allow armored vehicles to cross).[16]

The next day, March 14, 1,200 troops from the Saudi Arabian National Guard—the king's men—crossed the King Fahd causeway with armored personnel carriers to prop up the Khalifa dynasty. An additional 800 troops from the United Arab Emirates joined them. The Bahraini government had officially requested their intervention. Using helicopters and tanks, the Bahraini security forces crushed the demonstrations and cleared the financial district and Pearl Circle. At least thirty people died. Obama called Abdallah to urge restraint, and the king replied: "Saudi Arabia will never allow Shia rule in Bahrain—never."[17] When Clinton called Prince Saud, he was implacable, blaming Iran for all the island's problems.[18]

This was the first time Saudi Arabia had used force to stem the Arab Spring, and it exposed a massive break with Washington. The intervention in a close neighbor underscored the House of Saud's conclusion that the Arab Spring was an existential threat to its survival.

Abdallah also took measures to ensure there would be no demonstrations at home. In February he announced that $37 billion in new funds would be devoted to building homes, schools, and mosques across the country to stave off any unrest. In a TV broadcast in March he promised another $93 billion to build more housing and provide jobs. Public sector employees, the majority of Saudi workers, got pay bonuses. Abdallah was worried enough by the Arab Spring to spend $130 billion to keep it away. Only a few minor demonstrations took place.[19] James Smith, then American ambassador to Saudi Arabia, believes the massive aid package was the direct result of the king's fear that the revolutionary wave would hit the Kingdom sooner rather than later and needed to be bought off.[20]

The king took other steps to buy insurance. Oman and Bahrain, the two poorest Gulf Cooperation Council members, each got $10 billion in aid from the Saudis, Kuwaitis, Qataris, and Emirates in 2011 to ensure stability.[21] Prince Bandar bin Sultan bin Abdul Aziz, who had left Washington under a cloud for misinterpreting George Bush, had been given a job as national security adviser to the king. In March 2011 he was dispatched to Pakistan and China. In Pakistan Bandar asked for assurances that, if requested, Islamabad would send elite troops to the Kingdom to restore order if demonstrations got out of hand.[22] This was a repeat of King Khalid's request to Pakistani dictator Zia ul Haq in the 1980s for help after the takeover of the Grand Mosque in Mecca. Again the Pakistanis promised they would send troops if needed. More immediately they augmented the battalion of troops they had in Bahrain with a recruiting drive that hired experienced Pakistani soldiers to join the Bahrain Defense Forces, giving it more muscle to quell Shia unrest.[23]

In Beijing, where Bandar had secretly negotiated the East Wind missile deal two decades earlier, he pressed for Chinese political support for the Saudi counterrevolution. It was an easy sell since the Chinese were no fans of democracy, and Bandar could also promise that future investment and business deals would be steered toward China.[24] The trip restored Bandar's stature in the king's eyes. The next year Abdallah would promote Bandar to be chief of Saudi intelligence, a much more important job. His task would be to coordinate the clandestine counterrevolution.

Yemen, Saudi Arabia's traditional nemesis to the south, had its own version of an Arab Spring. Ali Abdullah Saleh, who had backed Iraq in 1990 and who the Saudis had tried to overthrow in 1994, faced massive demonstrations calling for an end to his decades of misrule. The opposition was deeply divided, however. Some were democracy advocates and wanted to end corruption and misrule. Others were southern separatists who wanted to restore South Yemen's independence, which Saleh had ended in 1990. In the north, the Zaydi Shia tribes that Saudi Arabia had backed in the 1960s had found a new leadership in the Houthi family, which sought to restore Zaydi dominance and flirted with Iranian support. The Saudis and Houthis had engaged in border clashes for years. Saleh fought six major military campaigns against the Houthis before 2011.

Working with the other Gulf states, a prolonged political process finally edged Saleh out of power, to be replaced by his former deputy, a southerner named Abdrabbu Mansour Hadi. The formal ceremony was held in Riyadh in November 2011 with King Abdallah presiding. Hadi then began a complex national dialogue to develop a stable government for Yemen. For the Saudis it was a tolerable outcome, though it proved to be short-lived.[25]

Revolutions in Syria and Libya provided a different choice for the Kingdom. Bashar Assad and Muammar Qaddafi were not long-standing Saudi allies. The Syrian regime had been an Iranian ally since 1980. The Saudis had pursued the Middle East peace process with Damascus in part to woo Damascus away from Tehran. They had helped resolve the Pan Am 103 case, not to help Tripoli but to ease tensions between the Arab world and the United States. Prince Bandar had been at the center of both efforts.

So when revolutions broke out in Syria and Libya, King Abdallah backed the revolutionaries. He was not hoping for democracy in either case; rather, he hoped new Sunni Arab strongmen would replace the existing tyrants but would be more inclined to accept Saudi influence. But the Saudis made clear to Washington that their assistance in getting rid of Assad and Qaddafi depended on America accepting the outcome in Bahrain.

After refusing to see Gates during the Bahrain crisis, Abdallah met him a month later when it was settled. They met at the king's palace office in Riyadh, which Gates noted was ten times larger than his own office in the Pentagon and was decorated with eight crystal chandeliers. The king had a carefully prepared message for Gates to take to Obama. Saudi Arabia and the United States had been partners in a strategic relationship for seventy years, but he said American behavior in Egypt and Bahrain had threatened that partnership. Some Arabs were saying America had treated its allies like it treated the shah when he was deposed. It was imperative for America to "listen to its friends" in the region. Finally, the king told Gates, "Iran is the source of all problems."[26]

Secretary Clinton got a similar warning from Prince Saud, the foreign minister. Saudi Arabia could help in Syria and Libya only if it was not being criticized at the same time for its occupation of Bahrain.[27] If the United States pushed a "freedom agenda" for the Arab Spring, the relationship with Riyadh would be endangered. If Washington was more pragmatic, cooperation could continue. In May 2011 Obama gave a long-awaited speech on the Arab Spring. He never once uttered the words "Saudi Arabia," but he urged pragmatism and dealing with each country based on its own circumstances.

The revolutions in Syria and Libya turned into bloody civil wars that continue today with no end in sight. The Saudis have been particularly active in Syria, where Abdallah took a personal interest in the revolution. He appointed as head of Saudi intelligence Prince Bandar, who, ironically, had a long history with the Assads. When Hafez Assad died in 2000, shortly after the failed summit with Clinton in Geneva, Bandar rushed to Damascus to persuade Syria's generals to back the young son, Bashar, to be president. By 2012 Bandar and King Abdallah had soured on Bashar al-Assad and hoped to recreate the Afghan model in Syria—that is, an insurgency armed and paid for by America and Saudi Arabia that would topple a pro-Iranian regime.[28]

The Kingdom clandestinely bought arms for the Syrian Sunni rebels, particularly in Croatia, and smuggled them to the rebels through Jordan. One study assessed that the Saudis bought arms for the Syrian rebels worth more than $1 billion from East European sources between 2012 and 2016.[29] But Obama was not very enthusiastic about the mission. U.S. support was slow in coming and limited in scale. Jordan proved a weak ally, as well. Some elements within Jordanian intelligence took some of the arms intended for the rebels and sold them on the black arms market; in the end, some even ended up in the hands of terrorists who killed two Americans in Amman in November 2015.[30]

The Saudi clerical leadership publicly urged all Muslims to support the revolution against the Iranian and Hezbollah-supported Alawite government of Assad. The grand mufti, Shaykh Abd al Aziz ibn Abdullah al Shaikh, publicly endorsed the war against Assad and his allies in May 2013. Saudis began to join the rebel camp and travel to Syria to join the fight.[31]

But Egypt was and remains the Saudis' main concern after the Arab Spring. After the fall of Mubarak, elections brought to power a government that was dominated by the Muslim Brotherhood. Although the Saudis had years of experience dealing with members of the Brotherhood, Riyadh was profoundly uneasy about a freely elected Islamic government ruling the most populous Arab state. If an Islamic democracy, however flawed, could successfully govern Egypt, it would set an example for every Muslim country. Saudi citizens would ask, if democracy worked in Egypt, why might it not work in Saudi Arabia? In short, success for the democratic process in Egypt would pose an existential threat to the Kingdom itself and would be a powerful argument for reform, if not revolution, in all the monarchies.

The new Egyptian government led by Mohammad Morsi had many enemies at home. The army was especially worried that the Brotherhood would begin to chip away at its prerogatives. Those who had benefited from the Mubarak regime wanted a restoration of a military-dominated government. The economy did not improve, and many who had demonstrated for democracy became disillusioned.

The Saudis had an important ally in the counterrevolutionary camp. General Abdel Fattah al-Sisi had been Egypt's defense attaché in Riyadh before the revolution, who was well known to Bandar and Saudi intelligence. In April 2012 he was promoted from head of Egyptian military intelligence to minister of defense. Rather than backing up Morsi, al-Sisi began plotting his ouster. The army privately encouraged demonstrations to undermine the legitimacy of the government. A year later, in July 2013, after increasingly large and disruptive demonstrations against the government of President Morsi, General al-Sisi gave the president a forty-eight-hour ultimatum to give up power. When the ultimatum expired, al-Sisi and the army took power, arrested Morsi and hundreds of Muslim Brotherhood supporters, and ruthlessly cracked down on any opposition. The Egyptian revolution was over; a counterrevolution and coup had bent "the arc of history" back to authoritarianism.

King Abdallah issued a public endorsement of the coup less than two hours after al-Sisi announced Morsi had been deposed and the constitution suspended. Saudi Arabia was the first government to back the takeover, and Abdallah followed his public statement a few hours later with a phone call to al-Sisi, which was made public. The counterrevolution had an overt foreign backer. Within a week Saudi Arabia organized a $12 billion aid package for Egypt. The Kingdom provided $5 billion, Kuwait $4 billion, and the United Arab Emirates the remaining $3 billion. The aid came with no strings attached and no requirement that al-Sisi restore democracy, ever.[32]

The clock had been turned back in Egypt. Obama and his new secretary of state, John Kerry, were unwilling to take any serious action to stop the coup and counterrevolution. Sisi was elected president in carefully controlled elections held a year after the coup. In his victory speech, al-Sisi mentioned only one foreign leader by name, King Abdallah, praising the king for the help Saudi Arabia had provided Egypt. Abdallah called al-Sisi fifteen minutes after his election to thank him for leading Egypt from the "strange chaos" of the Arab Spring.[33]

On June 20, 2014, the king did a victory lap in Cairo. It was a very unusual state visit. He flew to Cairo from Morocco, where he had been getting medical attention, but did not leave his special executive jumbo jet; instead, Sisi joined him inside for a thirty-minute meeting, then the king flew home. He spent no time in Egypt other than in his own aircraft. The ninety-year-old king was the first head of state to visit Egypt after the coup. Accompanying Abdallah was Foreign Minister Prince Saud and Chief of Intelligence Prince Bandar. Bandar's presence was highlighted in the Saudi press, a thank-you gesture from the king to the coup master.[34] The king's eldest son, Minister of National Guard

Affairs Prince Mitab, followed up the brief summit with a longer visit to Cairo later in 2014 to solidify ties with the military government.

Perhaps the major beneficiary of the failure of the Arab Spring was, ironically, al Qaeda. At first the revolutions threatened the narrative and ideology of the jihadists. When Mubarak and other dictators were toppled by mass popular movements, it appeared for a brief moment that there was a real and tangible path for democratic change in the Arab world. Twitter and social media had helped topple Mubarak, not terror. Al Qaeda suddenly seemed out of date. But not for long.

When the counterrevolution took control of Bahrain and Egypt and civil war wracked Syria and Libya, al Qaeda could argue its ideology had been upheld. Only jihad could change the Arab states. America was not a friend of change, the jihadists charged, because it did not really stand up for change at all. The ideology of Osama bin Laden was validated by the outcome of the Arab Spring in the eyes of its supporters and many others.

But bin Laden himself did not live to see the Arab Spring's failure. In May 2011 United States Navy SEAL commandoes brought justice to the mastermind of 9/11. The Central Intelligence Agency, using good analysis and sophisticated collection means, had found bin Laden hiding in a specially built house less than a mile from the Kakul Military Academy, Pakistan's equivalent of West Point or Sandhurst; he had been there at least five years. When Obama was told by the CIA that they believed bin Laden was present at this hide-out in Abbottabad, Pakistan, the president decided that no Pakistanis would be told. Obama rightly decided that Pakistan could not be trusted with the information, that it was all too likely that if the Pakistanis learned that the CIA had found bin Laden in Abbottabad, he would be alerted and flee. It was a remarkable decision given that, in the decade since 9/11, Obama and Bush together had provided over $25 billion in aid to Pakistan to fight al Qaeda.

Without bin Laden's charismatic leadership, the al Qaeda movement splintered. The most potent faction was the one in Iraq that Abu Musaib al Zarqawi had created after the American invasion. Al Qaeda in Iraq had been mauled by the surge in American troops that President Bush ordered in 2007 (and Zarqawi himself was killed in 2006), but it was not defeated. In 2014 the group's new leader broke with bin Laden's heir, the Egyptian Ayman Zawahiri, and announced that his group, the Islamic State of Iraq and al Shams (Syria) was the rightful heir to bin Laden. Abu Bakr al Baghdadi al Husseini al Hashemi al Quraishi, as he called himself, claimed to be a descendant of the Prophet Muhammad. He proclaimed himself caliph in June 2014 shortly after his group seized the Iraqi city of Mosul. At its peak, the Islamic State controlled an area across Syria and Iraq larger than Britain.

In naming himself the caliph, Ibrahim Baghdadi implicitly was announcing he was the rightful custodian of the two holy mosques in Mecca and Medina. He was quick to follow up this proclamation of a new caliphate with a call for the overthrow of the House of Saud and the end of the monarchy. The group's Internet magazine *Dabiq* showed a picture of the Kaaba in Mecca with the Islamic State flag flying over it.[35]

King Abdallah hosted an international conference in Jidda in September 2014 that formed an international coalition to fight the Islamic State. On September 22, 2014, the Royal Saudi Air Force joined the United States Air Force and other coalition allies in bombing Islamic State targets in Iraq and Syria.[36]

Abdallah's health deteriorated steadily after the Arab Spring. He continued to be a chain smoker and suffered from an assortment of illnesses. He had outlived two of his designated heirs: Prince Sultan had been crown prince from 2005 until 2011, and Prince Nayef bin Abdul Aziz was crown prince from 2011 until his death in June 2012. On Nayef's death, Abdallah's half-brother, Prince Salman bin Abdul Aziz al Saud, ascended to the office of crown prince, then on January 23, 2015, Abdallah passed away and Salman became king of Saudi Arabia.

Abdallah was a cautious reformer by Saudi standards. He had allowed a limited electorate to help choose municipal councils in the Kingdom, the first time ever Saudis were given a vote. The councils had strictly limited powers, but they represented a first step toward political reform. Abdallah also promoted female education and even appointed a woman to be deputy minister of education, the first and only time a woman had held such a high office in the Kingdom (she was ousted after Abdallah died). The king promised women would gain the right to vote in municipal elections and even run for office, a promise realized only after his death. Within the stark limits of the Kingdom's Wahhabi Islam, Abdallah was more advanced in this thinking on reform than archconservatives such as his brother Prince Nayef, who opposed any change in the status quo.

King Abdallah had ruled Saudi Arabia either de facto while Fahd was incapable or as king in his own right for two decades. A cautious and risk-averse man, Abdallah dealt with three U.S. presidents and forged the post–Desert Storm Saudi-American partnership. That partnership survived two near-death experiences on his watch: the quarrel with Bush over Palestine in 2001 and the quarrel with Obama over Egypt and Bahrain in 2011.

Salman

Salman was born on December 31, 1935, in Riyadh. His mother was Ibn Saud's favorite wife, Hassa bint Ahmad al Sudairi, which makes him a member of the Sudairi clan inside the royal family. He outlasted his two full brothers, Sultan and Nayef, to become king. Salman was appointed governor of Riyadh province by Faisal in 1963, and he would remain governor for almost a half-century. During that time the capital was transformed from a backwater town of fewer than 100,000 residents into a modern city of 7 million people, with skyscrapers, modern highways, a metro system, hospitals, and universities. He oversaw this transformation while maintaining excellent relations with the Wahhabi clerical establishment and ensuring the city retained its Islamic identity. It is the most Wahhabi city in the world.

Because most of the royal family lives in Riyadh, as governor, Salman was also the sheriff of the family. If a young prince or princess got into trouble with the law or into alcohol or drugs, it would be Salman's job to discreetly resolve the issue. The same would be true for older members of the family and their allies in business or religion. This gave him enormous power within the royal family and a reputation for being fair, pious, and efficient.

Salman was also in charge of raising funds for jihadist causes that the family supported. As noted earlier, King Faisal made him chairman of a committee to raise money to support the Palestinians after the 1967 war, and he still holds that title. King Khalid and King Fahd put him in charge of raising money for the Afghan mujahedin, and he worked closely with the senior clerics to support their cause at home and abroad. Crown Prince Abdallah sent him to Bosnia to raise support for the Bosnian Muslims in the 1990s. Again this fundraising role reinforced his position as a champion of Wahhabi causes and his close relations to the clerics.

American diplomats working in the Kingdom got to know Salman well as governor. The American embassy, like every foreign diplomatic post, was originally in Jidda, but as the capital grew it moved to Riyadh, where all foreign embassies are housed in a special diplomatic quarter. Salman oversaw their security. Especially during the troubled 1990s and early 2000s, when the Kingdom faced serious terrorist threats, Salman was an important interlocutor for American ambassadors seeking to ensure security for their staff and installations.

On Salman's accession to the throne in January 2015 Deputy Crown Prince Muqrin bin Abd al Aziz moved up to become crown prince. Muqrin, born September 15, 1945, is the last surviving acknowledged son of Ibn Saud. His mother was a concubine of Ibn Saud named Baraka al Yamanyah, a Yemeni girl. This maternal bloodline set Muqrin apart from the more "pure" Saudi siblings of Ibn Saud and was held against him by many all his life. But his father did acknowledge his son as his own and, thus, Muqrin had a claim to the line of succession.

Muqrin is a pilot who was trained at the Royal Air Force academy in Cranwell in England. In 1965 he joined the Royal Saudi Air Force as a jet pilot and he remained until 1980, when he was appointed governor of Hail province. During this time, while both were in the air force, he and Prince Bandar became close friends. In 1999 Abdallah moved him to be governor of Medina province. Abdallah was fond of his younger half-brother, whom he undoubtedly saw as another outsider from the Sudairis.[37]

In 2005 Muqrin became the head of Saudi intelligence. He was Prince Mohammad bin Nayef's partner in the war with al Qaeda, although his responsibility was external intelligence, not internal security. In interviews with key intelligence chiefs in the United States, Europe, and the Arab world during Muqrin's tenure, I was told that Muqrin was a professional, if not outstanding, chief. Bandar took the place of his friend Muqrin in July 2012, when Abdallah began grooming Muqrin to be a future crown prince. He became deputy prime minister in 2013 and formally moved to be deputy crown prince later that year.

In a shocking and unprecedented move, King Salman removed Crown Prince Muqrin from his position as the heir apparent on April 21, 2015, only three months after Abdallah died. No explanation was offered for the change, and Muqrin himself has never explained why he was removed from office. There is no reason to believe he was either unfit for the job or did not want to serve. Even before Muqrin's ouster, his friend Prince Bandar had been stripped of his remaining official positions in the government.[38]

Removing Muqrin ended the line of succession established by King Faisal upon his ascension to the throne more than a half-century earlier. No longer would succession pass among the sons of Ibn Saud, since Muqrin is the last acknowledged capable son. Instead, succession would pass to a crown prince lacking the legitimacy of being a direct heir and son of the founder of the modern Saudi Kingdom. That was, of course, inevitable, sooner or later, but Salman advanced the moment dramatically in April 2015. His move may well prove to have been a major mistake if succession quarrels damage family unity in the years ahead. Leaving Muqrin, a thoroughly qualified heir, in place would have put off the legitimacy issue for years, maybe decades.

Muqrin was replaced by Prince Muhammad bin Nayef, who is, without question, the most qualified member of his generation of Saudi princes to take up the throne. He is brave, smart, effective, and popular. He is also the epitome of the Saudi "deep state," as one commentator has written—the man who knows how to fight terrorism and suppress dissent in the Kingdom. There is little risk of political reform on his watch. Nayef controls "this deep state, now an empire of intelligence services, police agencies and emergency forces, in addition to a vast number of civil servants, judges, prison officials and Wahhabi loyalist circles."[39] There is one other important fact about Crown Prince Muhammad bin Nayef: he has no sons, only daughters.

To replace Muhammad bin Nayef as the third in line, Salman picked one of his own sons, Muhammad bin Salman. Only twenty-nine when selected to be deputy crown prince, Muhammad bin Salman is not the king's oldest or most experienced son. His elder brothers include Saudi Arabia's only astronaut, province governors, wealthy businessmen, and media moguls. But the king clearly favors this prince.

Muhammad bin Salman is different in many ways from the thousands of other Saudi princes today, while at the same time similar to a large part of the

President Barack Obama with Crown Prince Muhammad bin Nayef and Deputy Crown Prince Muhammad bin Salman at the White House, May 13, 2015. (Getty Images News/Chip Somodevilla)

overall population. He is far younger than most of his potential rivals for the throne. By picking this son, Salman has skipped a whole generation of Saudi princes. Muhammad was not educated abroad, but, instead studied at a Saudi university. He is not fluent in English, although he understands some, or believes he does. He sports a beard, unusual among the royals. His youth makes him popular with the majority of the population which, like him, is thirty or younger.[40]

The king quickly moved his favorite son into important positions of power. On Abdallah's death, Muhammad bin Salman was appointed by his father to be defense minister and chief of the Royal Court. This gave him command over the armed forces and access to the royal court and the king. Less than a hundred days later he became third in the hierarchy as deputy crown prince. He was also made chairman of an interagency committee to decide all economic and financial policy, including all issues related to petroleum policy. It is an extraordinary and unprecedented accumulation of power in the hands of one very young prince.

The first major challenge for the king and Defense Minister Muhammad bin Salman was Yemen. The political process that replaced Ali Abdallah Saleh with Abdrabbu Mansour Hadi dragged on into a prolonged national dialogue that culminated in a proposal to turn the country into a federation of six regions, four in the north and two in the south. The rebellious Houthis rejected the proposal because their region was landlocked and isolated. Saleh, who refused to go into exile, made an alliance with the Houthis against Hadi. In September 2014 the Houthis and Saleh loyalists seized control of the capital Sana'a.

By January 2015 the Houthis and Saleh had taken control of most of north Yemen, including the major port at Hodeidah. Hadi was placed under house arrest and parliament dissolved. The rebels signed an agreement with Iran to establish direct commercial flights between Tehran and Sana'a four times a day, and Iran agreed to build an electrical power plant in Yemen. Hadi fled to Riyadh, and the rebels began to march on Aden, the former capital of the south and the largest port on the Arabian Sea.

For the new king and his young defense minister, the deteriorating situation in Yemen seemed to suggest Iran was about to gain a foothold on the Arabian Peninsula in the Kingdom's backyard. The Houthis had long-time connections with Iran's Revolutionary Guards and Hezbollah. Small numbers of advisers from both the Iranian guards and Hezbollah had come to Yemen to assist the Houthis, especially with their ballistic missiles. It is estimated, as of this writing, that Iran provides $10 million to $20 million in aid to them each year.[41] Iranian newspapers trumpeted that four Arab capitals—Beirut, Damascus, Baghdad, and Sana'a—were under Iranian influence. In truth, neither Saleh nor the Houthis were Iranian pawns or even allies, but for the Saudis the situation was intolerable.

Riyadh quickly put together a coalition of its fellow Gulf monarchies (minus Oman), Egypt, Jordan, Morocco, Sudan, and some African states to restore Hadi to power. On March 25, 2015, the new coalition led by Muhammad bin Salman announced the beginning of Operation Decisive Storm, and the Saudis began bombing Saleh and Houthi forces across Yemen. The rebels responded with missile attacks on Saudi border cities and battles erupted on the Saudi-Yemeni border.

The air war was not decisive by any means. Although it imposed terrible suffering on the poorest country in the Arab world and created an enormous humanitarian crisis for Yemen's 25 million people, it did not restore Hadi to power. Instead, he moved to Aden, which became the de facto capital of his state. Backed by small contingents of Saudi and Emirati troops, Hadi gradually took control of the south.[42] The war became a bloody stalemate, with no end in sight, while tens of thousands of Yemeni civilians suffered the consequences of fighting, bombing raids, famine, and disease.

The United Nations Security Council, dominated by Saudi friends and oil customers, adopted a resolution on April 14, 2015, endorsing the Saudi position and demanding the Houthis "withdraw their forces from all areas they seized" and "immediately and unconditionally relinquish all additional arms seized from military and security installations, including missiles." Only Russia abstained on resolution 2216, arguing that it was unbalanced and unenforceable.

The hastily formed alliance was not joined by Pakistan. The Saudis had expected the Pakistanis to provide troops for the ground war in Yemen and summoned Prime Minister Nawaz Sharif to meet with the king and his ministers. The Pakistanis found the king and his court in a state of near panic. They were frightened by the Houthis' successes and determined to stop the Iranians but had no plan for how to defeat the enemy. The mood was reckless, one senior Pakistani told me later. There was no plan for an endgame, an achievable outcome at a reasonable price.

Despite Saudi assumptions, Sharif wanted no part of a war between Sunnis and Shias. His own country had a large Shia minority and a long border with Iran. He convened the Pakistani parliament to debate the Saudi request. In a stunning rejection, the parliament voted unanimously against sending any troops to Saudi Arabia. A half-century of Saudi courtship of Pakistan had failed to secure Pakistani support at a crucial moment. The Pakistani press was filled with angry articles about Saudi arrogance and recklessness.

Pakistan's rejection of Saudi troop requests raised another issue. For decades many outside observers had wondered whether Riyadh and Islamabad had a secret understanding that, in case of a dire external threat to the Kingdom, Pakistan would provide nuclear weapons to Saudi Arabia. The Saudi purchase of Chinese intermediate-range ballistic missiles in the 1980s had added meat to the question. Why would the Saudis buy missiles expressly designed to carry nuclear bombs without having nuclear warheads? Publicly, Saudi officials avoided any discussion of the question, but Prince Saud and others, in private, were more disposed to suggest that some kind of discreet understanding did exist. In 2014 the Saudis displayed their Chinese CSS2 missiles in public for the first time ever in a military parade. The guest of honor at the parade was the Pakistani army chief of staff. Saudi officials were eager to encourage observers like me to make the connection.

If there is a real connection, the Pakistan refusal to join the war in Yemen would suggest any such understanding is based on weak foundations. With Pakistan unwilling to send troops to fight the Houthis, how reliable was any vague promise to provide a nuclear warhead? The war that was designed to strengthen Saudi deterrence had, unintentionally, appeared to erode it.

Defense Minister Muhammad bin Salman was the face of the war, at least in the beginning. He was seen everywhere on Saudi television and in the newspapers meeting with the troops and chairing meetings of the generals. Saudi radio stations broadcast songs praising his leadership. Critics, on the other hand, dismissed him as the young general in over his head.

The king's promotion of his son and the war has its critics within the royal family. In 2015 several Saudi watchers, including myself, received unsolicited emails from unidentified members of the royal family harshly critical of Muqrin's demotion, Muhammad bin Salman's promotion, and the handling of Saudi policy toward Yemen. Some alleged the king was mentally unfit for office and was being used by his son. In time these letters came into the public domain and got widespread attention in the media then, gradually, they ceased to appear.[43]

The war is an expensive proposition for the Kingdom. Not only is there the military expense of a modern air war, but Riyadh also props up the Hadi government in Aden and funds the contributions of many poor allies, such as Sudan. The United Arab Emirates and Kuwait help significantly with the expenses.

Saudi Arabia has achieved significant territorial advantages from the war. The Hadi forces control Aden, the largest port and city in the south. They also control Perim Island, which sits in the middle of the strategic Bab al Mandab Strait that divides Africa and Asia at the mouth of the Red Sea. The island of

Socotra in the Indian Ocean is also in the hands of the pro-Saudi forces. In May 2016 Saudi-backed troops took control of the port city of Mukkala and the province of Hadramawt in southwest Yemen, giving Saudi Arabia a land connection directly to the Indian Ocean. Al Qaeda in the Arabian Peninsula had taken Mukkala during the confusion at the start of the war. While all of these territories remain under nominal Yemeni sovereignty, Saudi Arabia certainly has access to them and has military forces based in some of them.

The United States and United Kingdom provide crucial support for the Saudi war. Since the Royal Saudi Air Force is equipped entirely with American and British aircraft and equipment, the war could not go on without the backing of Washington and London.

When Abdallah passed away, Obama was quick to develop a dialogue with the new king. He cut short a trip to India to visit the Kingdom right after the succession occurred. He invited Salman to visit Washington for a summit with the Gulf Cooperation Council leaders. Salman instead sent Muhammad bin Nayef and Muhammad bin Salman, in what was seen by many at the time as a snub of the president. But later in 2016 the king did visit Washington for talks with the president. Muhammad bin Salman made a visit, as well, touring not only Washington but also San Francisco and New York to lay out his plans for Saudi economic reform, what is billed as Saudi Vision 2030.

Much of the discussion between the king and the president focused on Iran. The Saudis are increasingly concerned about the expansion of Iranian influence in the Arab world. In their eyes Iran is the dominant power in Iraq, Syria, and Lebanon, and it aspires to turn Yemen into a proxy. Iran also supports terrorist groups like Hezbollah and subversion in Bahrain and the Eastern Province.

Riyadh was critical of the nuclear accord negotiated between the five permanent members of the Security Council plus Germany and Iran in the spring of 2015. The deal strictly limits Iranian nuclear activity in return for lifting most of the economic sanctions on Iran imposed by the UN in the decade before 2015. The Saudis preferred keeping the sanctions in place permanently and keeping Iran isolated as a pariah nation.

Israel also strongly opposed the nuclear deal with Iran, creating an awkward overlap of interests for the Saudis, who do not want to appear to be working with Israel. King Salman kept his critique of the deal mostly behind closed doors in 2015, leveraging his silence in exchange for American and British support in Yemen.

The Saudi-Iranian rivalry has steadily escalated on Salman's watch. First there was the Yemen war. Then Saudi Arabia organized a coalition of Sunni Muslim states to form a military alliance based in Riyadh against terrorism. Three dozen states joined the entente, but Iran and Iraq were conspicuously absent. Large military maneuvers practiced repelling a mock Iranian invasion of northern Saudi Arabia from Iraq in the winter of 2015–16.

In the summer of 2015, in Lebanon, Prince Muhammad bin Nayef's security forces captured the mastermind of the 1995 Khobar Towers attack. Ahmed Ibrahim al Mughassil was just off a flight from Tehran to Beirut. The Saudis quickly took him from Lebanon to the Kingdom. It was a major coup for the prince.[44]

In January 2016 the Saudis executed several dozen alleged terrorists. Most were members of al Qaeda but one was a prominent Shia cleric, Nimr al Nimr, from the Eastern Province. Protests in Iran turned into an attack on the Saudi embassy. King Salman broke diplomatic relations with Iran in return. The Kingdom encouraged other Arab and Muslim states to do the same, and Bahrain, Sudan, and the Maldives did so. In July 2016 former intelligence chief Prince Turki al Faisal attended a conference in Paris hosted by the anti-clerical Iranian opposition group known as the Mujahedin e Khalq and called for the overthrow of the Islamic government in Iran. Iranian pilgrims were excluded from the hajj to Mecca on the grounds that without diplomatic relations they could not get the proper credentials.

The Saudi-Iranian rivalry and the Sunni-Shia sectarian war crossed the boundaries of the Middle East and helped nurture civil wars in Syria, Iraq, and Yemen. Never before has the sectarian conflict within Islam burned as fiercely as it does today.

Egypt remains at the top of Saudi concerns. In April 2016 the king paid a five-day visit to Egypt to support General Sisi. The Saudis promised $16 billion in additional investment in the economy. The Egyptians ceded control to the Saudis of two strategic uninhabited islands in the Straits of Tiran, named Tiran and Sanafir, and the king promised to build a bridge across the straits through the islands to provide a land corridor from Egypt to Saudi Arabia. The acquisition of the two islands gives Saudi Arabia nominal control over both

Israel's and Jordan's access to the Red Sea, and the Kingdom was quick to announce it would guarantee free access. Together with the acquisition of bases in Yemen, the acquisition of Tiran and Sanafir expands Saudi influence in the Red Sea. Technically the Egyptians maintained they were only returning the islands to Saudi control after Ibn Saud had asked Egypt to protect them in 1948 from Israel. However, this explanation was unpopular in Egypt, where many saw the affair as a pay-off for Saudi support for Sisi's coup.[45]

On the surface, Obama's relations with Salman were marred by some scratchy public spats. Saudi papers printed harsh indictments of Obama's policy toward Iran and, especially, his unwillingness to intervene boldly in the Syrian civil war against Bashar Assad. Obama was critical of the Saudis for not doing more to fight the Islamic State and for encouraging sectarian strife. In one interview he suggested the Saudis were "free riders" on American security, prompting a furious response from Prince Turki. Turki wrote that perhaps Obama was "petulant about the Kingdom's effort to support the Egyptian people" in the coup against Morsi. He harkened back to the good old days of George H. W. Bush and the liberation of Kuwait.[46]

Behind the public war of words, however, the Saudi-American connection remained strong in critical areas. Obama and his aides defended the Kingdom against continued accusations of being involved in the 9/11 plot, dismissing a long-classified 2002 Senate report on the alleged Saudi role as having been overtaken by later, more thorough, investigations. CIA director John Brennan stated publicly that "Saudi Arabia is among our closest counterterrorism partners" and praised Crown Prince Muhammad bin Nayef as "a very close partner."[47]

The arms relationship expanded considerably on Obama's watch. While some areas of discord remain, the military-to-military relationship is stronger than ever, if measured in arms sales between Washington and Riyadh. According to a Congressional Research Service study, the Kingdom purchased arms worth a total of $111 billion on Obama's watch.[48] A considerable portion came in the deal Defense Secretary Gates negotiated with King Abdallah, but the war in Yemen has added billions more. There has been some criticism in Congress over the wisdom of these massive arms sales, particularly by Connecticut senator Christopher Murphy, but the Obama administration defended them as crucial to maintaining the health of the special relationship with the Kingdom.

Barack Obama understood the importance of Saudi Arabia before he was elected president, and he made reaching out to its kings a high priority during his entire term in office. He was quick to offer his condolences in person when King Abdallah died and Salman ascended to the throne. Obama had at his side a genuine Saudi expert, John Brennan, who had served in the Kingdom twice while he was in the CIA. The relationship between the two countries occasionally was stormy, but it was one the president knew mattered a lot.

No president since Franklin Roosevelt courted Saudi Arabia as zealously as did Obama. He traveled to the Kingdom more than any of his predecessors and more than any other country in the region, including Israel. But by 2016 the Saudis had soured on Obama. Part of the reason was Obama's perceived desire to reduce America's role in the region. He did want to get out of Iraq and not get dragged into Syria. He also failed to deliver on his promises of an Israeli-Palestinian agreement.

But the key reason for Saudi disenchantment was the Arab Spring. Faced with a potential existential threat to the Kingdom's survival, Obama wavered on backing autocrats and monarchies. He seemed to be ready to let revolution topple American allies or at least result in major political reforms. The Saudis, instead, want any American president to stay away from awkward and difficult issues like religious freedom, freedom of the press, gender equality, and political reform. In November 2016 the Saudis got a U.S. president who would avoid such issues, Donald J. Trump.

Trump Visits Salman

Trump has courted the Kingdom even more zealously than Obama, and the Saudis reciprocated. He sent his director of the Central Intelligence Agency, Michael Pompeo, to Riyadh on his first trip abroad to see the Saudis. Pompeo awarded Crown Prince Muhammad bin Nayef the George Tenet Medal for excellence in fighting terrorism. Deputy Crown Prince Muhammad bin Salman next visited the White House and had lunch with the president and his senior team.

On May 20, 2017, Trump traveled to Riyadh as his first destination on his first trip abroad. It was a striking example of the importance Saudi Arabia holds for American national security. The Saudis rolled out the red carpet with an impressive reception at the airport and huge posters with the president's image on skyscrapers.

There were three summits in Riyadh. First, King Salman met with the president, then leaders of the six Gulf Cooperation Council states had a summit with Trump, and finally, forty Muslim leaders from around the world met with the president, who delivered a speech about Islam. Among those attending were the president of Egypt, prime minister of Pakistan, king of Jordan, and the amirs of Kuwait, Bahrain, Qatar, and the United Arab Emirates. All the key figures in the Saudi hierarchy met with the president, as well; even former crown prince Muqrin had a session with the president's daughter Ivanka.

Unlike Obama, Trump next flew to Israel for a meeting with Netanyahu. Trump told the prime minister that King Salman was ready for a comprehensive Arab-Israeli peace agreement along the lines of the Arab peace plan originally put forward by Fahd in 1981 and repeated by Abdallah in 2002.

The backdrop to the president's trip was growing scandal at home. The president had fired his first national security adviser, Michael Flynn, for misleading comments about his meetings with Russian officials, and then after the summit, Trump fired the director of the Federal Bureau of Investigation because of his investigation of the administration's connections with Moscow. The president's son-in-law was also tainted with the scandal. It was all reminiscent of Nixon's visit to the Kingdom in 1974.

The two-day visit to the Kingdom was long on ceremony and symbolism and short on substance. A major arms deal worth $110 billion was promised, but no contracts were signed and the joint statement of the two countries made no mention of any deal. A new center for countering violent extremist propaganda was inaugurated with a bizarre photo-op of the king, President Trump, and Egyptian president al-Sisi putting their hands on a glowing orb. The joint statement highlighted "the strong historical and strategic relations" between the two countries and promised cooperation on international terrorism and regional issues. The strongest language was reserved for "the need to contain Iran's malign interference in the internal affairs of other states." No specifics were addressed.[49]

There also was no mention of human rights, democracy, or political reform. The issues that had troubled Saudi-American relations under Obama were left off the table and not discussed. Trump embraced the Bahraini amir and the Egyptian president enthusiastically. Instead, the emphasis was on forging a new strategic partnership for the twenty-first century. The American-Saudi partnership, at least on paper, was stronger than ever.

In short the Saudis played Trump like a fiddle, flattering him and giving his first foreign trip a glittering start. Just like FDR and Ibn Saud in 1945, the summit was more symbol than substance. The Saudis were happy to be rid of Obama and to get an unqualified endorsement for their campaign against Iran from the American president.

Just a few weeks later the king moved to secure his favorite son's position in the hierarchy. Muhammad bin Nayef was fired on June 21, 2017, and replaced by Muhammad bin Salman. As with Muqrin, no explanation was given for the unprecedented step of removing a sitting crown prince. Nayef was also ousted from the Ministry of the Interior. The house of Saud and the house of al Shaykh were quick to endorse the change. No successor was announced immediately to be the new deputy crown prince. The Saudi media hailed it as a triumph for the younger generation in the Kingdom. Trump called and congratulated the new crown prince. The news was greeted much less enthusiastically elsewhere. The *New York Times* editorialized that the "young and brash" prince was not "ready for the top leadership post." It cited the Yemen war as a sign that the "prince acted without thinking through the consequences" of his decision.[50] *The Economist* criticized the young man as imperious and a "callow, hot headed prince," even "dangerous."[51] But he is now the future of the Kingdom and will be the next king for presidents to deal with.

Chapter Seven

WHITHER SAUDI ARABIA

It was October 1999 and I was in Geneva, Switzerland, with Assistant Secretary of State Martin Indyk to see Ambassador Prince Bandar. Bandar was hosting a secret meeting between representatives of the United States and Libya at his father's palatial home on Lake Geneva. It was the latest in a series of secret meetings that year hosted by the Saudis to broker a deal where Libya would turn over those responsible for blowing up Pan Am 103 over Lockerbie, Scotland, for trial in The Hague in return for an easing of sanctions. President Bill Clinton and Crown Prince Abdallah had explicitly authorized this secret diplomacy.[1]

After a day of discussions with the Libyans, Bandar took us out to an unforgettable dinner. He chose La Perle du Lac, perhaps the most elegant restaurant in the city, with a fabulous wine cellar. We certainly tested it that night.

I had another issue to discuss with Bandar unrelated to Libya. Only days earlier, Pakistan's elected prime minister Nawaz Sharif had been overthrown in a coup d'état by his military chief of staff Pervez Musharraf. The origins of the coup began earlier in 1999, when Musharraf had ordered Pakistani troops to cross the so-called line of control between Pakistani-controlled Kashmir and the Indian-controlled part of Kashmir. This troop movement forced a major confrontation between the two nuclear weapons states and resulted in a bloody war in the Himalayas around a town named Kargil. In the end, Sharif came to Washington on July 4, 1999, and reluctantly but bravely agreed to pull his army back behind the line of control. The war was over but the controversy over responsibility for the debacle produced a showdown in Pakistani politics that Musharraf won and Sharif lost.

Bandar had been helpful on July 4 in resolving the crisis. I had briefed him the night before on how the Kargil war was approaching a climax and the danger Clinton believed it posed of escalating into a nuclear exchange, which would have been the first-ever war between two states with nuclear weapons. Bandar had met Sharif at Dulles Airport when his flight arrived from Islamabad and urged him to find a way out of the crisis on the ride from the airport to Blair House, where the summit with Clinton was to take place. For decades Saudi Arabia had been a major source of aid and support for Pakistan, and together with Washington the two countries had won the war against the Soviet Union in Afghanistan in the 1980s.

In Geneva I reminded the prince of his role on July 4 and asked him to help again. Clinton was worried that Musharraf would have Sharif executed for treason or some other trumped-up charge. In 1979 General Zia ul Haq had overthrown and then executed his civilian boss Zulfiqar Bhutto in a coup. The execution had poisoned Pakistani politics for decades and helped destabilize the country.

The United States had little leverage with Musharraf. Clinton had denounced the coup as a break in Pakistani democracy. Under U.S. law, Washington had immediately cut off all assistance to Pakistan, especially military aid and contacts. These sanctions were added to those imposed when Pakistan tested nuclear weapons in 1998. Musharraf was unlikely to listen to Clinton.[2]

Clinton had directed me to find a way to stop another execution. I knew the Saudis had clout with the Pakistani army and could help; if Abdallah weighed in with Musharraf and offered to take Sharif into exile in the Kingdom, the general would almost certainly have to agree. The offer of exile would provide a way out of the problem of what to do with the ousted prime minister. The Saudis could assure Musharraf that Sharif would not engage in plotting his return to power from the Kingdom. While it would not make Pakistan stable, given its enormous problems, Sharif's exile in Saudi Arabia would give the country a better chance than would the execution of another civilian leader. Moreover, Sharif had been a good friend of Saudi Arabia on many issues during his two tenures in office, and Abdallah valued that bond.

Bandar agreed to help. He urged Crown Prince Abdallah and King Fahd to offer exile to the Pakistanis. Bandar's friend, Prince Muqrin, and his father, Prince Sultan, also weighed in to help convince Musharraf to let Sharif go into exile. It took several months to work out. The White House and the Royal Court worked closely to coordinate the exile agreement. Sharif was tried on charges of terrorism but Saudi intervention finally worked. In his memoirs, Musharraf credited the Saudis with saving Sharif from being executed like Bhutto.[3]

The episode is a good example of how the Saudi-American relationship can be used to produce positive outcomes, not just for the two countries

President Donald Trump and First Lady Melania Trump opening the World Center for Countering Extremist Thought in Riyadh, Saudi Arabia, May 2017, with King Salman bin Abdul Aziz al Saud (center) and President Abdel Fattah al-Sisi of Egypt (far left). (Saudi Press Agency via AP)

themselves but for broader regional reasons. Fahd and Bandar were not particularly worried about preserving democracy in Pakistan, but they were very worried about instability in a nuclear-armed ally. Like Clinton, they worried that Nawaz Sharif would be considered a martyr if he was executed, leading to riots and perhaps even a general breakdown in law and order. With Sharif safely in the Kingdom, the Saudis would have one of Pakistan's most important politicians beholden to them for the rest of his life. It was a long-term bet that eventually paid off. In 2008 Musharraf was forced from office by popular demand, Sharif returned from exile, and today he is again prime minister of Pakistan. He later wrote to thank me for my role in his avoiding the noose.

History of Tension and Unease

Like every president since Richard Nixon, Donald Trump sought to court the Saudis as soon as he entered the Oval Office. Trump sent his director of central intelligence, Mike Pompeo, to Riyadh on his first foreign policy trip as director with a message for the royal family that the new administration wanted to "reset" American-Saudi relations on a positive basis. Pompeo gave Crown Prince Muhammad bin Nayef a medal, named after former CIA director George Tenet, for fighting terrorism; it was a symbol of American respect for the prince's work on counterterrorism. Deputy Crown Prince Muhammad bin Salman came to Washington in March 2017 to see the president and other senior officials. Trump then made the Kingdom his first foreign stop in May. The visit was widely hailed in the Kingdom as a positive signal that the two states were back on track. There were the compulsory allusions to President Franklin Roosevelt and King Ibn Saud on the USS *Quincy* in 1943, yet beneath the public signs of amity longstanding differences and tensions remain in the relationship.

The relationship between the world's last absolute monarchy, Saudi Arabia, and the world's foremost democracy, the United States, has been troubled since its birth at the summit on the *Quincy*. Saudi kings and American presidents have little in common. They share no common cultural or historical past and have no shared political heritage or practices. Absolute monarchs running a theocracy have little sense of the complexities of modern elections or the checks and balances of a complex government with hundreds of lobby groups and competing political interests. Presidents, by contrast, have little experience in the complexities of Islamic jurisprudence and governance and few insights into the mechanics of an enormous royal family that jealously guards its secrets.

Yet Roosevelt and Ibn Saud had a successful meeting, which is why it is still lionized whenever Saudi kings and U.S. presidents meet. They struck the essential bargain that remains at the core of the relationship more than seven decades later: American security guarantees for the Kingdom and Saudi guarantees of affordable oil for the world economy.

But this crucial initial meeting also came close to failure because of fundamental differences over the fate of Palestine. The president's efforts to convince the king to support the creation of a Jewish state, either in Palestine or in Libya, were completely rebuffed. No amount of presidential charm could change the king's abject rejection of the notion of Israel. If Roosevelt had continued to make the case for a Zionist state, the summit would have collapsed. The president was smart to let it go.

For the next twenty-five years Saudi Arabia was a backwater for American presidents. None visited the Kingdom even though two visited Iran (Eisenhower and Nixon). Secretary of State John Foster Dulles was the only secretary of state to visit the Kingdom during this period, and no secretary of defense did so. While American oil companies expanded their critical role in the development of the Saudi petroleum business and got support from their government for doing so, the White House, from 1945 to 1973, saw Saudi Arabia as a backward and remote corner of the world, nowhere near the top of its priority list. The United States military presence in the Kingdom at Dhahran air base was allowed to end in 1962 without much attention or fanfare.

John F. Kennedy did have an important engagement with then Crown Prince Faisal in 1962. Their meeting produced a rare presidential intervention in Saudi domestic politics and society, when Faisal agreed to several reforms at home, most notably the abolition of slavery. Kennedy succeeded in persuading Faisal to take these steps because the Kingdom was under severe threat. The Soviet and Egyptian intervention in Yemen threatened the Kingdom with a dangerous hostile neighbor in its backyard, while the internal situation in the Kingdom was imperiled due to King Saud's weak and inconsistent leadership.

The Arab world was in the midst of a revolutionary upheaval as monarchs fell in Yemen and Iraq.

Kennedy's manner was also deliberate and low-key. He did not castigate the Kingdom in public. While he believed it was badly out of date and archaic, he kept those views to himself. With Faisal he provided security assurances in public and raised his concerns about the internal health of the Kingdom only in private in the residential quarters of the White House, far from the media and even most of his own administration.

Faisal was also receptive to the advice. He understood the kingdom needed to reform. He wanted to remove his brother from the throne and take the necessary actions to save the monarchy and preserve the House of Saud.

Kennedy's successors, Lyndon Johnson and Richard Nixon, left Saudi Arabia in the backwater. Johnson tilted American diplomacy in the Middle East decisively toward Israel in 1967. Nixon ignored the region when he came into office and kept ignoring it until 1973, with the exception of Iran. Nixon made the Iranian shah America's preferred ally in the region and provided him with an enormous quantity of American arms.

King Faisal's decision to impose an oil embargo against America in November 1973, following the Arab-Israeli war, fundamentally changed the arc of Saudi-American relations. The king did more damage to the American economy than the Soviet Union was able to do during the entire Cold War. The recession that followed the oil embargo and the rise in oil prices, coupled with severe inflation, put millions of Americans out of work. The Saudis had finally gotten the attention of the White House. First, Secretary of State Henry Kissinger and then President Nixon traveled to Riyadh to implore the king to lift the embargo and to put the Saudi-American relationship back on track.

The king insisted the relationship could only get back on track if the president made securing a comprehensive Arab-Israeli peace a priority. Faisal also insisted that East Jerusalem be returned to Arab sovereignty. He grew increasingly disillusioned with Secretary Kissinger and Presidents Nixon and Gerald Ford. Had he not been assassinated in 1975, another oil embargo would have been likely.

The partnership between kings and presidents has endured despite other near-death moments since 1973. In 1978 and 1979, the conclusion of a separate Egyptian-Israeli peace deal and the collapse of the monarchy in Iran deeply shook Saudi confidence in American diplomacy and security guarantees. King Khalid, who succeeded Faisal, believed President Jimmy Carter was ignoring Saudi concerns about Jerusalem and Palestine while doing nothing to keep a fellow monarch, the shah of Iran, on his throne. Only the Soviet invasion of Afghanistan in 1979 and the start of the Iran-Iraq war in 1980 salvaged the relationship.

President Ronald Reagan's flirtation with Iran in 1986 produced another crisis in the relationship. After promising American support for Iraq and de-livering critical intelligence to save Saddam Hussein from defeat, the president engaged in one of the most foolish and dangerous foreign policy adventures in American history, one that could have led to his impeachment. Reagan man-aged to restore a measure of Saudi confidence in America by engaging in an undeclared naval war with Iran in 1988; this step helped persuade Ayatollah Ruhollah Khomeini to end the long war with Iraq. King Fahd played a crucial behind-the-scenes role in persuading Saddam to accept a cease-fire and not seek total victory.

The 1990s were the golden age of Saudi-American relations. President George H. W. Bush's decision to send hundreds of thousands of American troops to defend the Kingdom in 1990 and then to liberate Kuwait in 1991 changed the arc of the relationship once again. The Saudis knew America had saved them from an Iraqi invasion and the partition of the Kingdom. Although the American military presence helped inspire jihadist radicalism inside the Kingdom, it was very popular among the top princes of the House of Saud royal family.

Bush's determination, after the Persian Gulf War, to pursue a comprehen-sive Arab-Israeli peace settlement through negotiations starting in Madrid further solidified Saudi confidence in American leadership. By making the first steps toward recognizing legitimate Palestinian aspirations, Bush prom-ised King Fahd that his concerns about addressing the root cause of the Arab-Israel problem were shared by the American president.

Bill Clinton took the peace process and the relationship with Saudi Arabia to new levels of cooperation during his administration. King Fahd, and then Crown Prince Abdallah, supported Clinton's hands-on approach to Middle East peacemaking. The Saudis, especially Prince Bandar, became important behind-the-scenes players in encouraging Syria and the Palestinians to reach

accommodation with Israel. At the same time Saudi Arabia was a robust partner with America on a wide range of issues, including the containment of Iraq
and Iran; maintaining peace and stability in South Asia; resolving the issue of
Libya's role in the 1988 bombing of Pan Am flight 103; and keeping world oil
prices low.

But the disastrous failures of Clinton's peace diplomacy in 2000 left a
damaging mark on Saudi-American relations. The relationship had another
near-death moment in 2001 when Crown Prince Abdallah refused President
George W. Bush's repeated requests for a summit. At the peak of the crisis, Abdallah threatened a fundamental break in the relationship and even hinted at
using the oil weapon again. Only Bush's promise to support a two-state solution
to the Israeli-Palestinian conflict prevented a breakdown.

The terrorist attacks in the United States on September 11, 2001, posed another fundamental danger to the Saudi-American relationship. Many Americans blamed the Kingdom for playing some role in the attacks, either through
funding al Qaeda, actively conspiring in the plot, or gross negligence in fighting the terrorist group. Those concerns linger today and remain a source of
friction in the relationship.

President Barack Obama had his own near-death moment with King
Abdallah in 2011 as a result of the Arab Spring. Obama's support for regime
change in Egypt deeply shook Abdallah's confidence in the president's judgment and reliability. The crisis in Bahrain and the Saudi intervention on the
island immediately brought the danger home to the king. Obama backed off
from his support for reform in the region, and the crisis passed.

On the positive side, this list of crises in the relationship underscores its
fundamental importance and resiliency. Kings and presidents have surmounted
difficult moments and challenging times and reaffirmed in every case the importance and benefits of working with each other. Nixon resisted hawks who
wanted a military response to the oil embargo. Carter and Reagan worked
closely with King Fahd to fight Soviet aggression. Bush senior and Clinton
found common ground with Riyadh on a global agenda. Bush junior and Obama
defended the Kingdom from accusations of involvement in 9/11 and helped it
fight al Qaeda and the Islamic State at home. The importance of good ties with
the Saudi kings has become bipartisan common ground in Washington even
when many other foreign policy issues are hotly contested.

On the other side, the near-death moments in the partnership reflect some fundamental and deep-seated differences between kings and presidents that challenge the relationship and could endanger its survival. Despite its seven-plus decades, the relationship lacks deep roots and ballast. The two countries have shared interests but no shared values. Just as kings and presidents have little in common personally, the two countries have almost nothing in common, except, on occasion, common enemies.

In contrast, the United States and France, America's oldest ally, share a common commitment to democracy and the rule of law. They share a common history in the Western community of nations and a common faith. While their political institutions differ, their fundamental politics have many similarities. When their leaders meet and agree on common objectives or disagree on what to do, there is always a reservoir of deep understanding between the two nations to help keep temporary disputes from unraveling the long-term relationship.

The absence of similar common values and deep roots means the relationship between the United States and Saudi Arabia is a far more transactional one, based on overlapping, often temporary, interests. These interests can be compelling, like fighting the Soviet Union or Saddam's Iraq, but they are not likely to last when the immediate threat changes or evaporates.

One measure of the volatility of the relationship is the pace at which American ambassadors to Saudi Arabia are turned over. Since 1940, twenty-seven U.S. ambassadors or chargés have been accredited to the Kingdom. At first they resided in Cairo, then Jidda, and today Riyadh. On average they have spent about two-and-a-half years in the assignment. Only a handful (Herman Eilts, John West, and Wyche Fowler) spent more than three years. The turnover rate reflects the difficulty of making a strong personal connection with the princes, as well as the frequency of irritants in the dialogue. In contrast, Saudi Arabia has sent ten ambassadors to the United States.

The strongest advocates of close ties with Saudi Arabia are, of course, the oil companies, arms dealers, and financial interests that make so much of their money doing business with the Kingdom. This is a strong and powerful lobby. Faisal tried to use it in 1973 to get Nixon involved in the Arab-Israel conflict, but pro-Saudi business interests lacked the clout to get his attention. These interests can help sell the American Congress on arms sales to Saudi Arabia, but only if a president is inclined to fight for such sales over the frequent op-position of Israel and its powerful allies on Capitol Hill.

The United States is far less dependent on Saudi oil today than it was in 1973. But other countries still depend heavily on Saudi oil, including Japan, China, and much of Western Europe. Since the U.S. economy needs growth in those economies to prosper itself, the global dependence on Saudi oil makes the Kingdom as important as ever.

Three Stumbling Blocks

Three fundamental issues hamper the relationship between Saudi Arabia and the United States. On these issues kings and presidents have basic disagree-ments about core goals and objectives. Interest and mutual accommodation can overlap, but it is difficult to find them. The three issues—the Israel-Palestine conflict; the role of Wahhabi Islam in Saudi policy at home and abroad; and the pursuit of political reform in the Arab world—are likely to be disruptive factors in the relationship in the years ahead and will require cre-ative diplomacy to manage.

The question of whether Palestine should be the home of a Jewish state, which preoccupied Roosevelt and Ibn Saud in 1945, has now changed into the issue of how to create a Palestinian state that will live in peace with Israel. The change has been slow in coming and has deeply troubled the U.S.-Saudi partnership. In 1948, when President Harry Truman recognized Israel only minutes after it declared its independence, then Prince Faisal recommended to his father Ibn Saud that the Kingdom break diplomatic ties with Washington. Ibn Saud realized his poor desert state was too dependent on American secu-rity to do so, and he protested Truman's decision but took no action.

After the Arab-Israeli war in 1967, then King Faisal joined an oil embargo against the United States and United Kingdom to press Washington and London to force Israel to withdraw from the territories it had seized. The em-bargo was a failure. Six years later, after the 1973 war, Faisal imposed a much more damaging oil embargo and succeeded in compelling Richard Nixon to become a mediator in the region.

Three decades of American diplomacy followed, with repeated efforts to secure a just, lasting, and comprehensive resolution of the Arab-Israel question. Successive Saudi kings had doubts about America's commitment to a just solution for the Palestinians. King Khalid concluded President Carter had opted for a separate Egyptian-Israeli peace at Camp David in 1978, thus forsaking the Palestinians, and broke relations with Cairo. Egyptian-Saudi ties resumed only after Anwar Sadat was assassinated in 1981. King Fahd concluded President Reagan was dodging the issue in the 1980s, but their common interest in thwarting Soviet and Iranian threats became higher priorities than the peace process—until the first Palestinian uprising, or intifada, began in 1988.

George H. W. Bush and Bill Clinton devoted considerable political effort and their own direct involvements in the peace process for more than a decade. The Saudis backed the Madrid and Oslo processes behind the scenes. They undoubtedly could have done more and been more proactive, but their contribution was important in giving the processes the blessing of the wealthiest Arab state and the protector of the holy mosques.

When the Oslo process failed in 2000 and George W. Bush showed little or no interest in trying to revive it Abdallah was prepared to fundamentally shake up the relationship. Events—the 9/11 attack in the United States and the al Qaeda insurgency in Saudi Arabia—intervened and the relationship staggered ahead.

This recitation of the ups-and-downs of the impact of peace diplomacy on the American-Saudi relationship illustrates two important points. First, the saliency of the Palestinian issue is, in part, a reflection of events in the broader Arab-Israel conflict. When there are wars, the Palestinian question, obviously, is more urgent, and when there is peace or a protracted stalemate, the issue recedes but never goes away.

The history also illustrates a second point that is more germane to the Saudi-American dialogue. Much depends on the passion of the sitting Saudi king about the Palestinian cause. Faisal was especially passionate about the importance of creating a Palestinian state and restoring Arab sovereignty in Jerusalem. For him, the issue became his top priority. King Abdallah was equally passionate in his own way. For much of the 1990s he believed American diplomacy was the means to secure his end. When that failed in 2000, he was deeply distressed and eventually made his own effort to produce a peace plan.

Kings Khalid and Fahd were also passionate about the Palestinian issue, but the record demonstrates they did not assign it the same overwhelming priority. It is too soon to make a judgment about King Salman.

An open question is whether the sons and grandsons of Ibn Saud will have the same commitment as their fathers and grandfather. It is likely they will. The Palestinian cause is deeply popular in Saudi society, especially within the clerical establishment. The House of Saud has made creating a Palestinian state, with Jerusalem as its capital, a signature policy since the 1960s. Generational change is unlikely to alter that fundamental posture.

It is also important to note that, despite profound differences over the question of Palestine and Jerusalem, the Kingdom has been prepared to collude, quietly, with Israel against common foes since at least the 1960s. Faisal accepted Israeli arms aid to the Yemeni royalists because it helped weaken Egypt's Nasser. The convergence of interests was temporary, however, and never compromised the Saudi position on Palestine or Jerusalem.

Behind the scenes there is, also, private cooperation today on some security issues. Discreet sales of Israeli high-technology counterterrorism equipment via third parties have been reported.[4] The Saudis and Israelis have overlapping interests in the containment of revolutionary Iran. There is circumspect cooperation, or at least indirect collaboration, in pressing Washington to do more to confront and contain Iran and its Shia allies, Hezbollah and the Houthis. Israeli officials are quick to make these connections and speak openly about them. Saudis are much less eager.

Today, Saudi Arabia is more willing than ever before to allow a handful of its citizens to interact with Israelis in public. A few Saudis have visited Israel (not government officials), always also traveling to the Palestinian Authority in Ramallah. The Saudi government has publicly disowned these Saudi visitors to Israel, but taken no serious action against them.[5] A handful of Saudis have appeared alongside Israelis at think tanks, Prince Turki being the most prominent. He always stresses at such meetings that Israel should accept the Arab peace plan developed by Abdallah and withdraw from the West Bank and East Jerusalem. He also makes clear that there will be no recognition of

Israel and no normalization of relations with Israel until there is a full and just peace.

For American presidents it is vital to understand the centrality of the Palestinian issue in Saudi national security policy. A vibrant and effective peace process will help cement a strong relationship between king and president; a stalled or exhausted process will damage their connection. The Saudis emphasized the Palestinian issue in their public statements about Trump's meeting with Prince Muhammad bin Salman. Trump has promised he will seek a deal.

The best approach for America to take is to pursue a peace agreement between Israel and the Palestinians, with the endorsement of Saudi Arabia and the rest of the Arab world when a deal is made. Of course, history shows that success in this arena is very difficult to achieve and, therefore, unlikely. Nonetheless, working toward such a deal is the right course of action.

The second major disruptive issue in U.S.-Saudi relations is more complex and less susceptible to direct diplomacy. Saudi Arabia has a unique connection with a unique form of Islam. The Kingdom is founded on the alliance between the House of Saud and the House of al Shaykh, the descendants of Muhammad Ibn 'Abd al Wahhab. This alliance is at the center of what makes Saudi Arabia the special country it is: an absolute monarchy combined with a strongly conservative theocracy.

This alliance between the royal family and the clerical establishment has evolved over the decades. The kings have tended to push the process to ensure the survival of the state. Ibn Saud was ready to work with the United Kingdom and then the United States, two foreign Christian powers, which his predecessors would have regarded as the epitome of evil and just targets for jihad. He accepted borders for his state, something the first Saudi state in the eighteenth century would never had accepted, even from a fellow Muslim state, the Ottoman Empire. King Faisal introduced reforms, such as female education and the abolition of slavery, that were questioned by many clerics. He was assassinated for introducing television. Fahd and Abdallah were both reformers in their own ways. So the Saudi family has successfully nudged the al Shaykh establishment into a more tolerant and modern world.

But there are limits to how far and how fast change can be made, and every Saudi king is acutely aware of them. The clerics are popular. For example, the eleven most popular Twitter handles in the Kingdom are those of conservative Wahhabi clerics.[6] Saudi Arabia cannot abandon Wahhabism and survive in its current form. Nor does the royal family want to abandon its faith. King Salman built the capital city to be a symbol of the alliance with the *ulema*. Salman has devoted his life to raising funds to promote the cause of the mujahedin from Afghanistan to Palestine.

The importance of Saudi religious belief is especially critical on the question of gender equality in the Kingdom. As one Saudi expert has written, the status and place of women "are what makes Saudi Arabia unique and different from other Arab and Muslim countries."[7] The Saudi Wahhabi interpretation of Islam is founded in a large corpus of religious legal findings. An estimated 30,000 fatwas or religious decrees have been blessed by the clerics in the last half-century to regulate every aspect of female life in the Kingdom and cement its gender policies.[8] Women live segregated from the public space for the most part, and they wear black while men wear white.

Some change has occurred for Saudi women. King Abdallah promised they could vote in the municipal elections, and King Salman lived up to that promise in 2015. Women ran for office and some of them won. More women are studying in university than ever before. But very few women can aspire to jobs in the workforce, and the rate of polygamy in the Kingdom has actually gone up since the oil boom of the 1970s.[9] According to a Saudi study, over half a million Saudi men have more than one wife.[10]

The status of Saudi women is a unique phenomenon in the Muslim world. Even its neighbor Qatar, which is also a Wahhabi state, allows Qatari women to drive and provides employment for many women in public service. Saudi women live sedentary lives and spend little time outside the home. As a consequence 80 percent have a vitamin D deficiency.[11] The Saudi treatment of women is also a serious barrier to American-Saudi relations and is likely to become an even more significant complication as gender politics change in America much faster than in the Kingdom.

Saudi religious beliefs also play a role in the issue of terrorism. There is no question that Saudi Arabia is a target of Islamic radical jihadist groups like al Qaeda and the Islamic State. Saudi Arabia has been, for over a decade, a crucial partner with America in the battle against the global jihadist network of terrorist groups. In 2010 the Saudis provided critical intelligence information that foiled an al Qaeda plot to blow up a commercial delivery aircraft over Chicago. The Saudi deep state that fights any dissent at home is effective in fighting terrorism, as well. Former crown prince Muhammad bin Nayef is the epitome of the deep state and its counterterrorism successes.

But there is also no question that the lack of tolerance inherent in the Saudi Islamic faith, especially in its severe attitude toward the Shia, has played a role in the development of the extreme views of Osama bin Laden and Abu Bakr al Baghdadi. The extremist ideology and narrative of al Qaedism has a connection to some of the extremes of Wahhabism. As one senior counterterrorist expert has noted, both al Qaeda and the Islamic State are "rooted in the hate-filled religious doctrine, curriculum material and money that Saudi Arabia pumped out to the wider Muslim world to counter its Shia rival, Iran."[12]

John Brennan, President Obama's Saudi expert, characterizes the issue this way: The Saudi intelligence services "are really very close partners with us. But . . . the Saudi government and leadership today have inherited a history whereby individuals have embraced a rather fundamentalist extremism in their version of the Islamic faith." The former CIA director argues that "these very fundamentalist realms of Saudi supported organizations fully exploited them as a spring board for militancy, extremism and terrorism."[13]

The challenges posed by Saudi Arabia's unique vision of Islam for the American partnership with the Kingdom are complex and have changed over time. When Saudi Arabia was a backwater, these problems could easily be ignored. The challenges also could largely be ignored during the Cold war, when Saudi Arabia and America were allies against the Soviet Union. It is much more difficult to do so when the enemy consists of al Qaeda and other extremists who have based some of their core ideology on the official Saudi belief system that is enforced by the Kingdom's clerics.

American presidents will have to deal with these complexities in the years ahead. Obama famously said the U.S.-Saudi relationship is "complicated," which, of course, is an understatement. Differences over gender are bound to become an increasing part of any conversation between kings and presidents in the future. Differences over the causes of violent sectarian tension are becoming more apparent in the region. The Kingdom remains xenophobic in many ways, resistant to opening up to outsiders except those with special skills, and even then resists bringing them into closed zones. The Holy Cities remain closed to the vast majority of Americans who work in the Kingdom (and 99 percent of Americans in general) simply because they are for Muslims alone. The most experienced Saudi experts in the U.S. government have never visited the two cities of greatest historical and societal importance in Saudi Arabia. That is a unique aspect of a very complicated bilateral relationship.

All these issues are for diplomats and security experts. They go well beyond the standard comfort zone for most diplomats, generals, and spymasters when engaging with their counterparts. Kings and presidents will need more than a phone conversation or a few hours in the Oval Office or the Royal Palace to cope with the complexity of these matters. As Brennan puts it, "There has been explosive growth in Saudi Arabia in terms of all the trappings of modernization but yet the environment, the culture, the society and the religious traditions have not yet adapted to the twenty-first century world" that Americans live in.[14]

The third area of disharmony is newer in many ways than the long-term differences over Israel and Wahhabism. In the last decade it has become clear to many Americans and also to many Arabs that the Arab world needs fundamental political and social reforms. The revolutionary explosions that shook the Arab world in 2011, in what was called the Arab Spring, embodied the concern that the status quo in Arabia is unsustainable. Except for Tunisia, the revolutions failed, ending either in a return to autocracy or in civil war and failed states.

Saudi Arabia was the leading player in the counterrevolution. As we have seen, it sent its own troops into Bahrain to prop up a Sunni monarchy against the wishes of the Shia-majority population. They are still there. In Egypt, the Saudis helped engineer a military coup that removed a democratically elected government. They have spent billions since to keep the military in power. In Yemen they tried to keep the old regime in power but with a new leader, swapping out Ali Abdallah Saleh. As usual Yemen proved to be more difficult, and a bloody and lingering civil war followed.

At home King Abdallah spent over $100 billion to buy off potential dissent. There is no doubt that he feared the revolutionary contagion could come to the Kingdom itself. Muhammad bin Nayef's deep state has gotten larger since 2011 to ensure order and stifle any dissent. The Ministry of the Interior, in 2017, numbers close to 1 million employees.

The Kingdom does have plans for large-scale economic reforms. Muhammad bin Salman, while serving as deputy crown prince, commissioned a series of task forces to review how to reduce and even eliminate the Kingdom's dependence on oil income. The result is a plan called Saudi Vision 2030. Some of its proposals are highly visionary in the Saudi context; for example, opening up a small portion of Aramco to outside stock ownership. Others are very smart moves to better utilize existing resources, such as encouraging more religious tourism to the holy cities year-round so that the hotels and other accommodations for hajj tourists are filled more than just once a year.

Saudi Vision 2030 is only the latest in a long series of projects by the Saudi leadership to reduce a near-total dependence on oil that dates from the 1970s. None of these ideas has had any appreciable impact on reducing the government's dependence on oil income. Various schemes have also tried to encourage more Saudi participation in the labor market, which would both give more Saudis jobs and keep their wages in the Kingdom, rather than relying so heavily on foreign workers who send much of their income home to their families. This, too, has been a failure, and foreign workers today number almost 10 million, or one for every two Saudis.

Important as it could be, Saudi Vision 2030 is only an economic reform package and has no political dimension. It provides no promise of opening up the opaque political process or giving non-royals any role in decisionmaking. The plan also makes no provision for giving rights to women, including the right to drive. At a seminar at the Brookings Institution, one of the drafters of Saudi Vision 2030 said allowing women to drive was not on the agenda. Then King Salman issued a decree announcing women will be allowed to get drivers licenses after June 2018.

Inevitably the Saudi determination to maintain the old order in the Arab world will lead to more unrest, not less. The reasons the Arab world exploded into revolution in 2011 have not gone away or been resolved. Rather they have been repressed and stifled more than ever. Many Arabs may well be horrified with the results of the Arab Spring in Syria and Libya, for example, but they also do not want a return to the harsh dictatorships of Assad and Muammar Qadhafi.

Superficially, then, it appears Saudi Arabia is a force for order in the region, one that is trying to prevent chaos and disorder. But in the long run, by trying to maintain an unsustainable order enforced by a police state, the Kingdom may, in fact, be a force for chaos. If there is no movement toward political reform, opening up the political process and reining in the deep state, then another revolutionary tidal wave is all but inevitable and is likely to be more violent and disruptive.

Bahrain and Yemen are good examples. The Saudi military intervention in Bahrain in 2011 saved the Sunni monarchy from collapse, or at least from having to enact major reforms. But the Shia majority are even more angry today at the Khalifas and the Saudis than ever before. The Shia are becoming more radicalized, not less. Iran has more opportunity to meddle because more and more Bahraini Shia are desperate for reform. In Yemen the war has brought huge suffering for the majority Zaydi Shia population, with mass starvation caused by the Saudi blockade and many deaths from the Saudi bombing campaign. Whatever the eventual outcome of the war, a generation of Yemenis are certain to hate the Kingdom and want to seek revenge.

American presidents have generally preferred order in the Middle East to political reform. The Eisenhower Doctrine promised American support for regimes that resisted Nasser's call for revolution. Successive American presidents, both Democrats and Republicans, have backed military strongmen like Sadat and Mubarak and absolute monarchs like the Saudis and the Gulf shaykhdoms. Only Kennedy tried to encourage reform in the Kingdom, because he recognized that without change and reform the House of Saud would probably be swept aside like the monarchies of Iraq and Yemen. Trump already has expressed enthusiastic support for autocratic regimes, a major reason the Saudis are enthusiastic about his presidency.

A better approach would be for the president to treat Saudi Arabia as the United States has treated autocratic regimes in the past. In the 1980s, we did arms control deals and managed conflicts with the Soviet Union while also pressing our human rights agenda and meeting with dissidents. We helped give dissidents a platform to express their dissent. We have continued doing the same with Russia and China, engaging with the dictators in Moscow and Beijing on issues of mutual interest while also promoting the cause of liberty and freedom.

Promoting reform and change is in our national interest. In the long run it is also in the Saudis' interest. We should not avert our attention from the brutality of the Saudi deep state, nor should we avoid commenting on the gender inequality in the Kingdom or its fierce sectarian approach to the Shia minority. As *The Economist* wisely commented when Barack Obama visited the Kingdom after Abdallah's death, "Western leaders should maintain the ties but ditch the sycophancy. Their friendship should be more conditional on reform—specifically the taming of Saudi Arabia's savage religious judiciary."[15]

The Saudi leadership of counterrevolution in the Arab world is bound to cause tension over time between their kings and American presidents. Managing that tension will be increasingly difficult, especially if some Arab states do find a way to progress toward more democratic governments and open their political space to allow greater freedom.

The American-Saudi relationship, which has always been troubled, is likely to face more challenges in the years ahead. Presidents and kings will see more near-death moments in the partnership, not less.

Will the Kingdom Survive?

All of this raises one more question. How stable is the Kingdom itself? The best answer to that question was provided by King Abdallah in 2011. When the Arab Spring began he rushed home from vacation in Morocco and spent more than $130 billion to prevent an uprising in the Kingdom. There had already been trouble that winter in Jidda because of severe flooding and a botched government response. Abdallah decided to take no chances and he spent a fortune to ensure the Arab Spring bypassed his country.

Many of the reasons Tunisia, Egypt, Yemen, Bahrain, and Syria experienced upheaval in 2011 are common to Saudi Arabia, as well. It is a closed police state that allows for little or no dissent. The press is controlled by the government. There is no systematic mechanism for the population to participate in the political process aside from the municipal councils. Nearly everything about the senior leadership is opaque.

While it has made many royals fabulously wealthy, the economy has failed to provide a good standard of living for many Saudis. One expert has concluded that 300,000 Saudis enter the job market every year, but there are far too few jobs for them; in 2015 private employers added only 49,000.[16] Unemployment among young Saudi males between twenty and twenty-four, according to the official figures, is 40 percent, and overall unemployment is 20 percent. The private sector employs nine foreign workers at minimal wages for every Saudi employed.[17] If women were to enter the job market in significant numbers, the jobs problem would only get worse.

Saudis do not pay taxes; rather they live on handouts from the government, which gets 90 percent of its revenues from oil. One of the most experienced Saudi watchers concludes that "handouts abound: for the military, a major employer of Saudis; for the religious establishment whose support legitimizes the al Saud; for education, healthcare and social welfare; and more recently for a minimum wage and unemployment payments. The result is at least three generations of Saudis addicted to benefits they see as a right."[18]

Abdallah was able to dispense $130 billion in 2011–12 because of high oil prices. Prices have declined considerably since then. The Kingdom had $600 billion in reserves when he died in 2015. Some $100 billion was spent in King Salman's first year on the throne as he handed out big bonuses to Saudis to welcome his reign and embarked on an expensive war in Yemen.[19]

Military spending is an enormous burden for the country. In 2015 the Stockholm International Peace Research Institute, a globally respected think tank that studies arms spending, reported that Saudi Arabia spent $87.2 billion on defense, making it the third-largest defense spender nation in the world, exceeded only by the United States and China. With only 20 million citizens, Saudi Arabia spent more on its military than Russia, the United Kingdom, India, or France.[20] Per capita defense spending is over $6,900 per year. Saudi Vision 2030 plans to cut the percentage of foreign purchases of military equipment for the military from 98 percent today to 50 percent by 2030, but few if any experts believe that is possible given the lack of a major industrial base in the Kingdom. The Yemen war only increases the burden on the defense budget. There are no public Saudi figures on the cost of the conflict, but a detailed study by a British think tank concluded they are substantial.[21]

Many in the younger generation recognize the current system is unsustainable. Half the population is under twenty-five. Crown Prince Muhammad bin Salman recognizes the system needs reform, which is why he is pushing Saudi Vision 2030 so aggressively.

Saudi Arabia also has significant regional tensions that could help produce discontent. Residents of the Hijaz and Asir have never fully been reconciled to

Nejdi dominance. The Eastern Province, with its Shia-majority population, is always a source of concern. Sixty percent of the employees of Aramco are Shia. If economic problems create discontent, it could take on regional dimensions as well.

The Achilles heel of any absolute monarchy is the succession issue. For sixty years the House of Saud resolved the question by transferring it among the sons of Ibn Saud. Each enjoyed complete legitimacy because he could trace his power directly back to the founder of the modern Saudi state. Only once did the system fail, when Ibn Saud's eldest son proved incompetent for the job and was ushered out of office, during the course of a decade, by his brother Faisal. This was a brilliant system that ensured family unity for the most part, provided legitimacy to each successor, and avoided the succession infighting that doomed the second Saudi state in the nineteenth century— but it would, inherently, run out of heirs. By removing two crown princes over the course of two years, first Muqrin, then Nayef, and then installing his own son as designated heir, King Salman seems to have resolved the succession question in favor of the next generation.

Muhammad bin Salman, who could rule as king for several decades, is the foremost proponent of change in the Kingdom today. His Saudi Vision 2030 is a stark commentary that the current system is unsustainable. But he is also the architect of the war in Yemen, a reckless and impulsive decision to go to war without an endgame in mind. If the Yemen war is his long-term legacy, then he will not be fit for the tough job of managing Saudi domestic and foreign policy.

The crown prince was also the prime advocate for cutting Saudi Arabia's land border with Qatar in July 2017 allegedly to punish Qatar for sponsoring terrorism. Bahrain and the United Arab Emirates joined the blockade, as did Egypt, effectively splintering the Gulf Cooperation Council. Iran and Turkey backed Qatar. The GCC has been a key supporter of American interests in the Gulf for decades and Qatar houses the largest American military base in the region.

All of this has enormous implications for America. Saudi Arabia has been America's partner in the Middle East since 1943. Every president since Franklin Roosevelt has understood the importance of building a bond with his counterpart, the king of Saudi Arabia. The relationship has often been strained, with moments of near-death, but its importance has never been in doubt.

With the region in more chaos than ever before, due to the failure of the
Arab Spring and the rise of extremist terrorists like al Qaeda and the Islamic
State, Saudi Arabia's importance has only gotten greater. America's other
Arab partners, like Egypt and Iraq, are weaker today than a decade ago. Other
partners, like Jordan and the United Arab Emirates, are valuable but lack the
clout of the Kingdom.

If there is regime change in Saudi Arabia—still very unlikely but not
impossible—who would take the place of the House of Saud? Al Qaeda and
other extreme groups have supporters in many Saudi cities despite Muhammad
bin Nayef's years of counterterrorism operations. They, undoubtedly, have
sympathizers in the clerical establishment at the grassroots level although not
in the top leadership. But the extremists have lost popular support over the last
decade by their acts of violence and are unlikely ever to gain power.

A more likely alternative might be the military. A succession crisis might
precipitate a move by the military to restore order. The Saudi Arabian National
Guard is deployed intentionally to forestall any attempt to overthrow the monarchy by rebels, whether they are Shia or Sunni extremists or the regular army.
National Guard commander Prince Mitab is King Abdallah's favorite son and
the only senior member of Abdallah's family to retain a powerful position of
authority after his death.

At the end of the day, it is important to remember that the House of Saud
is a survivor. Two previous Saudi states fell due to outside intervention and
internal family quarrels, and the family was forced into exile. But it came back.
It has since outlived its royal rivals, the Hashemites in Iraq and the Pahlavis in
Iran. It has outlived its secular rivals, Nasser in Egypt and Saddam in Iraq.
Since Faisal it has produced a succession of kings who have been effective rulers.
For presidents to come, the Saudi king will likely remain a crucial if difficult
partner.

In 2013 I wrote a memo for Barack Obama on the occasion of his reelection. It was titled, "Black Swan: Revolution in Riyadh" and was published by
the Brooking Institution.[22] I argued the Saudis are survivors and have considerable strengths, but I also suggested revolution is no longer unthinkable in the
Kingdom. I outlined all the arguments laid out in this chapter. I also suggested
there is little or nothing America can do to prevent a revolution in Saudi Arabia

if the circumstances make one likely. The short, four-page memo was translated into Arabic and posted on the Brookings website. The reaction in the Kingdom was astonishing. The Black Swan memo was read by tens of thousands of Saudis. It was among the most popular postings Brookings had ever posted on the Kingdom. Saudis know the relationship with America matters a great deal and that the future of the Kingdom is less certain today than at any time in the recent past. So should Americans, as well.

Appendix

THE OFFICIAL RECORD ON
SAUDI ARABIA AND 9/11

More than sixteen years after the terrorist attack of September 11, 2001, many Americans still believe Saudi Arabia had some role in the plot. Political leaders, survivors of the violence, relatives of those killed, and many average citizens suspect some Saudi hand in the attack on America. Fifteen of the nineteen terrorists were Saudis and so was the leader of al Qaeda, Osama bin Laden. But two American presidents, George Bush and Barack Obama, have both held that the Kingdom was not responsible for the attack or involved in the plot.

Part of the reason the suspicion has lingered so long despite two administrations' dismissal of the allegations involves a joint report prepared in late 2002 by the Senate and House Intelligence committees. One part of that report—which remained classified until July 2016—dealt with accusations of Saudi involvement in the attack. Because it had been kept secret, that section of the report attracted intense interest and speculation. What did the famous twenty-eight secret pages say about Saudi involvement? When it finally was released, the two opening sentences were damning: "While in the United States some of the September 11 hijackers were in contact with and received support or assistance from individuals who may be connected to the Saudi government. There is information primarily from FBI sources that at least two of these individuals were alleged by some to be Saudi intelligence officers."[1]

The 2002 report made clear, however, that its judgments were very preliminary and needed much more investigation.

The congressional report highlighted the role of three Saudis—Omar al Bayoumi, Osama Bassman, and Shaykh al Thumairy—who provided assistance to two of the al Qaeda terrorists when they first arrived in California in February 2000. The terrorists, Khalid al Mihdhar and Nawaf al Hazmi, were known to the CIA as al Qaeda operatives, but for reasons that have never been fully explained the CIA did not alert the FBI to their arrival in 2000. Al Thumairy is the most intriguing of the three Saudis because he was an accredited diplomat at the Saudi consulate in Los Angeles. He and the others allegedly provided assistance to the two terrorists as they looked for a place to stay in California. The Joint Inquiry also raised reports that Haifa bint Faisal, Prince Bandar's wife, had sent money to the wife of one of the Saudis allegedly in contact with the two terrorists.

The joint inquiry report made no connection between Saudi individuals and any of the other nineteen terrorists, nor does it claim any connection with Mihdhar and Hazmi once they left California as the plot matured. The report also found no connection to the hijackers' team captain, Muhammad al Atta, who arrived from Hamburg, Germany, later in 2000 to manage the plot. The report made clear that its conclusions as of late 2002 did not constitute a fully evaluated assessment of the information it does contain. That responsibility was given by the Joint Inquiry to later studies of the 9/11 plot.

The 911 Commission, established by the Congress in 2002, reviewed all the data available to the Joint Inquiry and concluded in its report in 2004 that there was no evidence to indicate the Saudi government or individual members of the Saudi government had any role in the plot. It dismissed the assertions of the Joint Inquiry as baseless. "The Commission staff found no evidence that the Saudi government as an institution or as individual senior officials knowingly support or supported al Qaida." The 911

Commission did find evidence of money going from individual Saudis to fund al Qaeda but no evidence that the Saudi government was involved in such financial support.[2]

The commission separately released a report on the funding of the plot, which looked at accusations about Haifa bint Faisal. It concluded, "despite persistent public speculation, there is no evidence that Princess Haifa bint Faisal provided any funds to the hijackers either directly or indirectly."[3]

In 2015 the FBI did an additional study of all the evidence available on the 9/11 plot. This included material found in bin Laden's hideout in Pakistan in 2011, additional interrogations of al Qaeda terrorists apprehended after 2004, and a further review of the material FBI sources had unearthed over the fifteen years since the first terrorists entered the United States. All additional allegations of Saudi involvement were reviewed, as well.

This FBI report was led by three outside experts on terrorism, chaired by Bruce Hoffman, a Georgetown University professor and one of the leading experts on al Qaeda in the United States. It validated the 911 Commission report, concluding that there is "no new information obtained since the 911 Commission 2004 Report that would change the 911 Commission's finding regarding responsibility for the 911 attacks."[4] The 2004 and 2015 reports are the most thorough assessments based on all the material available to the U.S. government, much of which is still classified, and they exonerate the Saudis. John Brennan, the CIA director in President Obama's second term, has said the earlier Joint Inquiry report is incorrect and that there is "no evidence to indicate that the Saudi government as an institution or senior Saudi officials individually had supported the 911 attacks."[5]

The existing evidence alleging Saudi involvement in the 9/11 plot, thus, has been reviewed carefully by the U.S. government more than once. The FBI keeps the investigation of the attacks open to evaluate any new material, but there is no smoking gun that points to any Saudi official.

Nonetheless, it is unlikely that the accusations will go away. Indeed, in the fall of 2016 Congress passed the Justice Against Sponsors of Terrorism Act, which authorizes court cases against the Kingdom and its officials for alleged involvement in 9/11. No other country has been given similar treatment. President Obama vetoed the act. The Congress overturned his veto, the only time

Congress overturned an Obama veto in his eight years as president. The Senate vote was 98 to 0. Donald Trump supported the bill. So the legal process will now have a chance to review what two independent commissions have already investigated. The families of victims of 9/11 have instigated a court proceeding in New York in 2017 to do just that. The case will almost certainly take years to resolve.

Notes

1. Martin Indyk, *Innocent Abroad: An Intimate Account of American Peace Diplomacy in the Middle East* (New York: Simon and Schuster, 2009), p. 57.

2. Ariel Ben Solomon, "Saudi King Blamed Mossad for 9/11," *Jerusalem Post*, August 4, 2015.

3. Robert W. Jordan, *Desert Diplomat: Inside Saudi Arabia Following 9/11* (Lincoln, Neb: Potomac Books, 2015), pp. 16, 53.

Chapter One: FDR and Ibn Saud, 1744 to 1953

1. FDR's 1945 travel to Yalta and Cairo is recounted in Susan Butler, *Roosevelt and Stalin: Portrait of a Partnership* (New York: Knopf, 2015), p. 342.

2. Rick Atkinson, *The Guns at Last Light: The War in Western Europe, 1944–1945* (New York: Henry Holt, 2103), pp. 498, 520–521.

3. Madawi Al-Rasheed, *A History of Saudi Arabia* (Cambridge University Press, 2002), p. 75; Alexei Vassiliev, *King Faisal: Personality, Faith and Times* (London: Saqi Books, 2015), p. 56.

4. Thomas W. Lippman, *Arabian Knight: Colonel Bill Eddy USMC and the Rise of American Power in the Middle East* (Vista, Calif.: Selwa Press, 2008), p. 126.

5. Aaron David Miller, *Search for Security: Saudi Arabian Oil and American Foreign Policy, 1939–1949* (University of North Carolina Press, 1980), pp. 122–24.

6. Sarah Yizraeli, *The Remaking of Saudi Arabia: The Struggle between King Saud and Crown Prince Faysal, 1953–1962* (Tel Aviv University Press, 1997), p. 151.

7. Alexei Vassiliev, *King Faisal of Saudi Arabia: Personality, Faith and Times* (London: Saqi Books, 2015), p. 156.

8. The first chargé was a career diplomat named James S. Moose Jr., who is most famous for saying "Arabic is a language that opens the door to an empty room." As late as 1937 the State Department had assessed American interests in the Arab world did not merit opening an embassy in the Kingdom; only in 1939 was the American consul in Egypt also given responsibility for representing America in the Saudi Arabia from his post in Cairo.

9. Stephen E. Ambrose, *Ike's Spies: Eisenhower and the Espionage Establishment* (New York: Anchor, 2012), pp. 21–22.

10. Michael Darlow and Barbara Bray, *Ibn Saud: The Desert Warrior Who Created the Kingdom of Saudi Arabia* (New York: Skyhorse, 2012), p. 433.

11. Butler, *Roosevelt, and Stalin*, p. 423.

12. Thomas Lippman, "The Day FDR Met Saudi Arabia's Ibn Saud," *The Link*, April-May 2005, p. 8

13. Darlow and Bray, *Ibn Saud*, p. 437.

14. Ibid., p. 437.

15. Lippman, "The Day FDR Met Saudi Arabia's Ibn Saud," p. 9.

16. Darlow and Bray, *Ibn Saud*, p. 439.

17. Ibid., p. 440.

18. William Eddy, "F.D.R. meets Ibn Saud" (Washington: America-Middle East Educational and Training Services, 1954), p. 12.

19. Lippman, *Arabian Knight*, p. 150.

20. Joseph A. Kechichian, *Faysal: Saudi Arabia's King for all Seasons* (University of Florida Press, 2008), p. 46.

21. Lippman, "The Day FDR Met Saudi Arabia's Ibn Saud," p. 9.

22. Darlow and Bray, *Ibn Saud*, pp. 441–42.

23. Lippman, "The Day FDR Met Saudi Arabia's Ibn Saud," p. 11.

24. Ibid., pp. 10–11.

25. Darlow and Bray, *Ibn Saud*, pp. 444–45.

26. Lippman, *Arabian Knight*, pp. 167, 180.

27. Darlow and Bray, *Ibn Saud*, pp. 32–35; David Commins, *The Wahhabi Mission and Saudi Arabia* (London: I.B. Tauris, 2013), p. 18.

28. Ian Timberlake, "Wahhabism Centre shows Conservatism Still Central to Saudi Soul," AFP, October 18, 2015.

29. Joseph A. Kechichian, *Succession in Saudi Arabia* (New York: Palgrave, 2001), p. 79.

30. Simon Ross Valentine, *Force and Fanaticism: Wahhabism in Saudi Arabia and Beyond* (London: Hurst, 2015), pp. 33–34.

31. Michael Crawford, *Ibn 'Abd al-Wahhab* (London: Oneworld, 2014), pp. 22–26.

32. Ibid., p. 22.

33. Ibid., pp. 29, 45, 60.

34. Ibid., p. 69.

35. Alexei Vassiliev, *The History of Saudi Arabia* (London: Saqi Books, 2000). Chapter 3 is the best history of the first Saudi state.

36. Crawford, *Ibn 'Abd al-Wahhab*, pp. 17, 108–12.

37. Joseph A. Kechichian, *Faysal: Saudi Arabia's King*, p. 12.

38. Darlow and Bray, *Ibn Saud*, p. 52.

39. Toby Matthiesen, *The Other Saudis: Shiism, Dissent and Sectarianism* (Cambridge University Press, 2015), p. 10.

40. Neil Partrick, "Saudi Arabia and Jordan," in *Saudi Arabian Foreign Policy: Conflict and Cooperation*, edited by Neil Partrick (London: I.B. Tauris, 2016), p. 166.

41. Aaron David Miller, *Search for Security: Saudi Arabian Oil and American Foreign Policy, 1939–1949* (University of North Carolina Press, 1980), p. 34.

42. Al-Rasheed, *A History of Saudi Arabia*, p. 52.

43. Miller, *Search for Security*, p. 37.

44. Darlow and Bray, *Ibn Saud*, p. 371.

45. Vassiliev, *King Faisal of Saudi Arabia*, p. 153.

46. Vassiliev, *The History of Saudi Arabia*, location 9077.

47. Department of State Bulletin of October 21, 1945, p. 623.

48. Miller, *Search for Security*, p. 200

49. Darlow and Bray, *Ibn Saud*, pp. 463–65.

Chapter Two: Faisal, Kennedy, Johnson, and Nixon, 1953 to 1975

1. Ishaan Haroor, "The Saudi Origins of Belgium's Islamist Threat," *Washington Post*, March 23, 2016.

2. Joseph A. Kechichian, *Faysal: Saudi Arabia's King for All Seasons* (University of Florida Press, 2008), p. 7.

3. Chams Eddine Zaougui, "Molenbeek, Belgium's Jihad Central," *New York Times*, November 19, 2015.

4. Haroor, "The Saudi Origins of Belgium's Islamist Threat."

5. Kechichian, *Faysal*, pp. 26–27.

6. Alexei Vassiliev, *King Faisal of Saudi Arabia: Personality, Faith and Times* (London: Saqi Books, 2015), p. 60.

7. Kechichian, *Faysal*, p. 29.

8. Ibid., pp. 32–36.

9. Madawi Al-Rasheed, *A History of Saudi Arabia* (Cambridge University Press, 2002), pp. 76, 107.

10. Kechichian, *Faysal*, p. 62.

11. Sarah Yizraeli, *The Remaking of Saudi Arabia* (Tel Aviv: Moshe Dayan Center, 1998), pp. 55–56.

12. Kechichian, *Faysal*, pp. 64–65.

13. Yizraeli, *The Remaking of Saudi Arabia*, p. 68

14. Percy Cradock, *Know Your Enemy: How the Joint Intelligence Committee Saw the World* (London: John Murray, 2002), p. 206.

15. Kechichian, *Faysal*, p. 70.

16. John F. Kennedy, "Imperialism—The Enemy of Freedom," July 2, 1957, can be found on the JFK Presidential Library website.

17. Warren Bass, *Support Any Friend: Kennedy's Middle East and the Making of the U.S.-Israel Alliance* (Oxford University Press, 2003), p. 4.

18. Harold Macmillan, *At the End of the Day, 1961–1963* (London: Harper and Row, 1973), p. 266.

19. Ibid., p. 276.

20. The CIA declassified hundreds of its daily reports to the White House in the 1960s in 2015. At first these were called Presidential Intelligence Checklists (PIC); later they became the President's Daily Brief (PDB). The PDB is the most highly classified product of the CIA. The declassified PICs and PDBs are available on the CIA website in its Electronic Reading Room and can be found by the date of issue.

21. PIC, October 6, 1962.

22. PIC, October 16, 1962.

23. Jesse Ferris, *Nasser's Gamble: How Intervention in Yemen Caused the Six-Day War and the Decline of Egyptian Power* (Princeton University Press, 2013), pp. 84–95.

24. Ibid., pp. 97–98.

25. Bass, *Support Any Friend*, p. 108.

26. Nigel Ashton, *King Hussein of Jordan: A Political Life* (Yale University Press, 2009), p. 92.

27. Bass, *Support Any Friend*, p. 63.

28. Ibid., p. 104.

29. Ibid., p. 104.

30. Kechichian, *Faysal*, p. 80.

31. Ibid., p. 80.

32. Vassiliev, *King Faisal of Saudi Arabia*, p. 236.

33. Ibid., p. 238.

34. PIC, October 19, 1962.

35. Daniel Yergin, *The Prize: The Epic Quest for Oil, Money and Power* (New York: Simon and Schuster, 1991), pp. 639–40.

36. Kechichian, *Faysal*, pp. 113–14.

37. Duff Hart-Davis, *The War That Never Was: The True Story of the Men Who Fought Britain's Most Secret Battle* (London: Random House, 2011), p. 96. See also Ferris, *Nasser's Gamble*, p. 132.

38. Ronen Bergman, "The Officer Who Saw behind the Top Secret Curtain," *Ynet Magazine*, June 22, 2015.

39. Hart-Davis, *The War That Never Was*, pp. 135, 139, 156; Yossi Alpher, *Periphery: Israel's Search for Middle East Allies* (London: Rowman and Littlefield, 2015), pp. 37–38.

40. Hart-Davis, *The War That Never Was*, p. 221.

41. PIC, September 26, 1962.

42. Ferris, *Nasser's Gamble*, p. 117.

43. Bass, *Support Any Friend*, pp. 129–30

44. Kechichian, *Faysal*, p. 88.

45. Joseph A. Kechichian, *Succession in Saudi Arabia* (New York: Palgrave, 2001), p. 44.

46. Kechichian, *Faysal*, p. 77.

47. Ibid., p. 108.

48. Ashton, *King Hussein of Jordan*, p. 102.

49. Thomas Hegghammer, *Jihad in Saudi Arabia: Violence and Pan-Islamism since 1979* (Cambridge University Press, 2010), pp. 20–22.

50. Gerald Posner, *Secrets of the Kingdom* (New York: Random House, 2005), p. 170.

51. Kechichian, *Faysal*, p. 117.

52. Stephane Lacroix "Understanding Stability and Dissent in the Kingdom: The Double Edged Role of the Jama'at in Saudi Politics," in *Saudi Arabia in Transition*, edited by Bernard Haykal, Stephane Lacroix, and Thomas Hegghammer (Cambridge University Press, 2015), p. 169.

53. Office of the Historian, U.S. State Department, Foreign Relations of the United States, 1964–1968, Volume XXI, Near East Region, Arabian Peninsula, Document 278, Memorandum from the President's Special Assistant (Rostow) to President Johnson, June 18, 1966, p. 1.

54. Office of the Historian, FRUS, Document 275, Memorandum of Conversation, June 21, 1966, p. 1.

55. Office of the Historian, FRUS, Document 283, National Intelligence Estimate, The Role of Saudi Arabia, December 8, 1966, p. 1.

56. David Robarge, "Getting It Right: CIA Analysis of the 1967 Arab-Israeli War," Studies in Intelligence, *Journal of the American Intelligence Community* 49, no. 1, 2005.

57. Al-Rasheed, *A History of Saudi Arabia*, p. 129; Samir A. Mutawi, *Jordan in the 1967 War* (Cambridge, U.K.: Cambridge Middle East Library, 1987), p. 128. The Saudi brigade deployed in Ma'an, the city formerly part of the Hejaz that Ibn Saud had ceded to Jordan.

58. Kechichian, *Faysal*, p. 130.

59. Bryan R. Gibson, *Sold Out? US Foreign Policy, Iraq, the Kurds and the Cold War* (New York: Palgrave Macmillan, 2015), p. 106.

60. Ibid., p. 109.

61. Ibid., p. 153.

62. Office of the Historian, Department of State, Foreign Relations of the United States, 1969–1972 Volume XXIV, Middle East Region and Arabian Peninsula, Document 127, Telegram from the Consulate General in Dhahran to the Department of State, February 5, 1969, pp. 399–404.

63. Robert Dallek, *Nixon and Kissinger: Partners in Power* (New York: Harper Collins, 2007), pp. 524–25.

64. Kechichian, *Faysal*, p. 135.

65. Ibid., p. 138.

66. Daniel Yergin, *The Prize*, p. 597.

67. Mohamed Heikal, *The Road to Ramadan* (New York: Quadrangle, 1975), p. 268.

68. Anwar el Sadat, *In Search of Identity: An Autobiography* (New York: Harper, 1977), p. 152.

69. Yergin, *The Prize*, p. 613.

70. Kechichian, *Faysal*, pp. 137–38.

71. Yergin, *The Prize*, pp. 591–94.

72. Ibid., p. 614.

73. Vassiliev, *King Faisal of Saudi Arabia*, p. 398.

74. Ibid., p. 400.

75. Dallek, *Nixon and Kissinger*, pp. 556–58, 562; Kechichian, *Faysal*, p. 161.

76. Richard Nixon, "Remarks of the President and King Faysal Ibn Abdul Aziz of Saudi Arabia at a State Dinner in Jidda," June 14, 1974. Online by Gerhard Peters and John T. Woolley, The American Presidency Project.

77. Ibid.

78. Kechichian, *Faysal*, pp. 168–69.

79. Andrew Scott Cooper, *The Oil Kings: How the U.S, Iran and Saudi Arabia Changed the Balance of Power in the Middle East* (New York: Simon and Schuster, 2011), pp. 233–35.

80. Yergin, *The Prize*, pp. 638–39.

81. Kechichian, *Faysal*, pp. 192–95.

82. Yergin, *The Prize*, p. 638.

Chapter Three: Khalid and Carter, 1975 to 1982

1. Office of Regional and Political Analysis, Central Intelligence Agency, "Saudi Arabia: An Assessment," RP 77-100003, January 14, 1977, in Department of State, Foreign Relations of the United States, 1977–1980, Volume XVIII, Middle East Region: Arabian Peninsula (Washington: Department of State, 2015).

2. Report Prepared by the Ambassador to Saudi Arabia (West), Jidda, August 1977, Foreign Relations of the United States.

3. Andrew Scott Cooper, *The Oil Kings: How the U.S., Iran and Saudi Arabia Changed the Balance of Power in the Middle East* (New York: Simon and Schuster, 2011), pp. 361–62.

4. Jimmy Carter, *White House Diary* (New York: Farrar, Straus and Giroux, 2010), pp. 56–57.

5. Memorandum of Conversation, Riyadh, December 14, 1977, Subject: The Secretary's Meeting with Crown Prince Fahd, Foreign Relations of the United States.

6. Carter, *White House Diary*, p. 156.

7. Ibid., p. 160.

8. Telegram from the Embassy in Saudi Arabia to the Department of State, Subject: Secretary's Meeting with Crown Prince Fahd, Jidda, February 22, 1977, Foreign Relations of the United States, Volume XVIII.

9. William Simpson, *The Prince: The Secret Story of the World's Most Intriguing Royal, Prince Bandar bin Sultan* (New York: Harper Collins, 2006), p. 53.

10. Briefing Memorandum from the Assistant Secretary of State for Near Eastern and South Asian Affairs (Saunders) to Secretary of State Muskie, Washington, December 18, 1980, Foreign Relations of the United States, Volume XVIII.

11. Carter, *White House Diary*, p. 161.

12. Ibid., pp. 137, 254, 255, 257, 262.

13. Cooper, *The Oil Kings*, p. 275.

14. Intelligence Memorandum Prepared by the Central Intelligence Agency, "The Impact of Iran on Saudi Arabia: Security Concerns and Internal Reaction," RPM 79-10053, Washington, January 26, 1979, Foreign Relations of the United States, Volume XVIII.

15. Don Oberdorfor, "Frustration Marks Saudi Ties to U.S.," *Washington Post*, May 6, 1979.

16. Patrick Seale, *Asad: The Struggle for the Middle East* (London: I.B. Tauris & Co., 1988), p. 313.

17. Joseph A. Kechichian, *Succession in Saudi Arabia* (New York: Palgrave, 2001), pp. 54–55.

18. Memorandum from Gary Sick of the National Security Council Staff to the President's Assistant for National Security Affairs (Brzezinski), Subject: Cracks in Saudi Façade, Washington, December 22, 1978, Foreign Relations of the United States, Volume XVIII.

19. Cambridge Reports National Omnibus Survey, April 1980, conducted by Cambridge Reports. Available at the Roper Center at Cornell University website.

20. Summary of Conclusions of a Presidential Review Committee Meeting, Washington, April 27, 1979, Foreign Relations of the United States, Volume XVIII.

21. Thomas Hegghammer and Stéphane Lacroix, *The Meccan Rebellion: The Story of Juhayman al Utaybi Revisited* (Bristol, U.K.: Amal Press, 2011), p. 18.

22. Yaroslav Trofimov, *The Siege of Mecca: The Forgotten Uprising in Islam's Holiest Shrine and the Birth of al-Qaeda* (New York: Doubleday, 2007). On his sources, see also Thomas W. Lippman, "A Missing Link in Terror's Chain," *Washington Post*, October 21, 2007.

23. Ziauddin Sardar, *Mecca: The Sacred City* (New York: Bloomsbury, 2014), p. 326.

24. Hegghammer and Lacroix, *The Meccan Rebellion*, p. 18.

25. Sardar, *Mecca*, pp. 328–29.

26. Trofimov, *The Siege of Mecca*, p. 52.

27. Sardar, *Mecca*, p. 330.

28. Toby Matthiesen, *The Other Saudis: Shiism, Dissent and Sectarianism* (Cambridge University Press, 2015), pp. 104–07. Between seventeen and twenty-six Shia died in the crackdown in 1979 and ten SANG soldiers.

29. Trofimov, *The Siege of Mecca*, p. 151.

30. Ibid., pp. 191–92, 209.

31. Ibid., pp. 170–72.

32. Ibid., p. 225; Hegghammer and Lacroix, *The Meccan Rebellion*, pp. 20–21.

33. Trofimov, *The Siege of Mecca*, p. 227.

34. Ibid., pp. 91, 119.

35. Telegram from the Embassy in Saudi Arabia to the Department of State and Multiple Diplomatic and Consular Posts, Jidda, November 21, 1979, Subject: Occupation of the Grand Mosque, Mecca. Foreign Relations of the United States, Volume XVIII.

36. Trofimov, *The Siege of Mecca*, p. 96.

37. Ibid., p. 139.

38. National Foreign Assessment Center, Central Intelligence Agency "Saudi Arabia: The Mecca Incident in Perspective," An Intelligence Memorandum. Approved for release November 2006, p. 1. Also cited in Trofimov, *The Siege of Mecca*, p. 243.

39. National Foreign Assessment Center, CIA, "Saudi Arabia," p. 1.

40. Ibid., p. 1.

41. Madawi Al-Rasheed, *A History of Saudi Arabia* (Cambridge University Press, 2002), p. 11.

42. Sardar, *Mecca*, pp. 337–38.

43. Basharat Peer, "Mecca Goes Mega," *New York Times*, June 12, 2016.

44. Sardar, *Mecca*, p. 339.

45. "Mecca versus Las Vegas," *The Economist*, June 26, 2010.

46. Bruce Riedel, *What We Won: America's Secret War in Afghanistan, 1979–89* (Brookings Institution Press, 2014), pp. 21–23.

47. Shuja Nawaz, *Crossed Swords: Pakistan, Its Army and the Wars Within* (Oxford University Press, 2008), p. 372.

48. Memo from Brzezinski to Carter, "Reflections on Soviet Intervention in Afghanistan," December 26, 1979, National Security Archives. See also Husain Haqqani, *Magnificent Delusions: Pakistan, the United States, and an Epic History of Misunderstanding* (New York: Public Affairs, 2015), p. 245.

49. President Carter was generous in offering me access to his private diary from his years in the White House in 2014. Parts of his diary have been published and have been previously cited. This reference is from his unpublished diary, December 28, 1979, and January 4, 1980.

50. Dennis Kux, *Disenchanted Allies: The United States and Pakistan* (Johns Hopkins University Press, 2001), p. 252.

51. Robert Gates, *From the Shadows: The Ultimate Insiders Story of Five Presidents and How They Won the Cold War* (New York: Simon and Schuster, 1996), p. 146.

52. Charles G. Cogan, "Partners in Time: The CIA and Afghanistan since 1979," *World Policy Journal* 10, no. 2 (Summer 1993), p. 79; Author interview with Cogan, August 12, 2009.

53. Carter diary, December 28, 1979.

54. Carter diary, January 4, 1980.

55. Zbigniew Brzezinski, *Power and Principles: Memoirs of the National Security Adviser, 1977–1981* (New York: Farrar, Straus and Giroux, 1983), pp. 448–49; Author interview with Brzezinski, October 16, 2013.

56. Summary of Conclusions of a Special Coordination Committee Meeting, Washington, February 6, 1980, Foreign Relations of the United States, Volume XVIII.

57. Author interview with Brzezinski, October 16, 2013.

58. Carter diary, February 6, 1980.

59. Nawaz, *Crossed Swords*, p. 386.

60. President Jimmy Carter, "The State of the Union Address Delivered before a Joint Session of the Congress," January 23, 1980.

61. Peter Tomsen, *The Wars in Afghanistan: Messianic Terrorism, Tribal Conflicts, and the Failures of Great Powers* (New York Public Affairs, 2011), p. 205

62. Mohammad Yousaf and Mark Adkin, *The Bear Trap: Afghanistan's Untold Story* (London: Leo Cooper, 1991), p. 106.

63. Tomsen, *The Wars in Afghanistan*, p. 248. Tomsen's source is CIA officer Milton Bearden.

64. The Saudis also provided considerable private financial aid to other Islamic causes. For example, Saudi Arabian private funds fueled the development of the Palestinian Islamic movement Hamas. See Ze'ev Schiff and Ehud Ya'ari, *Intifada: The Palestinian Uprising   Israel's Third Front* (New York: Simon and Schuster, 1989), p. 225.

65. Scheuer, *Osama Bin Laden* (Oxford University Press, 2011), pp. 22–29.

66. Ibid., p. 49.

67. Ibid., p. 51.

68. Ibid., pp. 62–64.

69. Ibid., p. 65.

70. Tim Wells, *444 Days: The Hostages Remember* (San Diego: Harcourt Brace Jovanovich, 1985), pp. 327, 357.

71. "Interview with Dr. Charles Cogan, August 1997," Soldiers of God Cold War Interviews, National Security Archives, George Washington University, p. 2. See also James Blight and others, *Becoming Enemies: U.S.-Iran Relations and the Iran-Iraq War, 1979–1988* (Lanham: Maryland, Rowman and Littlefield, 2012), p. 66.

72. Brzezinski, *Power and Principles*, p. 451.

73. Gates, *From the Shadows*, pp. 130–31.

74. Director of Central Intelligence Stansfield Turner, Alert Memorandum for the National Security Council, Iran-Iraq Conflict, September 17, 1980. Approved for Release January 22, 2004.

75. Carter, *White House Diary*, p. 469.

76. Mohamed Heikal, *Illusions of Triumph: An Arab View of the Gulf War* (London: HarperCollins, 1993), p. 81.

77. Summary of Conclusions of a Special Coordination Committee Meeting, Washington September 27, 1980. Foreign Relations of the United States, Volume XVIII.

78. Matthiesen, *The Other Saudis*, pp. 117–18.

79. Letter from the Ambassador to Saudi Arabia (West) to President Carter, Jidda, June 3, 1980, with a Report Prepared by the Ambassador to Saudi Arabia, Foreign Relations of the United States, Volume XVIII.

Chapter Four: Fahd, Reagan, and Bush, 1982 to 1992

1. Craig Unger, *House of Bush, House of Saud* (New York: Scribner, 2004), p. 87.

2. "Royal Flush," *Forbes* Magazine, March 4, 2002.

3. Gerald Posner, *Secrets of the Kingdom* (New York: Random House, 2005), p. 75.

4. David B. Ottaway, *The King's Messenger: Prince Bandar bin Sultan and America's Tangled Relationship with Saudi Arabia* (New York: Walker, 2008), p. 51.

5. Ze'ev Schiff and Ehud Ya'ari, *Israel's Lebanon War* (New York: Simon and Shuster, 1984), pp. 68–69. See also Posner, *Secrets of the Kingdom*, p. 180.

6. Lawrence Joffe, "Shlomo Argov," *The Guardian*, February 24, 2003. The Iraqi assassin was Colonel Nawaf al Rosan.

7. Schiff and Ya'ari, *Israel's Lebanon War*, pp. 96–100.

8. William Simpson, *The Prince: The Secret Story of the World's Most Intriguing Royal* (New York: Harper Collins, 2006), pp. 97–99.

9. Nasser Ibrahim Rashid and Esber Ibrahim Shaheen, *King Fahd and Saudi Arabia's Great Evolution* (Joplin, Mo.: International Institute of Technology, 1987), pp. 140–41.

10. James Blight, Janet Lang, Hussein Banai, Malcolm Byrne, and John Tirman, *Becoming Enemies: U.S.-Iran Relations and the Iran-Iraq War, 1979–1988* (Plymouth: Rowman and Littlefield, 2012), p. 113.

11. Memorandum for Geoffrey Kemp, Senior Staff, National Security Council From Henry Rowen Chairman, National Intelligence Council, July 20, 1982, in Blight and others, *Becoming Enemies*, pp. 311–12.

12. Memorandum for the President, Subject: An Iranian Invasion of Iraq: Considerations for U.S. Policy, July 1982, in Blight and others, *Becoming Enemies*, pp. 310–11.

13. Blight and others, *Becoming Enemies*, pp. 114–15.

14. Giandomenico Picco, *Man without a Gun: One Diplomat's Secret Struggle to Free the Hostages, Fight Terrorism and End a War* (New York: Times Books, 1999), p. 61.

15. Steven R. Ward, *Immortal: A Military History of Iran and Its Armed Forces* (Georgetown University Press, 2009), pp. 255–59.

16. Rashid and Shaheen, *King Fahd and Saudi Arabia's Great Evolution*, p. 154.

17. Ibid., p. 158.

18. Robert Gates, *From the Shadows: The Ultimate Insider's Story of Five Presidents and How They Won the Cold War* (New York: Simon and Schuster, 1996), p. 321.

19. Ibid., p. 349.

20. Ottaway, *The King's Messenger*, p. 67.

21. "Saudi Arabia: Will a Row over a British Arms Deal Affect Saudi Politics?," *The Economist*, June 11, 2007.

22. Richard Halloran, "2 Iranian Fighters Reported Downed by Saudi Air Force," *New York Times*, June 6, 1984, p. 1.

23. Ottaway, *The King's Messenger*, pp. 69–70.

24. Khalid bin Sultan with Patrick Seale, *Desert Warrior* (New York: Harper Collins, 1995), pp. 138–42.

25. Ibid., p. 143.

26. Ottaway, *The King's Messenger*, pp. 71–72.

27. Ibid., pp. 73–74.

28. Khalid bin Sultan, *Desert Warrior*, p. 141.

29. Cable from CIA Deputy Director John McMahon to CIA Director William J. Casey on Providing Intelligence to Iran, January 25, 1986, in Blight and others, *Becoming Enemies*, pp. 320–21.

30. Blight and others, *Becoming Enemies*, p. xii. Malcolm Byrne, *Iran Contra: Reagan's Scandal and the Unchecked Abuse of Presidential Power* (University of Kansas Press, 2014) is by far the best study of the scandal and the investigations that followed it.

31. E-mail message, William A. Cockell to Colin L. Powell, "Iran-Iraq," January 21, 1987, in Blight and others, *Becoming Enemies*, p. 324.

32. Toby Matthiesen, *The Other Saudis: Shiism, Dissent and Sectarianism* (Cambridge University Press, 2015), pp. 120, 134–35.

33. Ibid., pp. 136–38.

34. Blight and others, *Becoming Enemies*, pp. 205–06. See also Picco, *Man without a Gun*, pp. 94–95.

35. Mohamed Heikal, *Illusions of Triumph: An Arab View of the Gulf War* (London: HarperCollins, 1992), p. 123.

36. Ibid., p. 161.

37. Ibid., pp. 162–64.

38. Ibid., pp. 214–15.

39. Ken Pollack, *The Threatening Storm: The Case for Invading Iraq* (New York: Random House, 2002), p. 34.

40. George H. W. Bush and Brent Scowcroft, *A World Transformed* (New York: Knopf, 1998), pp. 310–13.

41. Heikal, *Illusions of Triumph*, p. 244.

42. Khalid bin Sultan, *Desert Warrior*, p. 4.

43. Interview with John Nixon, March 22, 2017.

44. Colin Powell, *My American Journey* (New York: Ballantine Books, 1995), p. 450.

45. Bush and Scowcroft, *A World Transformed*, p. 322. See also Jon Meacham, *Destiny and Power: The American Odyssey of George Herbert Walker Bush* (New York: Random House, 2015), pp. 421–22.

46. Khalid bin Sultan, *Desert Warrior*, p, 9.

47. Simpson, *The Prince*, pp. 191, 195.

48. Ibid., p. 188. Bandar was given Secret Service protection in 1990 because of the fear Iraq might try to assassinate him. This meant he had unprecedented access to the White House and other government buildings. No other ambassador received this special status.

49. Pollack, *The Threatening Storm*, p. 36.

50. Heikal, *Illusions of Triumph*, pp. 255, 277.

51. Meacham, *Destiny and Power*, p. 425.

52. Khalid bin Sultan, *Desert Warrior*, pp. 18–20.

53. Powell, *My American Journey*, p. 452.

54. Bush and Scowcroft, *A World Transformed*, p. 335.

55. Harris Poll, January 1991, Roper Center for Public Opinion Research (https://ropercenter.cornell.edu, February 11, 2016).

56. Madawi Al-Rasheed, *A History of Saudi Arabia* (Cambridge University Press, 2002), p. 166.

57. Ibid., pp. 165–66.

58. Ibid., 169–71.

59. Michael Scheuer, *Osama bin Laden* (Oxford University Press, 2011), p. 51.

60. Bruce Riedel, *The Search for Al Qaeda: Its Leadership, Ideology and Future* (Brookings Institution Press, 2008), pp. 47–49.

61. Khalid bin Sultan, *Desert Warrior*, p. 315.

62. Ibid., p. 116.

63. Heikal, *Illusions of Triumph*, p. 322.

64. Khalid bin Sultan, *Desert Warrior*, p. 324.

65. Simpson, *The Prince*, p. 220.

66. Khalid bin Sultan, *Desert Warrior*, p. 260.

67. Bush and Scowcroft, *A World Transformed*, pp. 410–11.

68. Khalid bin Sultan, *Desert Warrior*, p. 318.

69. Ibid., p. 326.

70. George N. Lewis, Steve Fetter, and Lisbeth Gronlund, *Casualties and Damage from Scud Attacks in the 1991 Gulf War* (MIT Press, 1993), p. 4.

71. Bush and Scowcroft, *A World Transformed*, p. 455.

72. Khalid bin Sultan, *Desert Warrior*, p. 350.

73. Ibid., p. 426.

74. Powell, *My American Journey*, pp. 477, 516.

75. Simpson, *The Prince*, p. 252.

Chapter Five: Abdallah, Clinton, and Bush, 1993 to 2008

1. Robert M. Gates, *Duty: Memoirs of a Secretary at War* (New York: Knopf, 2014), p. 184. Gates had lunch with the Crown Prince in the same room several years later.

2. Thomas Hegghammer, *Jihad in Saudi Arabia: Violence and Pan-Islamism since 1979* (Cambridge University Press, 2010), p. 114.

3. Martin Indyk, *Innocent Abroad: An Intimate Account of American Peace Diplomacy in the Middle East* (New York: Simon and Schuster, 2009), pp. 66–68.

4. Ibid., p. 56.

5. Efraim Halevy, *Man in the Shadows. Inside the Middle East Crisis with the Man Who Led the Mossad* (New York: St. Martin's Press, 2006), p. 116.

6. Bill Clinton, *My Life* (New York: Alfred Knopf, 2004), p. 627.

7. Indyk, *Innocent Abroad*, p. 256.

8. Ibid., p. 271.

9. Clinton, *My Life*, p. 886.

10. Indyk, *Innocent Abroad*, p. 276.

11. Clinton, *My Life*, p. 938.

12. Kenneth Pollack, *The Threatening Storm: The Case of Invading Iraq* (New York: Random House, 2002), p. 70.

13. Indyk, *Innocent Abroad*, pp. 153–55.

14. Pollack, *The Threatening Storm*, p. 92.

15. Ibid., p. 93.

16. Clinton, *My Life*, p. 582; Indyk, *Innocent Abroad*, p. 56.

17. David B. Ottaway, *The King's Messenger: Prince Bandar bin Sultan and America's Tangled Relationship with Saudi Arabia* (New York: Walker, 2008), pp. 117–18.

18. Ibid., p. 122.

19. Ibid., p. 137.

20. Joshua Teitelbaum, *Holier than Thou: Saudi Arabia's Islamic Opposition* (Washington: Washington Institute for Near East Policy, 2000), p. 90.

21. Ottaway, *The King's Messenger*, p. 120.

22. Ibid., p. 128.

23. Barbara Slavin, "Officials: U.S. Outed Iranian Spies in 1997," *USA Today*, March 29, 2004.

24. Richard Clarke, *Against All Enemies: Inside America's War on Terrorism* (New York: Free Press, 2004), pp. 120–21, 129.

25. George Tenet, *At the Center of the Storm: My Years at the CIA* (New York: Harper Collins, 2007), p. 124.

26. Suzanne Maloney, *Iran's Political Economy since the Revolution* (Cambridge University Press, 2015), p. 274.

27. Indyk, *Innocent Abroad*, pp. 224–27. Malcolm Byrne, "Secret U.S. Overture to Iran in 1999 Broke Down over Terrorism Allegations," National Security Archive, May 30, 2010, has copies of Clinton's letter and Khatami's response.

28. Ottaway, *The King's Messenger*, p. 131.

29. *United States of America v. Ahmed al Mughassil et al.*, United States District Court, Eastern District of Virginia, Alexandria Division, Criminal No: 01-228-A, Department of Justice, June 2001.

30. Bruce Lawrence, ed., *Messages to the World: The Statements of Osama bin Laden* (London: Verso, 2005), p. 9.

31. Ibid., p. 4.

32. Ibid., pp. 24–25.

33. Clinton, *My Life*, pp. 797–98.

34. Ibid., p. 799.

35. Ibid., p. 803.

36. Michael Scheuer, *Osama Bin Laden* (Oxford University Press, 2011), p. 109.

37. Ottaway, *The King's Messenger*, pp. 134–35; Ted Gup, *The Book of Honor: Covert Lives and Classified Deaths at the CIA* (New York: Doubleday, 2000), pp. 308–17.

38. Elliott Abrams, *Tested by Zion: The Bush Administration and the Israeli-Palestinian Conflict* (Cambridge University Press, 2013), p. 8.

39. Condoleezza Rice, *No Higher Honor: A Memoir of My Years in Washington* (New York: Crown, 2011), p. 50.

40. Ibid., pp. 17, 55.

41. Abrams, *Tested by Zion*, p. 14.

42. Craig Unger, *House of Bush, House of Saud* (New York: Scribner, 2004), p. 189.

43. Ibid., pp. 218, 224.

44. Abrams, *Tested by Zion*, p. 14.

45. Ottaway, *The King's Messenger*, p. 151.

46. Abrams, *Tested by Zion*, p. 8.

47. Ottaway, *The King's Messenger*, p. 149.

48. Abrams, *Tested by Zion*, p. 15.

49. Marwan Muasher, *The Arab Center: The Promise of Moderation* (Yale University Press, 2008), p. 110.

50. Abrams, *Tested by Zion*, p. 15, and Muasher, *The Arab Center*, p. 110.

51. Ottaway, *The King's Messenger*, p. 154.

52. The wedding party was also attended by the ambassadors from Algeria, Bahrain, Egypt, Israel, Lebanon, and India as well as Bandar, Tenet, and numerous friends. There were so many security personnel that the restaurant had to provide a room for them to wait. See Bandar's comment in Ottaway, *The King's Messenger*, p. 154.

53. Muasher, *The Arab Center*, p. 110.

54. "U.S. President Bush's Speech to United Nations," CNN.com, November 10, 2001.

55. Muasher, *The Arab Center*, p. 117. The full text of the Arab peace plan is at pp. 281–82.

56. George W. Bush, *Decision Points* (New York: Crown, 2010), p. 402.

57. Rice, *No Higher Honor*, p. 141.

58. Bush, *Decision Points*, p. 403.

59. Interview with Gamal Helal, June 15, 2016.

60. Abrams, *Tested by Zion*, p. 36.

61. Rice, *No Higher Honor*, p. 144.

62. Bob Woodward, *Plan of Attack* (New York: Simon and Schuster, 2004), p. 116.

63. Ibid., p. 164.

64. Ottaway, *The King's Messenger*, p. 259.

65. Woodward, *Plan of Attack*, pp. 228–30.

66. Ibid., pp. 263–67.

67. Ibid., p. 268. Abdallah said, "Mum is the word."

68. Ibid., p. 348.

69. Ottaway, *The King's Messenger*, p. 215.

70. Ibid., p. 239.

71. Yaniv Barzilai, *102 Days of War: How Osama bin Laden, Al Qaeda, and the Taliban Survived 2001* (Washington: Potomac Books, 2013), p. 2.

72. Bruce Lawrence, ed., *Messages to the World: The Statements of Osama Bin Laden* (London: Verso, 2005), p. 180.

73. The sermon is titled "Among a Band of Knights" and is translated in Lawrence, *Messages to the World*, pp. 186–206.

74. Thomas Small and Jonathan Hacker, *Path of Blood: The Story of al Qaeda's War on the House of Saud* (New York: Overlook Press, 2014), p. 70.

75. Ibid., p. 91.

76. George Tenet, *At the Center of the Storm: My Years at the CIA* (New York: Harper Collins, 2007), p. 248.

77. Nayef, who became crown prince before his death, repeatedly accused the Mossad of manipulating al Qaeda and orchestrating the 9/11 attacks.

78. Small and Hacker, *Path of Blood*, p. 100.

79. Tenet, *At the Center of the Storm*, p. 250.

80. Small and Hacker, *Path of Blood*, p. 396.

81. Ibid., pp. 396–97.

82. Ibid., pp. 310–11.

83. Ibid., pp. 163, 376.

84. Ned Parker, "The Conflict in Iraq: Saudi Role in Insurgency," *Los Angeles Times*, July 15, 2007.

85. Thomas Hegghammer, "Saudi Militants in Iraq: Backgrounds and Recruitment Patterns," Norwegian Defense Research Establishment paper, February 5, 2007.

86. Lawrence, *Messages to the World*, pp. 245–75.

87. "Saudi Religious Leaders Support Sunni Insurgency in Iraq," *Global Issues Report*, January 24, 2007.

88. Small and Hacker, *Path of Blood*, p. 399.

89. Ottaway, *The King's Messenger*, pp. 240–41.

90. Ibid., pp. 263–68.

Chapter Six: Obama and Trump, Abdallah and Salman, 2009 to 2017

1. Martin Indyk, Michael O'Hanlon, and Kenneth Lieberthal, *Bending History: Barack Obama's Foreign Policy* (Brookings Institution Press, 2012), p. 122.

2. Mark Landler, *Alter Egos: Hillary Clinton, Barack Obama, and the Twilight Struggle over American Power* (New York: Random House, 2016), p. 140.

3. Indyk, O'Hanlon, and Lieberthal, *Bending History*, pp. 120–22.

4. "Remarks by the President in Cairo on a New Beginning," June 4, 2009, Cairo University, Cairo, Egypt, White House Office of the Press Secretary, June 4, 2009.

5. Christi Parsons and Mark Silva, "Obama Starts Mideast Tour in Saudi Arabia, 'Where Islam Began,'" *Los Angeles Times*, June 4, 2009, p. 1.

6. Leon Panetta, *Worthy Fights: A Memoir of Leadership in War and Peace* (New York: Penguin, 2014), p. 244.

7. Robert Gates, *Duty: Memoirs of a Secretary at War* (New York: Knopf, 2014), p. 18.

8. Ibid., p. 387.

9. Ibid., pp. 394–97.

10. Panetta, *Worthy Fights*, p. 301.

11. Gates, *Duty*, p. 504.

12. Indyk, O'Hanlon, and Lieberthal, *Bending History*, pp. 147–48.

13. Ibid., p. 150.

14. Hillary Clinton, *Hard Choices* (New York: Simon and Schuster, 2014), pp. 355–56.

15. Indyk, O'Hanlon, and Lieberthal, *Bending History*, p. 154.

16. Clinton, *Hard Choices*, p. 357.

17. Indyk, O'Hanlon, and Lieberthal, *Bending History*, pp. 157–58.

18. Clinton, *Hard Choices*, p. 358.

19. Indyk, O'Hanlon, and Lieberthal, *Bending History*, p. 155.

20. Interview with Ambassador James B. Smith, October 22, 2012.

21. Imab K. Harb, "Oman's Needed Adjustment during the Trump Presidency," Policy Analysis Research Papers, Arab Center Washington, January 18, 2017.

22. "Pakistani Soldiers on Gulf Duty Alert," Paris Intelligence Online, March 31, 2011 (www.intelligenceonline.com).

23. Bruce Riedel, "Saudi Arabia: The Elephant in the Living Room" in Kenneth Pollack and others, *The Arab Awakening: America and the Transformation of the Middle East* (Brookings Institution Press, 2011), p. 163.

24. Ibid.

25. Ibrahim Fraihat, *Unfinished Revolutions: Yemen, Libya, and Tunisia after the Arab Spring* (Yale University Press, 2016), p. 39.

26. Gates, *Duty*, pp. 534–35.

27. Clinton, *Hard Choices*, p. 359.

28. Landler, *Alter Egos*, p. 217.

29. Ivan Angelovski, Miranda Patrucic, and Lawrence Marzouk, "Revealed: The £1bn of Weapons Flowing from Europe to Middle East," *The Guardian*, July 27, 2016.

30. Mark Mazzetti and Ali Younes, "CIA Arms for Syrian Rebels Supplied Black Market, Officials Say," *New York Times*, June 20, 2016.

31. Charles Lister, *The Syrian Jihad: Al Qaeda, the Islamic State and the Evolution of an Insurgency* (London: Hurst, 2016), pp. 106, 111, 137.

32. Rod Norland, "Saudi Arabia Promises to Aid Egyptian Regime," *New York Times*, August 19, 2013.

33. "Saudi King Abdullah Visits Egypt's Sisi," Al Jazeera.com, June 20, 2014.

34. "Saudi King Stops in Cairo to Visit Egypt's Sisi," Reuters.com, June 20, 2014.

35. Chris Zambelis, "To Topple the Throne: Islamic State Sets its Sights on Saudi Arabia," *Terrorism Monitor*, March 6, 2015.

36. Lister, *The Syrian Jihad*, pp. 284–91.

37. Simon Henderso, "Who Will Be the Next King of Saudi Arabia?" Policy Watch 2035, Washington Institute for Near East Policy, Washington, D.C., February 12, 2013.

38. Karen Elliot House, "Uneasy Lies the Head That Wears a Crown: The House of Saud Confronts Its Challenges," Belfer Center, Harvard University, March 2016. See also David Ottaway, "Bandar Out: Mohammad bin Nayef Washington's New Favorite Saudi Prince," *Viewpoints* No. 70, Wilson Center, Washington, D.C., January 2015.

39. Madawi Al-Rasheed, "Who's Next in Line for Saudi Throne? Don't Ask," Al-Monitor, July 1, 2016.

40. David Ignatius, "A 30-Year-Old Saudi Prince Could Jump Start the Kingdom or Drive It off a Cliff," *Washington Post*, June 30, 2016.

41. "Saudi Arabia Warns Trump: Iran Wants to Gain Legitimacy by Reaching Mecca," Al Arabiya, March 16, 2017. See also "Signaling Saudi Arabia: Iranian Support to Yemen's al Houthis," *Critical Threats*, October 12, 2016.

42. Fraihat, *Unfinished Revolutions*, p. 50.

43. Hugh Miles, "Saudi Royal Call for Regime Change in Riyadh," *The Guardian*, September 28, 2015, and Bel Trew, "Saudi Royals Want to Overthrow King and Embrace Democracy," *The Times*, October 1, 2015.

44. David Kirkpatrick, "Saudi Arabia Said to Arrest Suspect in 1996 Khobar Towers Bombing," *New York Times*, August 26, 2015.

45. "King Salman Talks 'Unity' at Egypt's Parliament," Al-Arabiya, April 10, 2016.

46. Prince Turki al Faisal, "Mr. Obama, We Are Not 'Free Riders,'" *Arab News*, March 14, 2016.

47. John Brennan, "CIA's Strategy in the Face of Emerging Challenges: Remarks by CIA Director John O. Brennan," Brookings Institution, July 13, 2016.

48. Christopher M. Blanchard, *Saudi Arabia: Background and U.S. Relations* (Washington: Congressional Research Service, April 22, 2016), p. 39. The $111.624 billion figure is for deals between October 2010 and November 2015.

49. Office of the Press Secretary, "Joint Statement between the Kingdom of Saudi Arabia and the United States of America," White House, May 23, 2017.

50. "The Young and Brash Saudi Crown Prince," *New York Times*, June 23, 2017.

51. "A Shake up in Riyadh: The Tasks Facing the New Saudi Crown Prince," *The Economist*, June 22, 2017.

Chapter Seven: Whither Saudi Arabia

1. Martin Indyk, "The Iraq War Did Not Force Gadaffi's Hand," *Financial Times*, March 9, 2004.

2. Saeed Shafqat, "The Kargil Conflict's Impact on Pakistani Politics and Society," in *Asymmetric Warfare in South Asia: The Causes and Consequences of the Kargil Conflict*, edited by Peter R. Lavoy (Cambridge University Press, 2009), pp. 280–308.

3. Pervez Musharraf, *In the Line of Fire: A Memoir* (New York: Free Press, 2006), pp. 268–90.

4. Jonathan Ferziger and Peter Waldman, "How Do Israel's Tech Firms Do Business in Saudi Arabia? Very Quietly," *Bloomberg Businessweek*, February 2, 2017.

5. "Saudi Government Distances Itself from Israel Visit," *Dawn*, July 28, 2016.

6. Martin Chulov, "Saudi Crown Prince's Ascendancy Gives Hope of Reform—But It May Be Premature," *The Guardian*, June 22, 2017.

7. Madawi al Rashid, "Caught Between Religion and State: Women in Saudi Arabia," in *Saudi Arabia in Transition: Insights on Social, Political, Economic and Religious Change*, edited by Bernard Haykal, Thomas Hegghammer, and Stephane Lacroix (Cambridge University Press, 2015), p. 301.

8. Ibid., p. 295.

9. Ibid., p. 299.

10. "Over Half Million Saudi Men Engaged in Polygamy, Report Shows," *Al Arabiya English*, October 27, 2016.

11. James Dorsey, "Sport, Culture and Entertainment: Driving Tricky Saudi Change," *International Policy Digest*, April 10, 2017.

12. Daniel Benjamin, "Threat Assessment," *Time*, October 6, 2014.

13. John Brennan, "CIA's Strategy in the Face of Emerging Challenges: Remarks by John Brennan," Brookings Institution, Washington, July 13, 2016, p. 10 (www.brookings.edu/wp-content/uploads/2016/06/20160713_cia_brennan_transcript.pdf).

14. Ibid.

15. "An Unholy Pact: The Accession of King Salman in Saudi Arabia," *The Economist*, January 31, 2015.

16. "Looking Forward in Anger, Briefing Arab Youth," *The Economist*, August 6, 2016.

17. David Ottaway, "Saudi Arabia's Race against Time," Middle East Program Occasional Papers Series, Summer 2012, Woodrow Wilson Center, Washington, D.C., p. 5.

18. Karen Elliot House, "Uneasy Lies the Head That Wears a Crown: The House of Saud Confronts Its Challenges," Harvard Kennedy School Belfer Center, Senior Fellow paper, March 2016, p. 10.

19. Ibid., p. 13.

20. Ishaan Tharoor, "Saudi Arabia Passes Russia as World's Third Largest Military Spender," *Washington Post*, April 5, 2016.

21. "Quantifying a 'Taboo' Subject: Saudi Arabia Counts the Cost of the Yemen War," *Gulf States News* 40, no. 1,025 (November 3, 2016).

22. Bruce Riedel, "Revolution in Riyadh," in *Big Bets & Black Swans: A Presidential Briefing Book*, edited by Martin Indyk, Tanvi Madan, and Thomas Wrights (Brookings Institution Press, 2013), (www.brookings.edu/wp-content/uploads/2016/06/big -bets-and-black-swans-a-presidential-briefing-book-20.pdf).

Appendix

1. Report of the U.S. Senate Committee on Intelligence and U.S. House Permanent Select Committee on Intelligence, Joint Inquiry into Intelligence Community Activities Before and After the Terrorist Attacks of September 11, 2001, December 2002, p. 415.

2. Ibid.

3. National Commission on Terrorist Attacks upon the United States, Monograph on Terrorist Financing, Staff Report to the Commission, 2004.

4. Bruce Hoffman, Edwin Meese, and Timothy Roemer, The FBI: Protecting the Homeland in the 21st Century, 9/11 Review Commission, Report to the Director of the FBI, March 2015.

5. Full Transcript of Al Arabiya's Interview with CIA director John Brennan, *Al Arabiya*, June 12, 2016.

Selected Bibliography

Allen, Charles. *God's Terrorists: The Wahhabi Cult and the Hidden Roots of Modern Jihad*. London: Little, Brown, 2006.

Alpher, Yossi. *Periphery: Israel's Search for Middle East Allies*. London: Rowman and Littlefield, 2015.

Ashton, Nigel. *King Hussein of Jordan: A Political Life*. Yale University Press, 2008.

Atwan, Abdel Bari. *After Bin Laden: Al Qaeda, the Next Generation*. London: New Press, 2012.

Badeeb, Saeed. *The Saudi-Egyptian Conflict over North Yemen, 1962–1970*. Boulder, Colo.: Westview Press, 1986.

———. *Saudi-Iranian Relations, 1932–1982*. London: Centre for Arab and Iranian Studies, 1993.

Baer, Robert. *Sleeping with the Devil: How Washington Sold Our Soul for Saudi Crude*. New York: Three Rivers Press, 2003.

bin Sultan, Khalid, and Patrick Seale. *Desert Warrior: A Personal View of the Gulf War by the Joint Forces Commander*. New York: HarperCollins, 1995.

Bronson, Rachel. *Thicker than Oil: America's Uneasy Partnership with Saudi Arabia*. Oxford University Press, 2006.

Catherwood, Christopher. *Churchill's Folly: How Winston Churchill Created Modern Iraq*. New York: Basic Books, 2007.

Cigar, Norman. *Saudi Arabia and Nuclear Weapons*. London: Routledge, 2016.

Clarke, Richard. *Against All Enemies: Inside America's War on Terror*. London: Free Press, 2004.

Cole, Steve. *The Bin Ladens: An Arabian Family in the American Century*. New York: Penguin, 2008.

Commins, David. *The Wahhabi Mission and Saudi Arabia*. London: Taurus, 2006.

Cooper, Andrew Scott. *The Oil Kings: How the U.S., Iran and Saudi Arabia Changed the Balance of Power in the Middle East*. New York: Simon and Schuster, 2011.

Crawford, Michael. *Ibn 'Abd al-Wahhab*. London: Oneworld, 2014.

Darlow, Michael, and Barbara Bray. *Ibn Saud: The Desert Warrior Who Created the Kingdom of Saudi Arabia*. New York: Skyhorse, 2012.

Delang-Bas, Natana J. *Wahhabi Islam from Revival and Reform to Global Jihad*. New York: Oxford, 2004.

Djerejian, Edward P. *Danger and Opportunity: An American Ambassador's Journey through the Middle East*. New York: Simon and Schuster, 2008.

Filiu, Jean Pierre. *Apocalypse in Islam*. University of California Press, 2011.

Gibson, Bryan R. *Sold Out? US Foreign Policy, Iraq, the Kurds and the Cold War*. New York: Palgrave Macmillan, 2015.

Gold, Dore. *Hatred's Kingdom: How Saudi Arabia Supports the New Global Terrorism*. Washington: Regnery Publishing, 2003.

Hart-Davis, Duff. *The War That Never Was*. London: Arrow Books, 2011.

Haykal, Bernard, Thomas Hegghammer, and Stephane Lacroix, ed. *Saudi Arabia in Transition*. Cambridge University Press, 2015.

Hegghammer, Thomas. *Jihad in Saudi Arabia: Violence and Pan-Islamism since 1979*. Cambridge University Press, 2010.

Hegghammer, Thomas, and Stephanie Lacroix. *The Meccan Rebellion: The Story of Juhayman al Utabi Revisited*. Bristol: Amal Press, 2011.

Heikal, Mohamed. *Illusions of Triumph: An Arab View of the Gulf War*. London: HarperCollins, 1993.

————. *The Road to Ramadan*. New York: Quadrangle, 1975.

Hourani, Albert. *A History of the Arab Peoples*. Harvard University Press, 1991.

House, Karen Elliot. *On Saudi Arabia: Its People, Past, Religion, Fault Lines and Future*. New York: Knopf, 2012.

————. *Uneasy Lies the Head That Wears a Crown*. Belfer Center for Science and International Affairs, Harvard University, 2016.

Jordan, Robert W., with Steve Fiffer. *Desert Diplomat: Inside Saudi Arabia Following 9/11*. Lincoln, Neb.: Potomac Books, 2015.

Kechichian, Joseph A. *Faysal: Saudi Arabia's King for All Seasons*. University of Florida Press, 2008.

————. *Succession in Saudi Arabia*. New York: Palgrave, 2001.

Lacey, Robert. *Inside the Kingdom: Kings, Clerics, Modernists, Terrorists and the Struggle for Saudi Arabia*. London: Arrow Books, 2009.

Lippman, Thomas. *Arabian Knight: Colonel Bill Eddy, USMC and the Rise of American Power in the Middle East*. Vista, Calif.: Selwa Press, 2008.

Matthiessen, Toby. *The Other Saudis: Shiism, Dissent and Sectarianism*. Cambridge University Press, 2015.

————. *Sectarian Gulf: Bahrain, Saudi Arabia and the Arab Spring That Wasn't*. Stanford University Press, 2013.

Miller, Aaron David. *Search for Security: Saudi Arabian Oil and American Foreign Policy, 1939–1949*. University of North Carolina Press, 1980.

Muasher, Marwan. *The Arab Center: The Promise of Moderation*. Yale University Press, 2008.

Murray, Williamson, and Kevin M. Woods. *The Iran-Iraq War: A Military and Strategic History*. Cambridge University Press, 2014.

Naimi, Ali Al-. *Out of the Desert: My Journey from Nomadic Bedouin to the Heart of Global Oil*. London: Penguin, 2016.

Ochsenwald, William. *The Hijaz Railroad*. University of Virginia, 1980.

Ottaway, David B. *The King's Messenger: Prince Bandar bin Sultan and America's Tangled Relationship with Saudi Arabia*. New York: Walker, 2008.

Partrick, Neil. *Saudi Arabian Foreign Policy: Conflict and Cooperation*. London: I. B. Tauris, 2016.

Picco, Giandomenico. *Man without a Gun: One Diplomat's Secret Struggle to Free the Hostages, Fight Terrorism, and End a War*. New York: Times Books, 1999.

Posner, Gerald. *Secrets of the Kingdom: The Inside Story of the Saudi-U.S. Connection*. New York: Random House, 2005.

Quandt, William. *Camp David: Peacemaking and Politics*. Brookings Institution Press, 1986.

Rasheed, Madawi Al-. *A History of Saudi Arabia*. Cambridge University Press, 2002.

Rashid, Nasser Ibrahim, and Esber Ibrahim Shaheen. *King Fahd and Saudi Arabia's Great Evolution*. Joplin, Mo.: International Institute for Technology, 1987.

Rogan, Eugene. *The Arabs: A History*. New York: Basic Books, 2009.

————. *The Fall of the Ottomans: The Great War in the Middle East*. New York: Basic Books, 2015.

Safran, Nadav. *Saudi Arabia: The Ceaseless Quest for Security*. Cornell University Press, 1988.

Sander, Nestor. *Ibn Saud: King by Conquest*. London: Selwa Press, 2008.

Sardar, Ziauddin. *Mecca: The Sacred City*. New York: Bloomsbury, 2014.

Scheuer, Michael. *Osama bin Laden*. Oxford University Press, 2011.

Scott-Clark, Cathy, and Adrian Levy. *The Exile: The Stunning Inside Story of Osama bin Laden and al Qaeda in Flight*. New York: Bloomsbury Press, 2017.

Simpson, William. *The Prince: The Secret Story of the World's Most Intriguing Royal, Prince Bandar bin Sultan*. New York: HarperCollins, 2006.

Small, Thomas, and Jonathan Hacker. *Path of Blood: The Story of al Qaeda's War on the House of Saud*. New York: Overlook Press, 2015.

Teitelbaum, Joseph. *Holier than Thou: Saudi Arabia's Islamic Opposition*. Washington: Washington Institute for Near East Policy, 2000.

Trofimov, Yaroslav. *The Siege of Mecca: The Forgotten Uprising in Islam's Holiest Shrine and the Birth of al Qaeda*. New York: Doubleday, 2007.

Unger, Craig. *House of Bush, House of Saud: The Secret Relationship between the World's Two Most Powerful Dynasties*. New York: Scribner, 2004.

Valentine, Simon Ross. *Force and Fanaticism: Wahhabism in Saudi Arabia and Beyond*. London: Hurst, 2015.

Vassiliev, Alexei. *The History of Saudi Arabia*. London: Saqi Books, 2013.

————. *King Faisal of Saudi Arabia: Personality, Faith and Times*. London: Saqi Books, 2015.

Woods, Kevin M. *The Mother of All Battles*. Annapolis: Naval Institute Press, 2008.

Yergin, Daniel. *The Prize: The Epic Quest for Oil, Money and Politics*. New York: Simon and Schuster, 1991.

Yizraeli, Sarah. *The Remaking of Saudi Arabia: The Struggle between King Sa'ud and Crown Prince Faysal, 1953–1962*. Tel Aviv University, 1997.

Index